CLASSIC
ROCK POSTERS

MICK FARREN AND DENNIS LOREN

CLASSIC ROCK POSTERS

SIXTY YEARS OF POSTERS AND FLYERS: 1952 TO 2012

OMNIBUS PRESS

London / New York / Paris / Sydney / Copenhagen / Berlin / Madrid / Tokyo

Copyright © Elephant Book Company 2012
www.elephantbookcompany.com

Published by Omnibus Press
(A Division of Music Sales Limited)

Editorial director: Will Steeds
Commissioning editor: Chris Stone
Project manager: Jane M. Struthers
Senior editor: Laura Ward
Book design: Paul Palmer-Edwards, www.gradedesign.com
Cover design: Oil Often Graphic Design
Production: Alastair Gourlay
Picture research: Dennis Loren and Chris Stone

ISBN: 978.1.78038.452.8
Order No: OP54670

Exclusive Distributors
Music Sales Limited, 14/15 Berners Street, London, W1T 3LJ
Macmillan Distribution Services, 56 Parkwest Drive, Derrimut, Vic 3030, Australia

A catalogue record for this book is available from the British Library

Visit Omnibus Press on the web at **www.omnibuspress.com**

Printed in China

Contents

Foreword

It has often been said, "Beauty is in the eye of the beholder." Art appreciation is a subjective pursuit. That endeavor asks nothing more of the "beholder" than that he or she truly loves, enjoys, or simply appreciates the image or object in question.

To illustrate what I mean, let me take a moment to tell you a story about my maternal grandparents. They owned an eighty-acre family farm, located halfway between Nashville and Memphis, near McEwen, Tennessee. Although my brother David and I were born and raised in Detroit, we spent many summer vacations on the farm. My grandparents weren't wealthy, sophisticated, or even that well educated, but in their own way they appreciated art.

As a young woman, my grandmother Eula cut pictures out of magazines and framed them to decorate her dining room. Some were actually full-page advertisements for Edison electric light bulbs. This may seem odd, but most of these pictures were illustrated or painted by Maxfield Parrish. My grandmother obviously had taste, a good eye, and recognized Parrish's style. She was simply drawn to his art, in whatever form was available to her.

My grandfather Ray loved and trained show horses as a hobby. He had a large, impressive sculpture of a horse on his desk. It was a noble steed with one hoof raised, head cocked, nostrils flaring, a wind-blown mane, and piercing eyes. I later discovered that it was a three-dimensional copy of an illustration by Western artist Frederic Remington.

This story has little to do with rock poster art, but it does explain how art—even commercial art—is loved by ordinary people. Early in the twentieth century, works by Maxfield Parrish and Frederic Remington were hugely popular. Parrish, unlike Vincent Van Gogh, sold millions of prints of his paintings and illustrations during his lifetime. This doesn't diminish the wonderful paintings of Van Gogh, but it does speak highly of the work that Parrish produced. The prints of Remington and Parrish were artworks that everyday folk could afford to hang in their homes. Those same people often collected advertising posters by Alphonse Mucha, Lucian Bernhard, and others. It was all popular art; pop art, if you will, long before Andy Warhol came along.

This book isn't an academic tome about rock posters. (We can let the art critics and art history scholars argue over what is fine art, commercial illustration, or "lowbrow" art.) What we want to show in these pages is the evolution of rock poster design over the last sixty years. The images in this book were chosen by the artists who created them, the musicians whose concerts they advertised, the people who printed them, and the collectors who love them (along with a little help from the authors and editors). The posters you see in this volume were chosen primarily for emotional reasons rather than intellectual ones, for the feelings and memories that the posters evoke.

In Paul Grushkin's 1987 book *The Art of Rock*, San Francisco's legendary concert promoter Bill Graham is quoted as saying, "These posters are so much more than just historical documents or promotional tools for our business, they are art, as the music itself is art, and in many cases they are very fine, high art."

Many of the poster images in this book have already stood the test of time; and many others will, we feel. Some are extremely rare, and have not been previously published in book form. Most of these posters are much loved by music fans in general, and sought after, often vigorously, by collectors around the world. And yes, many of these posters are now sold for a lot of money. And in some cases an extraordinary amount of money indeed.

DENNIS LOREN, OAKLAND, CALIFORNIA

A History of Poster Art

By very definition, a live performance is in the fleeting moment. It happens, and then it's gone. It may be a play, a concert, or a comedy show, but it can run for anything from a matter of minutes to a number of hours; and then the finale comes, and it's a part of history. This history may, on some occasions, be preserved for posterity, either as an audio or as a video recording, but at other times nothing remains, except the audience's memories, and perhaps a program, some photographs, and the advertising material used to promote the show. In the modern world, where a camera phone can be pointed effortlessly at anything and everything and then uploaded to YouTube, much that is preserved for posterity probably shouldn't be. But even in the midst of a digital revolution, printed ephemera still remains the most lasting and popular of event souvenirs—and of all of the printed ephemera, the poster is conceivably the favorite for collectors.

The use of the advertising poster as a piece of art dates back some two hundred years, since which time posters have come in all shapes and sizes, and covered a multitude of subjects. Among the earliest display posters to catch the public imagination were those created for operas, musical recitals, horse races, prizefights, and other sporting events. Circuses and carnivals were among the first to use color images in their promotional displays, and these fanciful and often garish representations of strong men, bearded ladies, high-wire acts, and trapeze artists are now highly prized and very valuable.

History fails to record exactly when posters were first used as a form of decoration or were considered worth collecting, but at some stage during the first half of the nineteenth century, taverns and alehouses began hanging posters and sporting prints on their walls. As the century moved on, the manufacturers of all sorts of products—from soap to tobacco—started producing more decorative advertising, of which posters were a major part. The works of well-known artists were even incorporated into these graphic campaigns. Thus in 1886 the Pears Soap company purchased the famous painting *Bubbles* by Sir John Everett Millais; the original title, *A Child's World*, was changed, and Millais's permission was sought for a bar of Pears soap to be painted into the sentimental picture of the little boy blowing soap bubbles. Initially Millais balked at the alteration, but 2,200 pounds changed hands, and the artist acquiesced. Francis Barraud, on the other hand, had no problem when his 1898 painting titled *His Late Master's Voice*, in which a black-and-white dog (called Nipper) apparently listens quizzically to an early gramophone, was purchased by the Gramophone Company. As with *Bubbles*, the original name was changed to the simpler *His Master's Voice* and the image would, in various modifications, survive to this day as the logo of RCA in the United States and HMV in the United Kingdom.

During the final decade of the nineteenth century, the interplay between fine art and poster art reached its peak when the French artist Henri de Toulouse-Lautrec was commissioned to create posters for the Moulin Rouge and other Parisian nightclubs and performers (as well as for the Simpson bicycle company in England and the photographer P. Sescau). Some in the Parisian avant-garde accused Lautrec of prostituting himself by working for commercial interests, but the physically handicapped, rebellious one-time aristocrat treated the charges with contempt, probably noting the irony that many of his closest friends and companions were, in fact, prostitutes.

Despite the sniping and bohemian snobbery, Lautrec's posters broke down barriers between fine and commercial art. Graphic derivations of art nouveau and later art deco quickly found their way into the design of promotional posters, which frequently made eye-catching use of stylized images of attractive and often scantily clad young women. Such fine art-influenced advertising was by no means confined to shows and nightclubs. Lingerie and perfume, food products and alcohol, footwear and automobiles—all made use of cutting-edge visuals. In the first half of the twentieth century, a more mobile population was creating a market for vacation travel that the advertising industry was quick to exploit. Railroad stations and travel agents came alive with sophisticated, full-color artwork—romantic representations of the Mediterranean island of Capri or of Havana, the Golden Gate Bridge, or the Eiffel Tower. Travel posters were among the first to be framed and hung on walls, lending a supposedly cosmopolitan touch to any home, with scenic views of majestic ocean liners, and elegantly streamlined versions of early commercial aircraft.

More decorative innovations in the early twentieth century were ushered in by the spread of cinema. Movie posters became a feature in towns and cities across the developed world. These posters were garish, eye-catching, and sexy, and they provided coveted souvenirs of the movies they advertised and of the early stars like Rudolph Valentino and Mary Pickford as they gained devoted fan followings. The movie poster as both a collectable item and worthy of display in the home, as part of the decor and as a reflection of the owner's taste and character, is a theme that survives to this day.

Not all posters that incorporated cutting-edge contemporary art were for commercial advertising, however. Political propaganda posters were equally groundbreaking, and at times had an even more powerful visual impact. The art generated by the Bolsheviks in Russia, the loyalists in the Spanish Civil War, the Maoist revolution in China, and the Cuban revolution quickly attracted collectors, and are now prized items. The famous portrait of revolutionary hero Che Guevara, titled *Guerrillero Heroico*, was shot in 1960 for the Cuban newspaper *Revolución* by photographer Alberto Korda and is now among the best-known images in the world. For decades Korda allowed the picture to be reproduced without charging royalties, but when Smirnoff Vodka used Korda's image in a 2000 advertising campaign, the photographer sued for $50,000, which he donated to supporting the Cuban medical system. A similar but less savory collectors' cult formed around the graphics of the Nazi Party to become part of a largely hidden but very extensive market for Nazi memorabilia, with dubious connections to neo-Fascist and white supremacist political groups.

Music-themed posters have existed for as long as posters have been printed, and those announcing recitals by the great classical composers or the opening performances of ballets or grand operas are now priceless museum pieces. Closer to the modern world, music and design increasingly interacted as the twentieth century progressed. In 1917, the Théâtre du Châtelet in Paris hosted the debut of *Parade* by Sergei Diaghilev's Ballets Russes, with music by Erik Satie, scenario by Jean Cocteau, and costumes and sets designed by Pablo Picasso. The result was a violent riot in the theater that spilled out into the streets. Not all multimedia cooperations, however, were quite so provocative. In the 1900s the lucrative trade in sheet music for ragtime—the immediate popular forerunner of jazz—developed

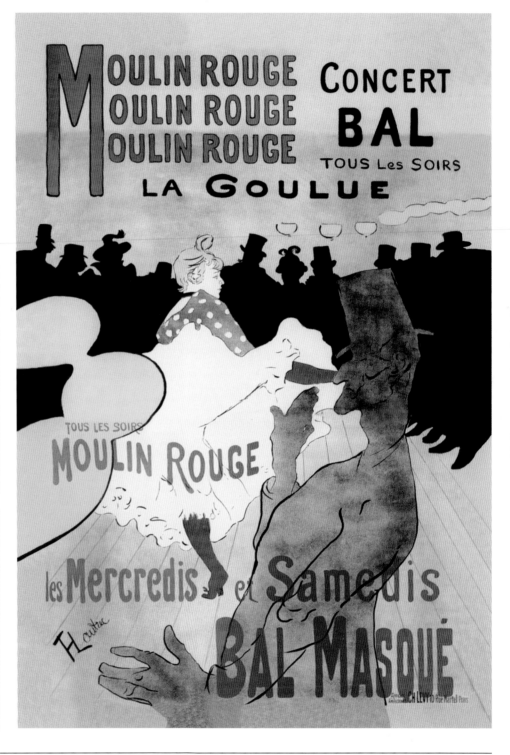

TOP LEFT Loyalist propaganda from the Spanish Civil War borrowed its style and threatening impact directly from the cutting-edge expressionist movement of the 1920s and 1930s, and the work of painters such as Edvard Munch.

BOTTOM LEFT This multicolored Ringling Brothers and Barnum & Bailey Circus poster, designed by artist Bill Bailey, was typical of the very direct "all-singing" style of American entertainment advertising of the twentieth century.

ABOVE RIGHT Henri de Toulouse-Lautrec's posters for the Parisian cabaret club the Moulin Rouge, as well as other nightclubs in bohemian Paris of the 1890s, brought art and advertising closer than had previously been considered possible.

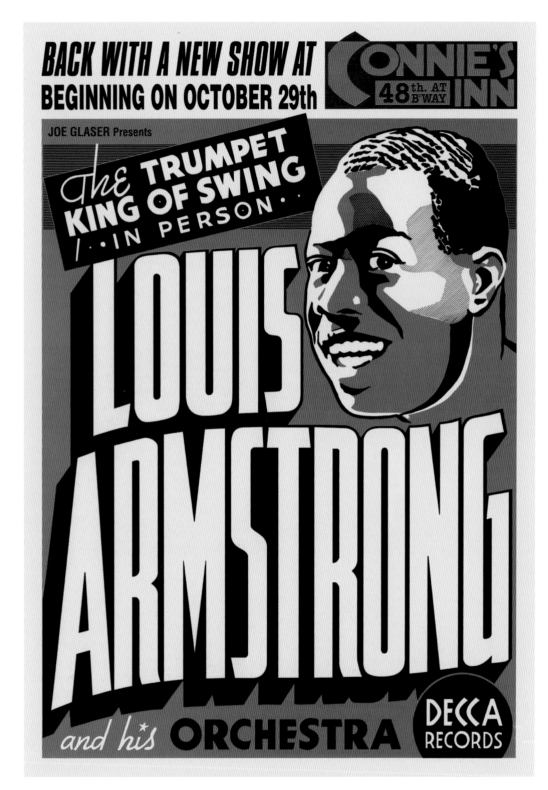

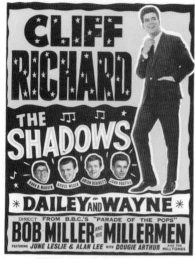

ABOVE LEFT While not sacrificing any of the bold type or ease of legibility, an art deco influence lent jazz-age posters such as this 1935 Louis Armstrong promotional poster an air of fashionable sophistication.

TOP RIGHT Early rock posters like this UK example, promoting a 1964 Sheffield concert by Cliff Richard and his band the Shadows, had little truck with either art or sophistication. They presented the information, without frills or pretension.

BOTTOM RIGHT This US poster for an early rock 'n' roll pioneer package tour from 1956 headlined Bill Haley & His Comets, the Platters, and Chuck Berry; it was equally direct and to the point.

illustrative styles, fonts, and letterforms that attempted to reflect the spirit of the music. Some of it was openly racist, but much of it represented genuine attempts to couple music with innovative graphic design.

Jazz and abstract art coexisted readily, and the energy and inspiration that fueled the Harlem Renaissance of the 1920s and 1930s extended not only to musicians like Jelly Roll Morton, Fats Waller, Duke Ellington, and Willie "The Lion" Smith, but also to painters such as Jacob Lawrence, Charles Alston, and Henry Bannarn. In the 1940s and 1950s, the jazz magazine *Down Beat* and the Blue Note record label were catalysts for a distinct school of jazz photography spearheaded by William P. Gottlieb and Francis Wolff. Black-and-white images became frozen moments, lit by the intense beams of the spotlights of a jazz club stage. The reflected highlights from polished brass instruments and even the baroque curls of cigarette smoke evoked a concentrated sense of atmosphere that was completely in tune with the music, and surpassed simple portraits of jazz legends such as Charlie Parker, Miles Davis, Dizzy Gillespie, and Thelonious Monk.

The advent of long-playing records brought music and graphic design even closer together. In the days of fragile 78 rpm singles, many record companies had introduced designs and letterforms into their record sleeves, labels, and advertising, which were supposed to reflect the spirit of jazz, blues, or country music. With the LP, however, each and every album that was released brought with it a chance to create a piece of art that was exclusive to the record. In the early days of LP vinyl, though, that opportunity was rarely seized with both hands; the majority of record labels perceived the record sleeve to be nothing more than the packaging it intrinsically was. An unimaginatively posed photo of the artist or maybe a model in a bikini was considered sufficient, and the outstanding jazz photography used by Blue Note was the exception rather than the rule.

In addition to Blue Note, another unexpected catalyst bringing innovative and intelligent graphic design to the music business was the "girlie" magazine *Playboy*. Its publisher, Hugh Hefner, was a longtime jazz buff and when he began devising what came to be known as the *Playboy* lifestyle, jazz—especially post-bebop and cool—played a major part in the image of the swinging, James Bond-perfect male-on-the-make, complete with the Brooks Brothers' suits, the Hathaway shirts, custom hi-fi, immaculate bachelor pad, and all of the other "toys" and products that were promoted as the *Playboy* route to sexual fulfillment. Decorating the walls of this male dream home played a crucial part in creating the desired ambience. Framed prints by contemporary artists like Piet Mondrian and Bernard Buffet were deemed suitable. Spanish bullfight posters and posters for championship boxing matches added Ernest Hemingway machismo, while posters for modern jazz concerts lent cool. For the first time in mass popular culture, posters for musical events were considered as both art and lifestyle accoutrements.

Sadly, in the 1950s this hipster fashion did not extend to rock 'n' roll. While jazz moved on from *Playboy* to inspire a wide-ranging "hepcat" style that was part cubism and part *Mad* magazine (and would be lovingly re-created some twenty years later by the legendary designer Barney Bubbles), rock never rose above the absolute basics. While rock 'n' roll would become the dominant force in music and a major influence on pop culture over the next half century, in its early days rock was treated with disdain. It was dismissed as a transitory fad and considered beneath contempt by devotees of "legitimate" music. Even Frank Sinatra condemned it as being "sung, played, and written by cretinous goons" and functioning as "the martial music of every side-burned delinquent on the face of the earth." (Although, this didn't stop Frank—just three years after making the

remark—from having Elvis Presley appear on his network TV show when he needed the ratings.)

To the amazement of everyone from Sinatra on down, rock 'n' roll not only refused to go away, but grew and flourished as the "cretinous goons" perfected their craft and caught the imagination of a new generation not only in the United States and Europe, but also in Japan and South America. With its roots in the blues and country music, it was able to cross boundaries of color and culture at a time when such barriers seemed insurmountable. The universal appeal of rock 'n' roll so scared the Ku Klux Klan that racists joined Sinatra in vitriolic denunciation. "Help save the youth of America. Don't buy negro records. The screaming, idiotic words and savage music is undermining the morals of our white youth. Call the advertisers of the radio stations who play this type of music and complain to them!"

The Klan, however, was no more able to stop rock 'n' roll than Frank, and the music also managed to survive payola (pay-to-play) scandals, hostile congressional hearings, Elvis Presley being drafted into the army, and Chuck Berry being jailed on morality charges. Rock simply went from strength to strength, exerting influences way beyond its original simple backbeat. It would infiltrate language, play a major part in fashion and personal style, and for a period in the late 1960s seriously impact on politics, especially the anti-Vietnam War movement. In many respects, however, rock 'n' roll's primary long-term influence was on the visual arts, although this might have been hard to believe back in the early 1950s.

The earliest posters for rock 'n' roll shows were simplistic to the point of crude, little different from those for boxing, professional wrestling, or stockcar racing. The general attitude was that anything was good enough for "sideburned delinquents," and no one imagined that the flyers and posters for rock 'n' roll acts could ever be anything but totally functional. To believe that half a century later original copies of those posters would change hands among collectors for hundreds of dollars would have been looked on as nothing short of insanity. The giant Alan Freed package tours elevated the standards of rock 'n' roll poster art, but only very slightly. Such shows might feature up to twenty acts, and the posters displayed the names and small photographs of the performers. The height of creativity was to sprinkle any unused space on the double-crown-size sheet with stars, musical notes, and guitar silhouettes.

The 1960s brought radical change, to every level of society—and to the image and visual promotion of rock music, too. At the core was the fact that rock musicians and their fans could no longer be dismissed as sideburned delinquents. A new generation of English rockers, including John Lennon, Pete Townshend, Ray Davies, and Ron Wood all benefited from the easygoing, laissez-faire education provided by UK art schools that placed emphasis on originality (and what would later be dubbed "thinking outside of the box") rather than academic qualifications. They were well aware of the pop art of Andy Warhol and Roy Lichtenstein, the flags and targets of Jasper Johns, and the op-art paintings of Bridget Riley and Victor Vasarely, and felt themselves to be very much a part of the same creative movement.

The Who, in particular, incorporated much of the new art they saw around them into the band's visual style, while at the same time embracing the culture of the emerging mod youth movement, with its emphasis on speed, fast-shifting fashion, and frenetic and symbolic violence. Their starkly classic, black-and-white poster for Maximum R&B at London's Marquee Club—designed by Brian Pike and showing Pete Townshend in his classic windmill pose—ushered in not only a new era in rock 'n' roll poster design, but also a new way of thinking about the rock musician. The poster hung on the bedroom walls of countless teenage mods from London and beyond.

A parallel but somewhat different change was taking place in the United States. The British Invasion spearheaded by the Beatles had shaken up the accepted package tour operations that had been bringing rock music to the majority of American fans. To present bands such the Kinks or the Animals, which were more than capable of playing sets of an hour or more, in the same fifteen-minute format as a manufactured one-hit wonder was plainly absurd, and so new show formats—and possibly even new venues—needed to be found. At the same time, all across the country local bands were coming out of the garage, and local promoters were opening up local clubs and dancehalls to the new wave of rock 'n' roll guitar bands, and the audiences who wanted to see them.

The major changes in the United States and Canada during the early 1960s, though, were happening under the guise of folk music. Running parallel with the British Invasion, a homegrown "hootenanny" boom was filling clubs and coffeehouses. Although imbued with a kind of self-conscious faux-bohemianism, and often harboring a definitely snobbish prejudice against old-school rock 'n' roll (which would climax when Bob Dylan was booed for appearing onstage at the 1965 Newport Folk Festival wearing a black leather jacket, toting a Stratocaster, and being backed by an aggressively loud electric band), it was an authentic grassroots phenomenon, effectively divorced from commercial pop. Indeed, icons of the mainly leftist folk movement such as Pete Seeger and Woody Guthrie had been wholly exiled from mainstream American music and were affected by the blacklistings of corporate radio during the Joe McCarthy anti-communist witch hunts of the early 1950s.

The venues that provided the working nuclei for the 1960s folk revival (established mainly in major cities like New York and San Francisco, and in college towns and on university campuses across the country) quite militantly did it themselves. With a noticeable anti-establishment air, and significant connections to the nuclear-disarmament and free-speech movements, they designed and printed their own posters and flyers, handled their own promotion, and generated their own publicity. These folk music venues—despite their distaste for rock 'n' roll—provided both a refuge and a launchpad for a generation of future rock musicians. Members of the Grateful Dead, the Mamas & the Papas, the Byrds, Jefferson Airplane, the Charlatans, and Buffalo Springfield all made their bones in and around the folk-club circuit before jumping the fence and going electric, and it would not be unfair to say that many folk performers, from Bob Dylan on down, had always had at least half an eye on the prize of rock 'n' roll stardom.

Despite all of its problems and prejudices, the hootenanny boom established that music could survive and even flourish without the support of the mainstream music business. Although few realized it at the time, it created precedents that would stand independent music in good stead in the years to come, and especially when a new factor entered the world of rock 'n' roll, and clubs that had previously featured performers looking to be the next Bob Dylan or Joan Baez began advertising something they called "the acid test."

The drug lysergic acid diethylamide ("LSD," "LSD-25," or simply "acid") was first synthesized by the Swiss chemist Albert Hofmann in the Sandoz Laboratories in Basel, Switzerland, in 1938, but five years passed before its psychedelic properties were discovered. Psychiatrists, the military, and the intelligence community all experimented with LSD, both as therapy and a potential chemical weapon. In 1965, however, acid started to appear on the same underground recreational drugs market as marijuana, amphetamines, and heroin—but with very different results. An acid trip produced an intense and occasionally mind-wrenching "psychedelic" experience that could include vividly overwhelming hallucinations and a state of euphoria at one

extreme, and abject and desperate fear at the other. The breakout city for what became dubbed "the psychedelic revolution" was San Francisco. Indeed, conspiracy theories claim that the drug use that triggered the 1967 Summer of Love and all that went with it was the result of a massive covert operation by the Central Intelligence Agency to see what might happen if an entire urban metropolis were exposed to large quantities of acid. These theories were fueled by the established fact that the highly secret, covert, and one hundred per cent illegal CIA human experimentation program MKULTRA conducted LSD experiments on volunteers at the Menlo Park Veterans Hospital in the Bay Area—volunteers whose numbers happened to include the writer Ken Kesey and the poet Allen Ginsberg.

Kesey would later form a group known as the Merry Pranksters, which, in the summer of 1964, took a lengthy road trip across the United States, traveling in a psychedelic-painted school bus with a rock band called the Warlocks (which would later change its name to the Grateful Dead) and members of the Hells Angels. Their adventures were chronicled by Tom Wolfe in his book *The Electric Kool-Aid Acid Test* as they presented impromptu multimedia, rock 'n' roll events with music, prototype light shows, and the liberal distribution of LSD. The shows staged by the Merry Pranksters set a pattern for all the psychedelic events that would follow. Like the folk boom that preceded it, the psychedelic revolution started out as a DIY affair, but taken to extremes that folkies could never have imagined.

The first San Francisco shows staged by promoters Bill Graham at the Fillmore Auditorium and Chet Helms at the Avalon Ballroom totally followed the precedents set by Kesey and the Pranksters—that is, that they should deliver much more than just the average rock concert. Although neither Graham nor Helms handed out free acid, the essential aim was the integration of every facet of the event; light and sound, design and theater, were all made part of the trip, and all were (in their own way) a simulation of the LSD experience. Everyone involved was pushing their respective envelopes to the extreme limit, and the results were like nothing that had ever been seen before. Although the Bay Area was ground zero for this psychedelic mushroom cloud, that same freeform formula was duplicated at the UFO and Middle Earth clubs in London, England, the Paradiso in Amsterdam, Holland, the Whiskey a Go Go in Los Angeles, the Café Au Go Go and the Electric Circus in New York, the Grande Ballroom in Detroit, and the Vulcan Gas Company in Austin.

Radical originality was the order of the day, and nowhere was this more prevalent than in the design of the posters for these events. They represented, in a way, the very starting point of the whole trip. Fly-posted on billboards, telephone poles, and storefronts, they broke all the rules of conventional advertising. Standard practice was to display the name of the venue and the headlining acts, boldly and clearly, in the largest possible type. The psychedelic posters did the complete reverse. They used custom-created letterforms that were more fanciful than legible and were made even more hard to read by the use of optically vibrating color combinations borrowed from Vasarely, and swirling light-show/acid-hallucination underlays. The message seemed to paraphrase Bob Dylan: Something was happening but you didn't know what it was; but if you wanted to be a part of it, get on down to the hard-to-read venue and see the even-harder-to-read band. When a new set of posters would go up around London or San Francisco, groups of hippies could be encountered, staring intently at them, attempting to puzzle out the names of the bands playing at London's UFO or San Francisco's Fillmore Auditorium.

Both the power and the paradox of psychedelic art was that the poster work—and, to a lesser extent, album sleeves, comic books, and the revolutionary layouts of underground newspapers—were the cutting edge

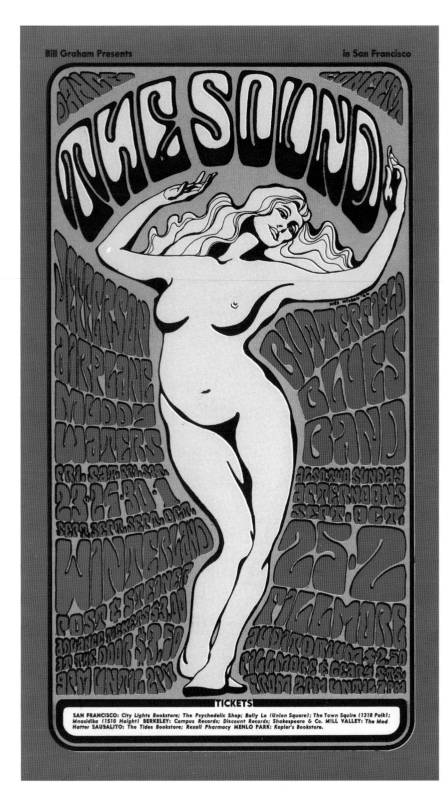

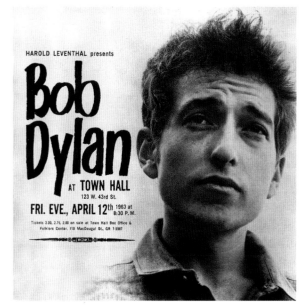

ABOVE LEFT During the psychedelic era, artists such as Wes Wilson, the acknowledged "father of psychedelic rock posters," pioneered the use of designed letterforms—influenced in no small part by the work of Viennese Secessionist artist Alfred Roller (1864–1935)—which actually challenged a stoner rock 'n' roll demographic to puzzle out the name of the venue and the featured bands.

TOP RIGHT Another example of creative letterforms, this time by the designer Randy Tuten. This poster is for a series of gigs featuring Creedence Clearwater Revival, Jethro Tull, and Sanpaku in March 1969 at the Fillmore West, San Francisco.

BOTTOM RIGHT When Bob Dylan graduated from coffeehouses to concert halls, he was still promoting an image of the "young Woody Guthrie," and the style of photography used for this poster for Dylan's concert at New York Town Hall in 1963 (and for the cover of *Times They Are A-Changin'*) deliberately recalls black-and-white images of the Great Depression.

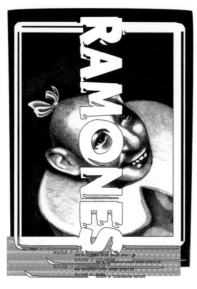

14 15 TOP In the wake of the psychedelic excesses of the late 1960s, the mood turned to one of more controlled surrealism, as evidenced in Paul Whitehead's art for Genesis' 1971 *Nursery Cryme* gatefold album sleeve and posters.

ABOVE LEFT In the case of this poster for Interpol's concert at the Sasquatchi Music Festival, Jeff Kleinsmith from design company Patent Pending went all the way to a blank, monochrome minimalism for this seventeen-by-twenty-four inch silkscreen print.

ABOVE CENTER Through his use of the famous pinhead from Tod Browning's 1932 movie *Freaks*, Thomas Scott from the design group Eye of Noise points up the punk and post-punk obsession with social distortion from various eras in this artwork created for the Ramones.

ABOVE RIGHT Victor Moscoso was a master of underground graphics who shuttled between poster design and cartoon work for publications such as Zap Comix. These twin influences are evident in this 1968 handbill for the Who's concert at the Shrine Auditorium, Los Angeles.

of the movement. Sure, there were psychedelic painters and kinetic artists, but by far the most significant work was (in its own highly idiosyncratic way) commercial art, which had a definite function and role in the larger youth revolt. Psychedelic posters, by turning the entire concept of advertising upside down, had made all things possible, especially an almost-infinite eclecticism. The influences borrowed by the leading artists (like Rick Griffin, Victor Moscoso, Stanley Mouse, Wes Wilson, and Alton Kelley in San Francisco; Michael English, Nigel Waymouth, and Martin Sharp in London; and Simon Posthuma and Marijke Koger in Holland) came from every direction. The work of comic book artists such as Jack Kirby, Steve Ditko, and Wally Wood were crazily combined with art nouveau works by illustrators like Aubrey Beardsley, the neoclassicism of Maxfield Parrish, the drag-strip stylings of Big Daddy Ed Roth, and even Disney characters and ancient Egyptian hieroglyphics—while underlying each surreal collage were myriad personal interpretations of acid hallucinations.

The psychedelic poster was an undisputed peak in music-related graphic design, but the wild and unfettered freedom of the late 1960s was impossible to sustain. The mainstream music industry had been largely taken by surprise by the psychedelic explosion, but, by the start of the 1970s, it had watched and learned, and even hired its own long-haired consultants (scornfully known as "house hippies") to help the corporate suits understand and exploit the radical new music and its accompanying imagery. The original, if simplistic, idealism of the psychedelic counterculture bent in the ill-wind of economic hard times, and the commercial rock business reasserted itself as the businessmen regained control.

The early '70s are remembered as an era of hot-tub, quaalude, polyester hedonism, during which everything of commercial value was looted from the '60s and the altruistic was left to wither. The rock poster was a perfect example of this kind of cultural carpetbagging. Bands like the Rolling Stones, Led Zepellin, and the Who drawing crowds in excess of 20,000 at stadium rock tours became viable, and these massive, high-profile, high-prestige tours required top-flight promotion and advertising. The posters for these shows were lavishly designed, had maximum impact, and the printing was of the highest quality. The stadium tour promoters had also learned an important lesson from psychedelic clubs. Rock posters were more than just advertising. The UFO Club and the Fillmore always printed far more posters than were needed for fly-posting, and the excess copies were distributed for sale at headshops, record shops, and bookstores. At the stadium shows, the posters could be bought at the official souvenir stands, along with the T-shirts, the baseball caps, and all the other merchandise. Rock posters were now a product in their own right and completely collectable.

In retrospect, the early '70s were a time when rock 'n' roll was dulled down and over-exploited, but one of the more positive aspects was the way in which close relationships were formed between bands and visual artists. Stanley Mouse and Rick Griffin had long been part of the Grateful Dead's extended family. Roger Dean supplied Yes with its trademark science-fiction images, and Storm Thorgerson, Aubrey Powell, and Peter Christopherson of Hipgnosis served the graphic needs of Pink Floyd. Joe Petagno designed the famous Motörhead war-dog logo, and went on to create the band's early design work. The tightest relationship between a band and a visual artist, however, was the bond between Hawkwind and Barney Bubbles.

Originally a light-show artist, Bubbles (who would later become the primary designer for Stiff Records) provided the highly unorthodox band with just about everything that wasn't music. He designed outstanding posters, highly inventive album sleeves, T-shirts, and badges, and even organized the custom painting of the band's stage equipment, proving that some

vestiges of the counterculture had managed to survive. But Hawkwind was the exception rather than the rule. Rock in the '70s seemed organized for the maximum commercial profit and the minimum creative risk. The fans who filed like sheep into huge sports arenas to watch the Who perform their anthem from *Tommy*, "We're Not Going to Take It," seemed willing to take just about anything. But something changed. Although the original punks would have furiously denied even the slightest similarity, the punk explosion in London and New York, and later Los Angeles and San Francisco, was effectively a repeat of the psychedelic upheavals a decade earlier. (Indeed, it was a well-kept secret that Malcolm McLaren of the Sex Pistols borrowed his ideas and philosophy from the French situationists of 1968.) The haircuts may have been different, the style more aggressive, the songs faster and shorter, and the drug of choice amphetamine sulphate rather than acid, but it was exactly the same kind of grassroots cultural revolution.

The influences behind punk visuals may have been totally different from those of the psychedelic, but they were equally eclectic. In their search for imagery that would shock, they seemed to leapfrog a generation, looking back to the underworld and underground of the '50s for their inspiration. Jamie Reid's ransom note typography for the Sex Pistols was straight out of '50s gangster movies. In *PUNK* magazine John Holmstrom borrowed from *fumetti* (the violent Italian photographic comic strips) and also evolved a cartoon style for his work with the Ramones that could only be described as "distorted *Mad* magazine." Where the hippie poster artists had primarily worked with offset printing, the punks had the Xerox machine to produce a smudged and muddy visual anarchy. In their quest for suitably outrageous images, punk designers, led by Vivienne Westwood, resurrected Bettie Page and the fetish photography of Irving Klaw, and the '50s homoerotic drawings of Tom of Finland. Even in Pennie Smith's famous photos of the Clash, the band members adopt both the clothes and poses of rock 'n' roll primal screamers like Eddie Cochran and Gene Vincent.

Like the hippies of the '60s, the punks of the late '70s were part of a cultural spike that was too intense and too extreme to sustain itself. As the first punk generation ran out of energy in an overdose of nihilism and heroin, it seemed as though the aftermath would follow the same pattern, and, to a great extent, it did. Mainstream commercial pressures came back into play. Punks were filtered to separate the acceptable from the unacceptable, with the acceptable being rebranded as new wave and the unacceptable consigned back to whatever tattooed, tongue-studded ghetto had spawned them. The new romantics came and went, grunge briefly made its mark—but nothing close to a seething teen mass movement was generated by the music. And without the jolt of a new and vibrant youth outbreak to inspire one more turn of the revolutionary wheel and trigger a much-needed seismic flip to the popular culture, the danger would seem to be that rock would turn into nothing more than one more product from the corporate entertainment conglomerates, with its posters and ephemera being created in advertising agencies rather than in the studios of stoner artists running free.

Except, as we moved toward the end of the twentieth century, something very interesting happened. Rock fragmented. While mainstream pop rock continued in a diminishing market, dozens of subgenres—each with its own dedicated following and its own unique style—orbited like angry satellites. The catalog was endless—death metal, thrash metal, speed punk, cow punk, various graduations of goth, hip-hop, and gangsta rap—and it multiplied constantly. The best artwork is now not being generated by major record labels. It comes from artists working for small genre bands and local clubs and, to find it, one actually has to go and look for it—and that may, in truth, be the most desirable road to stimulating art and cultural good health.

Early R&B, Rock 'n' Roll & Soul

1950s–early 1960s

In the Beginning…

To describe rock 'n' roll as the illegitimate child of a union between the blues and country music may be a cliché, but it is also effectively true. And, like a bastard child, early rock received very little in the way of mainstream approval; neither was it touched by any real business professionalism. Both blues and country were already looked on as the ragged-ass poor relations of more sophisticated popular music, such as big-band swing, or the music from Broadway and Hollywood musicals. With such a low-rent pedigree, it was inevitable that the early days of rock 'n' roll would be, for the most part, somewhat cowboy primitive.

Tours by the first generation of 1950s rock stars were wild and wooly affairs. Performers like Jerry Lee Lewis and Gene Vincent left behind them a trail of wrecked motels, shows that ended in near riots, and desperate dashes to leave town ahead of the law that more than rivaled any later outrages by bands like the Who and Led Zeppelin. The business end of rock 'n' roll was an unsavory stew of small record labels with limited distribution, fast-buck hustlers, bribe-taking disc-jockeys, fly-by-night promoters, and crooked managers who lacked both vision and imagination. Booze and pills played their part, just as they had done in the careers of bluesmen such as Robert Johnson and country stars such as Hank Williams. Although the word had yet to be coined, first-generation groupies acted out their good-time roles in the early rock 'n' roll after-hours circus.

Little wonder, then, that rock was held in contempt by all but its growing legion of fans. The new music was denounced by preachers, politicians, and even Frank Sinatra—condemned as the music of teenage misfits and sociopaths. In the United Kingdom, the BBC attempted to exclude rock music from state-controlled radio. Fortunately for British teenagers, it could be heard regularly on Radio Luxembourg, a maverick station that beamed out a powerful signal with English language, rock-friendly, commercial programming from a transmitter in the tiny European principality.

On both sides of the Atlantic, nice young people were supposed to stick to Doris Day and Perry Como. Rock 'n' roll was generally considered the gateway to fast cars, promiscuity, alcohol, and worse. As Little Richard more than once told it: "The kids left Pat Boone records on the turntable where their folks could see them, but they hid my records in the drawer." If contemporary accounts are to be believed, by far the majority of parents wished that the music would prove to be a brief fad and vanish like the Hula-Hoop or the Davy Crockett hat.

Even Elvis Presley—rock's first superstar—had his share of problems. Police in Florida filmed his stage act with a view to bringing charges of public lewdness, while in Lubbock, Texas—at a show attended by no less than the young Buddy Holly—he was attacked by a gang of local thugs angry that he was "getting their women in an uproar." Meanwhile, his manager, the dubious ex-carnie Colonel Tom Parker, saddled Elvis with washed-up comedians and Irish tenors such as Frankie Connors and Phil Maraquin as support acts, who drove Presley fans to impatient fury as they waited for their idol to hit the stage.

The posters that are the tangible legacy of these early live shows were rudimentary. Even those for a major star like Elvis were uncomplicated red and blue silkscreen or woodblock prints, not unlike those for boxing or professional wrestling events produced by firms such as Hatch Show Print and the Globe Poster Company, which had a history of producing posters for theatrical, musical, and carnival clients. Tom Parker—who had the posters for Elvis's 1950s shows printed by Hatch in Nashville—saw no reason to waste money on fripperies like custom design. The artwork was simply laid out at the printworks and then run off in the hundreds to be put on display in each town on the tour by Parker's advance men.

When lesser stars like Little Richard embarked on solo tours, the promotional material was produced even more cheaply and "cheerfully." A single run of posters would be ordered, usually featuring a photo of the artist and some bold, simple type. A blank strip would be left at the top or bottom of the poster on which the details of each stop on the tour could be overprinted by a local printer or even filled in by hand. This practice was known as using "tour blanks," and it dated back to the 1930s and the days of the touring big bands.

When multistar package shows became the favored vehicle for live rock 'n' roll, the posters became a little livelier, featuring more color, some thumbnail headshots of the acts, and sometimes other embellishments, such as clip-art silhouettes of guitars and musical notes. But in spite of such improvements, the posters were essentially still items of memorabilia rather than examples of significant design—more artifact than art.

OPPOSITE The archetypal rock 'n' roll manager, Colonel Tom Parker, pictured with the prototype rock star, Elvis Presley. Parker worked his charge hard, and the posters produced by Hatch to promote Presley were as hard-hitting and uncomplicated as the music he performed. Quantity, not sophistication, was the order of the day—but what an image to play with!

ABOVE Bill Monroe (right), pictured inside Hatch Show Print's headquarters with Jim Sherraden. He is being shown the final product of the carved wooden block in the foreground. Monroe, the legendary Father of Bluegrass, first began using Hatch posters to promote his roadshows in 1940, the year he joined the Grand Ole Opry, and continued to use them for decades thereafter.

CONCERT and DANCE

MEMORIAL AUDITORIUM
CHATTANOOGA

TUES. NOV. 16

8:00 'til 12:00

ADVANCE $1.50--LAST DAY SALE $2.00

5 ★★★★★ STAR RHYTHM & BLUES REVUE

THE SENSATIONAL "5-10-15 HOURS" GIRL

RUTH BROWN

"MAMA" "OH, WHAT A DREAM" "LOVE CONTEST"

Plus

CHARLES  BROWN

"GOOD TIME CHARLIE"   and his ORCHESTRA

 RAY "DON'T YOU KNOW" CHARLES AND HIS ORCH.

LOWELL FULSOM

'EVERYDAY I HAVE THE BLUES' "BLUE SHADOWS"

Plus

 MUDDY "HOOTCHY KOOTCHY MAN" WATERS

AND HIS BAND

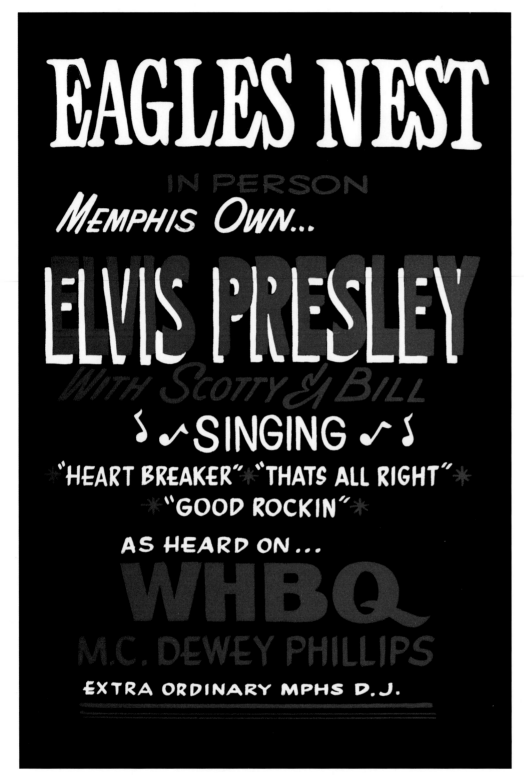

OPPOSITE This classic boxing-style poster from 1954 has a tour blank with a space for the venue to overprint local details. Clever use of colors and of solid and outlined fonts brings much variety to a fundamentally simple layout. The stellar lineup of this package tour illustrates the melting pot of blues, gospel, and R&B from which rock 'n' roll emerged that year.

ABOVE LEFT This unassuming example of the signwriter's art doesn't do justice to the significance of the event. Elvis played the Eagles Nest, on Highway 78 outside Memphis, sixteen times in 1954—the year he recorded "That's All Right" and helped to invent rock 'n' roll. Scotty and Bill were Messrs Moore and Black, Elvis's guitarist and bass player at the recording.

TOP RIGHT The Woolever Press of Los Angeles had been printing posters for exploitation movies since at least 1940. In 1952, the year this poster was created, expanding into the popular-music market was an obvious move. Percy Mayfield was a great early R&B songwriter— "Someone to Love" was later covered by the Rolling Stones, and Percy became a favorite of Ray Charles in the 1960s.

BOTTOM RIGHT This basic act-and-tour blank from 1952 has a yellow square on which to overprint the lineup, and a white strip for venue details. The Mambo Club was part of the chitlin' circuit of venues open to black performers during the era of segregation. The Ravens' pioneering doo-wop and Sonny Thompson's smoldering R&B had been delivering hits since the late 1940s.

IN PERSON
BILL HALEY

AND HIS
COMETS
OF "SHAKE RATTLE & ROLL" FAME
"ROCK AROUND THE CLOCK" "RAZZLE DAZZLE"
And Many Other Famous DECCA Recording Hits

MUNICIPAL AUD.
OKLAHOMA CITY - OAKLA.
SUN. OCT. 16
2 SHOWS MATINEE & NIGHT
TICKETS ON SALE AT YEATEY'S, DOWNTOWN

TONIGHTS the NIGHT
FROM 8:00-11:00PM
GRAND PRIZE
JAMBOREE
PRESENTS
ELVIS PRESSLEY
LOUISIANA HAYRIDE STAR
★HOOT GIBSON
FAMOUS WESTERN MOVIE STAR
★SONNY BURNS
★BROWN BROS.
★TOMMY SANDS
At Eagles' Hall
A Block South off Gray on Louisiana
With
BIFF COLLIE
as Master of Ceremonies!
Also Appearing on the Show will be...
James O'Gwynne, Coye Wilcox, the Dixie-
Drifters, Ernie Hunter and Herb Remington!
☆NEXT WEEK'S GUEST☆
TOMMY COLLINS

---

22   23   ABOVE LEFT Oklahoma City was the home of letterpress poster printers Litho Color Craft as well as the venue for this simply advertised 1956 appearance by Bill Haley and His Comets. Tickets were available at Veazey's drugstore, founded in 1900 and still going strong in Oklahoma City today as Bill Veazey's Party Store.

ABOVE RIGHT The hall of the Fraternal Order of Eagles in Houston, TX, was hired by local radio stations for their weekly jamborees. This hand-painted lobby card was for the March 19, 1955, event sponsored by Grand Prize Beer and broadcasted on KLEE. The misspelled Presley's co-star Hoot Gibson made his first movie in 1910 and his last, *Ocean's Eleven*, in 1960.

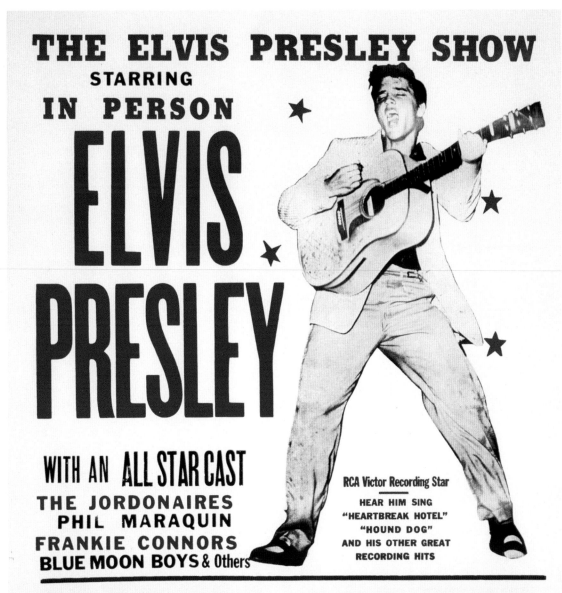

ABOVE LEFT Elvis's manager Colonel Tom Parker used Nashville poster shop Hatch Show Print (where, it's been said, he never paid his bill). The Hatch style, widely familiar to the huge country music community, made it easier to spread the rock 'n' roll gospel to the masses. The Elvis Pelvis is already a big selling point in this 1956 poster.

TOP RIGHT This is another vaudeville-style tour blank from the Globe Poster Company of Baltimore, featuring some of the giants of rock 'n' roll and early R&B in a racially mixed lineup. At the bottom of the bill, Shirley Gunter's brother Cornell sang in the Flairs—he had been in the original lineup of the Platters and would soon be a founder member of the Coasters.

BOTTOM RIGHT This poster is typical of Globe Posters' variety-style design, with its bangs and ovals of color behind the performers' names. Here is an early indication of the importance of the record charts. Not only is this 1956 package called the Top Ten Review, but almost every artist's billing also includes his or her record company.

TOP LEFT Another year, another package tour, another stylish four-color Globe circus-ring poster. The use of dot-etched headshots helps to emphasize the size of the package; the faces of so many of "America's greatest teen-age recording stars" were aimed squarely at 1958's target audience of excited bobby-soxers.

BOTTOM LEFT This no-nonsense two-color boxing-style bill from Globe still manages to convey the diversity of the lineup by adding photos of many of the acts. In 1957 Little Richard was at the height of his wild early fame, but two months after this concert he found God and retired temporarily to become a Seventh Day Adventist minister.

ABOVE RIGHT This restrained 1959 tour blank for hardworking veteran organist Bill Doggett comes from the E.J. Warner Poster Corp. of New York. Warner's began producing posters for theater, circus, and cinema in the 1930s. The company's work ranged from crude one-color announcements to full-color illustration; it created whatever the budget called for.

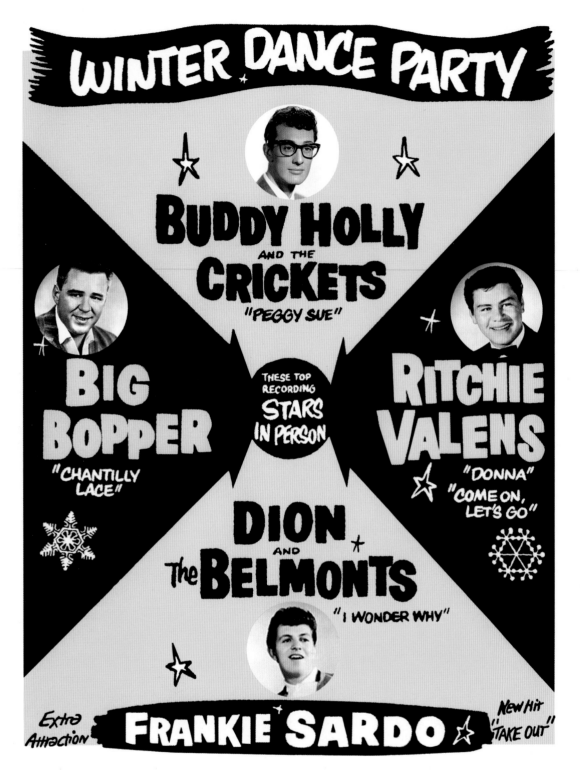

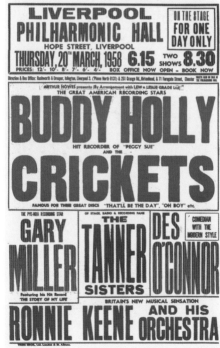

ABOVE LEFT The strong diagonals in this simple two-color design stress the presence of four great headliners in this package tour of early 1959. However, midway through the tour, three of the four attractions—Buddy Holly, Ritchie Valens, and the Big Bopper—were killed in a plane crash. It was, for many fans, the Day the Music Died.

TOP RIGHT The *Big Beat* was Alan Freed's ABC TV show in 1957, and it made sense for him to host this 1958 package tour of the same name. The TV series was unexpectedly canceled when, rumor has it, Frankie Lymon was seen on-screen dancing with a white girl, offending ABC's Southern affiliates. Freed is credited with inventing the expression "rock 'n' roll."

BOTTOM RIGHT This no-frills boxing-style poster from 1958 was for Buddy Holly's first and only British tour—consisting of twenty-five consecutive dates, with a minimum of two shows a day, and a minimal two-color design. Tribe Brothers, who printed it, had been producing playbills for London's West End theaters since at least the 1920s.

Freed, the DJ who championed early rock 'n' roll on WINS in New York City and Radio Luxembourg in Europe. Freed would, however, be replaced by TV personality Clay Cole when the former found himself disgraced during the radio payola scandals.

The concept of the rock 'n' roll package show grew from the fact that no one—except for a few million teenagers—expected rock 'n' roll to be anything but a nine-day wonder. The music industry of the mid-'50s viewed the majority of rock 'n' roll recording artists as nothing more than a parade of infinitely interchangeable one-hit wonders. No entertainment entrepreneur was about to invest in any kind of rock infrastructure. Embryonic rock 'n' roll wasn't even given the commercial respect accorded to jazz. There would be no rock clubs or purpose-dedicated concert halls. The "smart money" believed that the new music wasn't going to be around long enough to recoup that kind of investment.

No one denied, however, that in the short term there was money to be made. The rock 'n' rollers were selling records, and a solid demand existed for live performances. While crowds of kids were willing to stand in line for a rock show, the goal would be to stage them cheaply, easily, and in large numbers, and to reap the maximum profits for the minimum effort.

The result of this kind of huckster thinking was what became known as the rock 'n' roll "package show." Assembled under collective titles such as "Big Beat Jamboree," a bill of up to twenty recording stars with current or recent chart hits would be dispatched on tour, all backed by the same tour band, to play spots of no more than ten or fifteen minutes on stage, during which they'd perform their hits and, at most, two or three other songs. Featuring stars such as Chuck Berry, Bobby Vee, Bobby Darin, Connie Francis, the Everly Brothers, Sam Cooke, and Brenda Lee, the double-crown-size playbills for these package shows read like rosters of late 1950s rock 'n' roll talent.

Many of the posters for the US package shows were printed by the Globe Poster Company of Baltimore, Maryland. Established in 1929, Globe (much like Hatch Show Print) started out printing posters for theaters, vaudeville

The package shows played concert halls and old-style big-band ballrooms, but the most effective—and most lucrative—deals were made with cinema chains where the live rock shows could be rotated with movie screenings and run for four or even five shows a day. Although they started in the United States, the idea was quickly duplicated in the United Kingdom, with shows that combined current American stars with home-grown talent. The leading promoter—the flamboyant Larry Parnes—even maintained a stable of creatively named performers (Tommy Steele, Marty Wilde, Billy Fury, Vince Eager, and Duffy Power) with which to pack the bills on his tours. Toward the end of Globe's heyday, two names began to appear on its posters for package shows that, with hindsight, indicated that a massive change was coming—those names were the Beatles and the Rolling Stones.

ABOVE LEFT Tommy Steele, arguably Britain's first home-grown rock 'n' roll star, pictured with Svengali Larry Parnes (standing behind his protégé). Steele, born Thomas Hicks, was renamed in time-honored Parnes style and set on the road to '50s stardom by covering US hits for the British market. The UK-girdling package tours Parnes set up were scarcely as relaxing for performers as the pose suggests, however—they worked hard for their money.

ABOVE RIGHT DJ Alan Freed, who would later be convicted as a scapegoat for the payola scandal of paying for radio play, lent his name (and face) to package tours of up to twenty artists. This 1957 show combines the live spectacle with *Don't Knock the Rock*, a movie starring Alan Dale, advertised on posters as "the

OPPOSITE LEFT A typical lineup from the Larry Parnes stable of imaginatively named rockers from March 1961. Despite Parnes's implication that many of the artists in his show were American, all except for Davy Jones were British.

OPPOSITE RIGHT When Freed diversified into rock exploitation movies, the poster industry moved right along with him. Remarkably modern, hard-hitting typography hammers home the message of this early feature from 1956, the third in a series of five the impresario promoted. Paradoxically, given this

"The package tour was an extension of the old music hall idea of sending a number of acts on tour together."

CHRIS NICKSON, MINISTRY OF ROCK

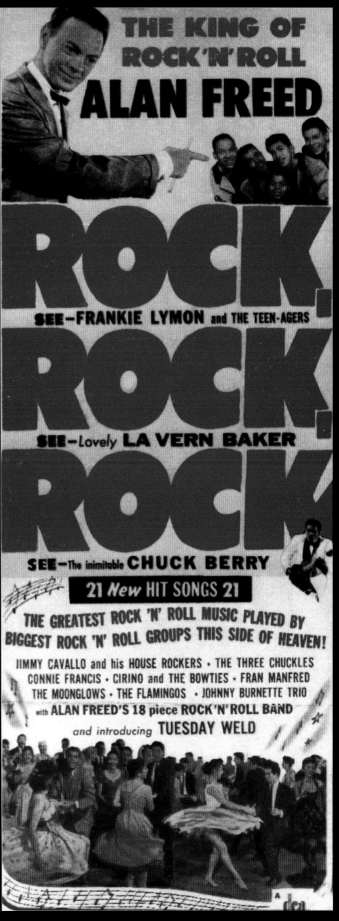

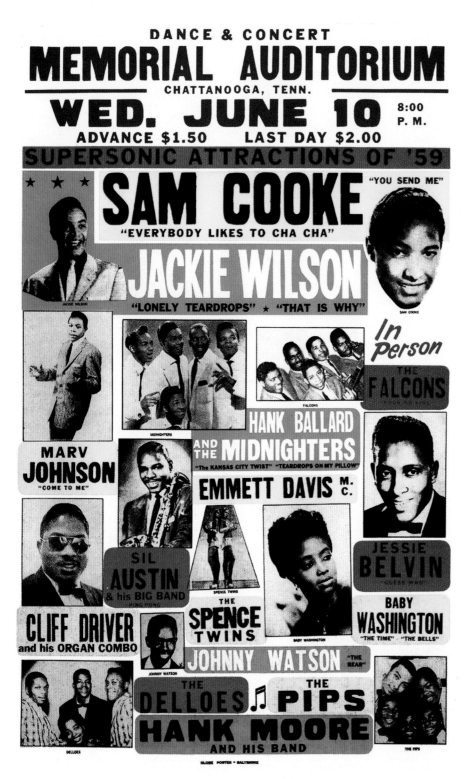

ABOVE LEFT This Globe poster for a strong soul package of 1959 shows how the photography was becoming as important as the lettering. Other versions of the same poster omitted the picture of the racy burlesque act the Spence Twins—perhaps so that it could be displayed in more "respectable" neighborhoods.

TOP RIGHT The sizzling flame motif is a nice touch on this 1959 Globe poster for a tour by "the hot 5." The Crests were riding high on "16 Candles," the biggest hit of their career; but Chubby Checker was yet to record the novelty twist dance hits which, from June 1960, would make his name.

BOTTOM RIGHT Leading West Coast printers Tilghman of Oakland, CA, produced this 1961 boxing-style effort. The simple two-color tour blank makes good use of large cropped photo images. Bobby Bland's charismatic mixture of blues and gospel was a powerful influence on Southern soul. Bland, Vi Campbell, and the Malibus all recorded for Houston impresario Don Robey's Duke/Peacock Records.

OPPOSITE, TOP LEFT A powerful R&B package is promoted on this 1962 Globe boxing-style poster. For Jackie Wilson, at the height of his success, the hits would soon start to dry up, but the Four Seasons were just getting started. Bo Diddley was already a rock 'n' roll legend; and Bunker Hill remains one of the great undiscovered R&B shouters in the Little Richard mold.

OPPOSITE, BOTTOM LEFT James Brown was a regular client of Globe Posters. In 1961 they made the most of this lineup with good use of color and geometry. The Flames were Brown's vocal group, the Brownies his dancing troupe, the Orchestra his backing band, and Nat their drummer (his hit was "Pig Eyes," not "Pigs Feet"). Even Sugar Pie DeSanto was a former member of Brown's Revue.

RIGHT The Ike and Tina Turner Revue padded out its lineup with local talent wherever it went. This Globe tour blank from 1961 cleverly leaves space for overprinting not only venue details (at the top) but also two hot local support acts (over the flame panels at the bottom).

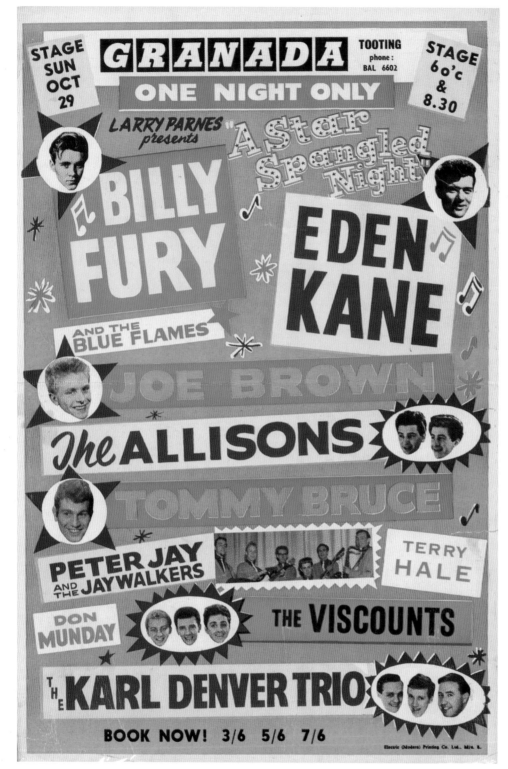

ABOVE LEFT British rock promoter Larry Parnes groomed a large stable of young stars that he regularly featured in his own package tours. From this candy-coated, all-British "Star-Spangled Night" in 1961 he managed Billy Fury, Joe Brown, Tommy Bruce, and the Viscounts; Fury's band the Blue Flames later backed another Parnes protégé, Georgie Fame.

TOP RIGHT The Beatles made their debut at Liverpool's Cavern Club in February of 1961, the first of 292 performances there over the next two years. It must have been a refreshing change from the claustrophobic cellar to play this evening river cruise event promoted by the club, on board one of the celebrated Mersey ferries.

BOTTOM RIGHT Disappointingly, the visual possibilities of prototype shock rocker David "Screamin' Lord" Sutch have been overlooked by this somewhat generic poster. The Queens Hall in the provincial Devon town of Barnstaple, UK, was redeveloped as the Queens Theatre in 1993 after forty years' service.

ABOVE LEFT This bold poster, by London theaterland printers Tribe, advertises an event that never happened. Just three performances into his 1958 British tour, Jerry Lee Lewis was forced to cancel and return to the US, following revelations about his third wife, who was also his thirteen-year-old first cousin.

TOP RIGHT This 1963 poster for a south London date reflects the Electric Modern Printing Company's background in variety-style entertainment. Variety developed out of music hall and, like its predecessor, featured a number of entertainers on one bill—a tradition mirrored here.

BOTTOM RIGHT This 1962 poster is in the landscape format and size more usually associated with movies. Bobby Vee's career launched when he stepped into the package-tour slot opened as a result of the death of Buddy Holly. Three years later, here, he headlined at a British cinema hall above Holly's backing band the Crickets.

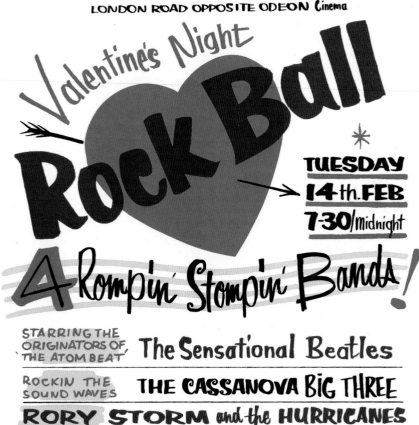

Die Not hat ein Ende!

Die Zeit der Dorfmusik ist vorbei!
Am Freitag, dem 13. April

eröffnet

★ Star-Club

die Rock n' Twist-Parade 1962

mit The Beatles   Tex Roberg   Roy Young   The Graduates   The Bachelors
zusätzlich ab Mai: Tony Sheridan-Quartett und Gerry and the Pacemakers

Eine Ballung der Spitzenklasse Europas

Hmb.-St.Pauli, Gr.Freiheit 39

At the "CASSANOVA CLUB"
SAMPSON AND BARLOW'S FABULOUS
NEW BALLROOM
LONDON ROAD OPPOSITE ODEON Cinema

Valentine's Night
Rock Ball
TUESDAY 14th FEB
7·30/midnight

4 Rompin' Stompin' Bands!

STARRING THE ORIGINATORS OF 'THE ATOM BEAT' — The Sensational Beatles
ROCKIN THE SOUND WAVES — THE CASSANOVA BIG THREE
RORY STORM and the HURRICANES
and Introducing MARK PETERS and the CYCLONES

LICENSED BAR AND BUFFET UNTIL 11·0 p.m

TICKETS 4'6
(INCLUDING REFRESHMENTS)
ON SALE AT
Rushworth's · Lewis's · Cranes

OPPOSITE The Beatles—listed second on the bill—and Rory Storm were engaged to play alternate ninety-minute sets at the Kaiserkeller, five times a day, in the fall of 1960. It was during this grueling Hamburg residency that drummer Ringo Starr of Storm's backing group the Hurricanes first sat in with the Beatles—the rest is history.

ABOVE LEFT Hamburg hardly lacked music clubs, but this 1962 announcement of the launch of the city's newest venue declares that "the famine is over, the age of folk music is dead." The Star-Club opened with a seven-week residency by the Beatles. When they returned later in the year, it was with a new drummer and a Parlophone recording contract.

ABOVE RIGHT A hand-painted lobby card for the first of two performances by the Beatles on the same date in 1961—from Liverpool's Cassanova Club, they raced to nearby Litherland Town Hall, where the stage was rushed by girls hoping for a kiss from Paul McCartney. The Atom Beat was then drummer Pete Best's signature rhythm.

Printers to the stars

One of the leading producers of early rock 'n' roll posters—most notably those for Elvis Presley—was Hatch Show Print in Nashville, Tennessee. Located at the time at 116 4th Avenue, close to the Ryman Auditorium—the original home of the Grand Ole Opry—Hatch was the "official printer" of world country music, creating posters for a range of stars including Roy Acuff, Eddie Arnold, Bill Monroe, and Hank Williams. When Colonel Tom Parker—who used Nashville as his base of operations in the mid-'50s—required posters for Elvis, Hatch was an obvious choice. Other rock 'n' rollers followed suit, and Hatch expanded out of country into the lucrative rock poster business.

The Hatch print shop had a long history. It was established in 1879 by brothers Herbert and Charles Hatch, who printed posters and other advertising for lectures, magicians, plays, minstrel shows, and vaudeville. The shop produced posters for the New York-based Orpheum Theatre chain, Charles Collier's *Silas Green from New Orleans* traveling show, and F. S. Wolcott's touring company Rabbit Foot Minstrels. Hatch also produced posters for blues singers Ma Rainey and Bessie Smith. The Hatch brothers specialized in letterpress printing using hand-set moveable metal or wooden type on a Babcock cylinder printing press. When illustrations and custom lettering were needed, they were initially hand carved on wooden blocks. Later, as print technology improved, line blocks and halftone screens came into play for the reproduction of pictures and photographs. In the 1950s, pictures of performers were preferred by clients, and raised-relief dot-etched metal plates were used to reproduce photographs.

Although the posters that Hatch printed for Elvis Presley are the company's greatest claim to fame, the brothers created posters for a galaxy of rockers. In the 1960s, they produced the posters for Johnny Rivers's Memphis Special package tour, which featured Chad & Jeremy, the Ventures, and others. Dick Clark also hired Hatch for the "Caravan of Stars" package tour posters. One 1965 Dick Clark poster featured the Byrds, Bo Diddley, and Paul Revere and the Raiders. More recently, the company has turned out print work for artists such as Bob Dylan, Cyndi Lauper, Emmylou Harris, Neil Young, the Beastie Boys, R.E.M., and the White Stripes.

The company has changed hands a number of times over the years and is now owned by the Country Music Hall of Fame and Museum. The museum not only runs Hatch as a commercial printer but also ensures the care and survival of its vast and priceless archive in what manager Jim Sherraden has called a "living museum," visited by more than 20,000 fans each year.

LEFT Bob Cicero of the Globe Poster Company and Jim Sherraden, manager of Nashville-based Hatch Show Print, show off two posters by Hatch. Americana artists such as John Hiatt are particularly fond of using retro print styles such as those displayed here.

ABOVE A printer of bygone days would readily recognize this "living museum" and commercial print shop at Hatch Show Print.

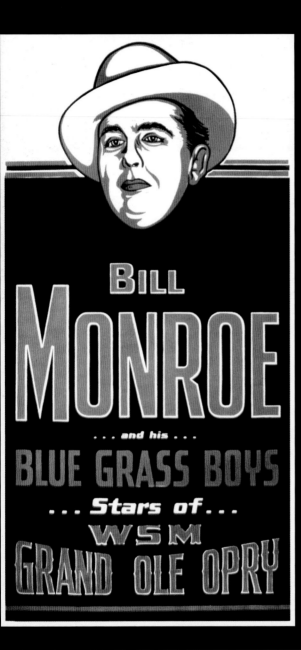

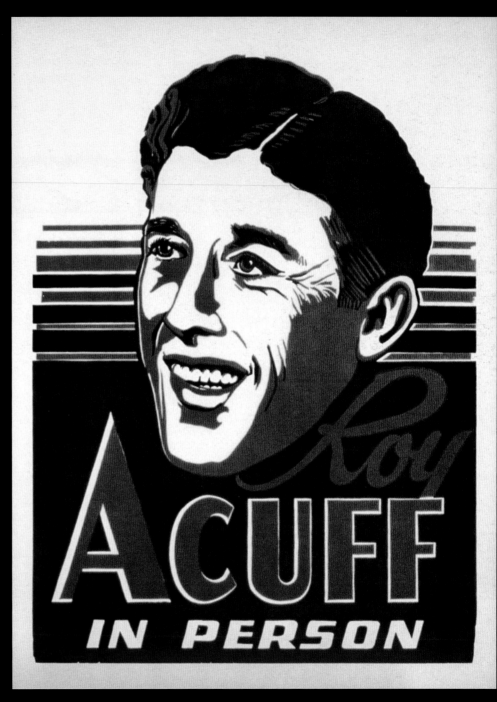

ABOVE LEFT In 1943, the Grand Ole Opry moved to the Ryman Auditorium, which was located one block from Hatch Show Print. The stars of the Opry hired Hatch Show Print to create posters for their tours. Will T. Hatch was an adept artist; he drew a reverse image on a block of wood and carved a raised relief image. When the surface was inked and pressed onto the paper, a positive image would appear. Bill Monroe is considered to be the "father of bluegrass music."

ABOVE RIGHT In the '40s and '50s, Roy Acuff appeared frequently at the Grand Ole Opry. Will T. Hatch carved the portrait of Acuff and the custom lettering into a block of wood, then made a second relief carving for the shadows and second color highlights—a skill learned as a boy from his father Charles and Uncle Herbert.

2

British Beat, Surf, Blues & Folk

Early to mid-1960s

The Times they Start a'Changin'

Buddy Holly was dead. Elvis was in the Army. Chuck Berry was in jail, Jerry Lee Lewis was ruined by scandal, and Little Richard had—at least temporarily—found Jesus and abandoned music. At the start of the 1960s rock 'n' roll's future seemed in doubt. No one seriously believed that the clock could be turned back to Doris Day and Perry Como as if rock 'n' roll had never happened; but the early years of the decade found popular music being recast in a form sufficiently bland to be acceptable to conservative white America, the arbiters (as they saw themselves) of national—and even international—taste.

The induction of Elvis Presley into the US Army symbolized the suppression of rock 'n' roll's more rebellious characteristics. The process was turned into a media emasculation with an almost biblical obsession over the cutting of Presley's hair. Elvis was shorn of his hoodlum pompadour and his rebel sideburns. His crazy clothes were exchanged for a uniform, and the provocative moves that had so offended Ed Sullivan would be drilled out of him as he learned to march in step.

Drafting Elvis was a public circus; but in the dark corridors of power, serious if less spectacular attempts were being made to reshape popular culture. Congressional hearings were linking rock music with juvenile delinquency and organized crime with the jukebox supply business. Rock 'n' roll was at the center of the so-called payola scandals, the much-trumpeted exposure of widespread bribery in the broadcast radio industry.

In Britain however, the influences of American soul and rock 'n' roll were fused together with a melodic sensibility in a radical new way by the Beatles. Like many British groups, the Beatles honed their performances through a string of hardworking residencies in Hamburg, appearing at the Indra, the Kaiserkeller, the Top Ten Club, and, most famously, the Star-Club. It was there that they sharpened their instincts for attention-grabbing energetic pop.

Their success introduced a new concept, Beatlemania, and gave the British scene as a whole an invigorating injection of confidence. After two decades of absorbing American cultural influences, young British musicians at last had role models of their own. They began to experiment, developing more sophisticated musical vocabularies, merging styles and crossing musical borders in the search for original sounds. Rock ceased to be merely an excuse to bring boys and girls together on the dance floor, and began to emerge as a medium in its own right.

The first fruit of this newfound self-awareness was the short-lived but highly influential mod movement. The mods' sharp, punchy style extended well beyond the music they played—to the suits and haircuts they wore, and even to the Italian scooters they rode. The mixture of Italian fashion, British beat, Jamaican ska, and American soul was explosive.

The Beatles unlocked the door to America in 1964, opening the way for the mods' Small Faces and the Who; for British bands such as the Rolling Stones, the Animals, and Them; and for more clean-cut bands such as Herman's Hermits. The Fab Four inspired a new generation of wannabe rock bands, all looking for a new sound and a place to play. According to writer and critic Charles Shaar Murray, the success of this "British Invasion" was

due in part to America's hunger for the vitality of rock 'n' roll after the trauma of the Kennedy assassination. Rock had been tamed in the US, but the youthful energy of the British beat reminded her of what was possible.

All over America, the British Invasion merged with local scenes to yield exciting new music, named garage rock after the places in which the young bands rehearsed. In the Midwest, garage showed marked soul influences in bands such as the Trashmen from Minnesota. In the Pacific Northwest, it combined mod with surf in a sound of almost punk immediacy through groups such as the Standells and Oregon's Don and the Good Times.

On both East and West Coasts, it fell to folk clubs to embrace the new British influences. On the East Coast, Greenwich Village was already home to radical theater performances and folk music, and had been a well-established bohemian area since the nineteenth century. Gerdes Folk City had opened there in 1960; it introduced Bob Dylan and Joan Baez to the world, and now presented early performances by future folk-rock giants such as the Byrds, and the Mamas and the Papas. On the West Coast, British influences merged with surf, blues and folk music, and eventually produced the sounds that defined the hippie era and the "Summer of Love."

The posters for the first wave of the British beat boom were as conventional as anything out of the '50s. But with the emergence of mod and other pop cultures, it became clear that rock 'n' roll was no longer just a matter of playing guitars and singing at live shows or on record. Rock was

ABOVE Beatlemania had swept across Europe, and on February 7, 1964, the boys disembarked to a tumultuous reception at New York's John F. Kennedy Airport. Formerly known as Idlewild, the airport had recently been renamed in honor of the fallen president, assassinated barely three months beforehand.

to be taken seriously as a creative form and as an integrated, marketable lifestyle. Its posters, too, could therefore be considered as works of art, rather than as mere vehicles for conveying information. Inspiration came from other forms of advertising, from other forms of visual art—and, particularly, from the contemporary pop art movement.

Many posters, in Britain at least, had been created by local printers or signwriters. But this was set to change when, in 1954, artist Tom Eckersley joined the teaching staff at the London College of Printing; Eckersley would later establish Britain's first undergraduate graphic design course at the college. Other art colleges followed suit, and it was the graduates that emerged from these new graphic design courses who would take British rock 'n' roll poster art to new levels.

Competition for audiences increased as new bands and clubs tried to build a following. The need grew for a strong identity to be conveyed on posters; and so rock logos began to appear. Signwriter Colin Duffield, who had no formal training in graphic design, incorporated the distinctive King Mojo logo on posters promoting British bands the Amen Corner and the Small Faces, among others, and American soul acts, including Wilson Pickett and Stevie Wonder, for their performances at the King Mojo Club in the northern English city of Sheffield. Other venues followed. The promoters of Ricky-Tick (originally a club based in a hotel in Windsor), Philip Hayward and John Mansfield, organized "Ricky-Tick"-branded events at twenty-seven locations across southern England and beyond. The Ricky-Tick nights were important platforms for new British beat and blues acts, and from 1963 all the club's posters carried the distinctive "screaming man" image by art student Bob McGrath, which gave it a strong and recognizable public image.

Individual bands began to draw upon the idea of the logo to create their own promotional material. Brian Pike designed the symbol that was to define the era—the aggressive, sharply defined, no-nonsense impact of the design and lettering on the Who's iconic Maximum R&B poster, which perfectly encapsulated not only the Who but also the whole mod sound.

The emergence of logos encouraged poster designers on both sides of the Atlantic to explore the possibilities of typography for demonstrating the character of individual acts and the diversity of a multiple bill of performers. As rock musicians began to cross borders with their music, so visual artists pushed the boundaries of lettering. Logos became ever more stylized, until their very illegibility as announcements of events became their abstract attraction as posters. Eventually hallucinogenic drugs liberated the music and the poster altogether, ushering in the psychedelic age.

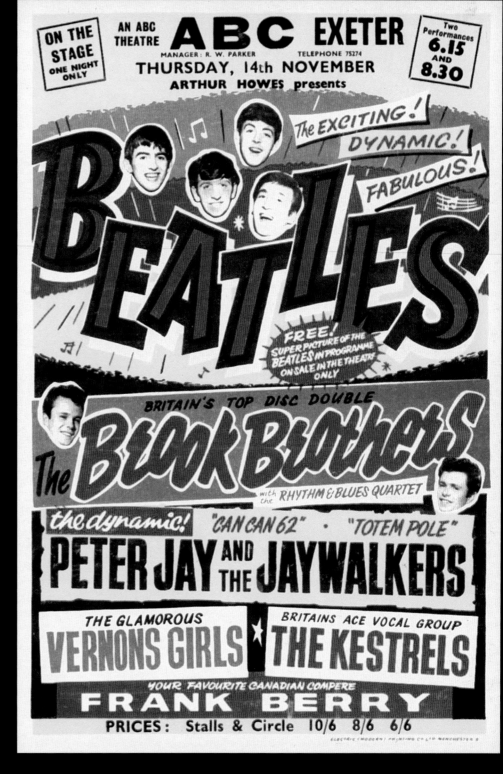

ABOVE The Electric Modern Printing Company was England's answer to the Globe Poster Company of Baltimore, adapting the old variety poster style to the demands of the new pop package tour. Frank Berry, compere of this 1963 tour, became a regular host on TV and stage and even appeared in the 1964 movie satire *Dr. Strangelove*.

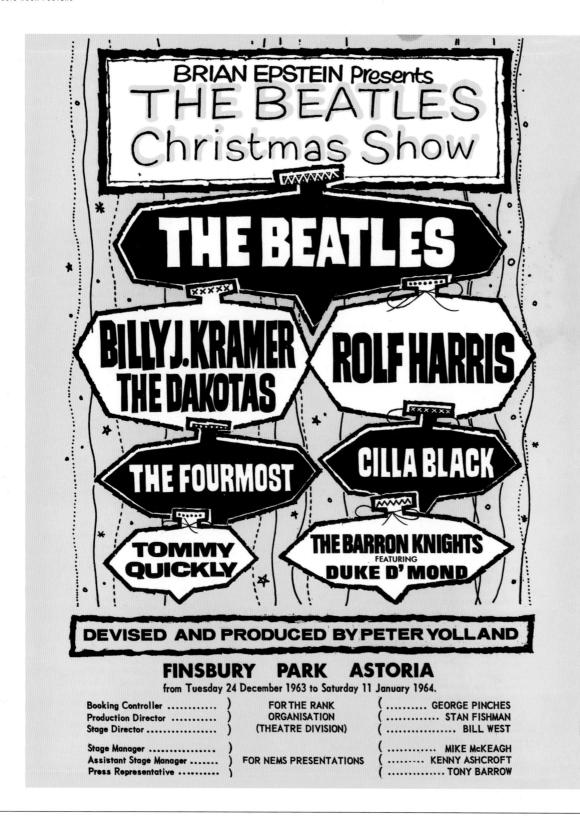

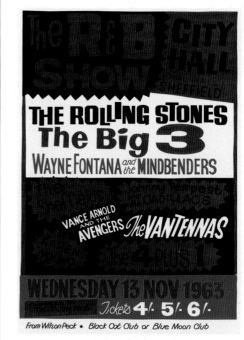

ABOVE LEFT The program cover for the Beatles' 1963 Christmas Show is in pure variety style, but the use of one font and the same shape for all the performers shows more than usual design flair. Of the seven acts, five were from Merseyside and the other two were comedy slots. Merseybeat had arrived.

TOP RIGHT It was early days for the groups in this package: the Oval Hall at Sheffield City Hall is a smallish room behind the main auditorium. Sheffield artist Colin Duffield produced many screenprint posters for local promoter Peter Stringfellow, an early pioneer of the new R&B music.

BOTTOM RIGHT The Rolling Stones' first hit "Come On" is used as an invitation to this 1963 Christmas party. The poster is a generic blank: the preprinted Top of the Pops banner and Vox guitar in one color could be overprinted in another as required, with the details of any event, at any venue.

THE HIGH NUMBERS

EVERY TUESDAY 3/6

RAILWAY HOTEL HARROW & WEALDSTONE!

RIGHT In February 1964 the Detours changed their name to the Who; but briefly that summer they changed their name again, to the High Numbers. Their residency at the Railway Hotel was due in part to Pete Townshend's friendship with the owner, Richard Barnes. Barnes also produced this screenprint poster, based on a design he'd seen in a British Sunday newspaper.

FOX & GOOSE HOTEL
HANGER LANE, EALING W.5

JIVING & TWISTING
FRIDAYS
FEATURING THE DYNAMIC
"DETOURS"

7.30–11.00 P.M.   4/- ADMISSION
LICENSED BALLROOM BAR
BUSES—83, 187 TO DOOR   112, 105 TWO MINUTES   TRAINS—HANGER LANE, PARK ROYAL

COMMENCING FRIDAY, 11TH JAN.

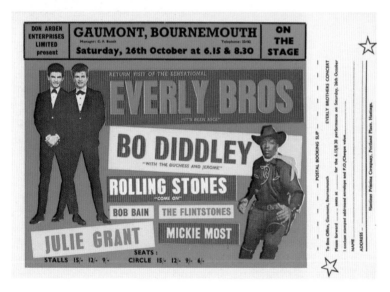

42 43 **TOP LEFT** A graphic-free 1963 poster in a rare landscape format, this poster advertises an early residency (in Ealing, west London) by the band that would become the Who. The Detours' Roger Daltrey, at this point playing lead guitar to Pete Townshend's rhythm and John Entwistle's bass, didn't take over lead vocal duties until the end of the year.

BOTTOM LEFT This 1963 flyer, by showbiz printers Hastings, advertises the first package tour to feature the Rolling Stones. The band refused to play its debut single, a cover of Chuck Berry's "Come On," in live sets, but their manager Andrew Loog Oldham used his knowledge of chart-return record shops to propel it to No. 21, earning the Stones their place on this tour.

ABOVE RIGHT Rod Stewart hooked up briefly with Southampton band the Soul Agents after he quit Long John Baldry's Hoochie Coochie Men in late 1964. They won a Thursday night residency at London's Marquee Club and the occasional support gig for visiting R&B stars like Buddy Guy. The unusual landscape format of this 1965 type-only poster comes from long-established letterpress printers Arthurs of Woodchester.

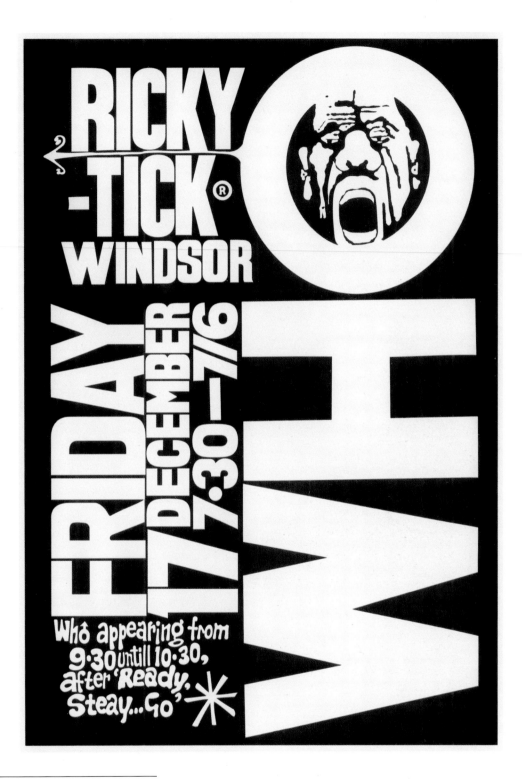

TOP LEFT A Hastings Poster Co booking-slip flyer printed for the performances at Colston Hall, Bristol. The basic variety layout is spiced up with some imaginative lettering, and the design's block spaces not only allow for changes of venue, but for variations in lineup—for example, a week later the tour went to Birmingham and Alan Bown's place on the bill was filled by the Small Faces.

BOTTOM LEFT A strong blues and R&B program for February 1966. Veteran jazz promoters Nanda and Ron Lesley switched to R&B in the early '60s and ran two Bluesvilles—the original in Ipswich, Suffolk, and this one in London's Finsbury Park district. They played a vital part in nurturing the '60s British blues boom.

ABOVE RIGHT The "screaming face" logo appeared on all Ricky-Tick Club posters from spring of 1963 onward, giving the club a strong and recognizable public image. Bob McGrath, who designed it, printed the early posters himself, but as the Ricky-Tick got busier he taught its promoters Philip Hayward and John Mansfield to screenprint his artwork themselves. This poster is from 1965.

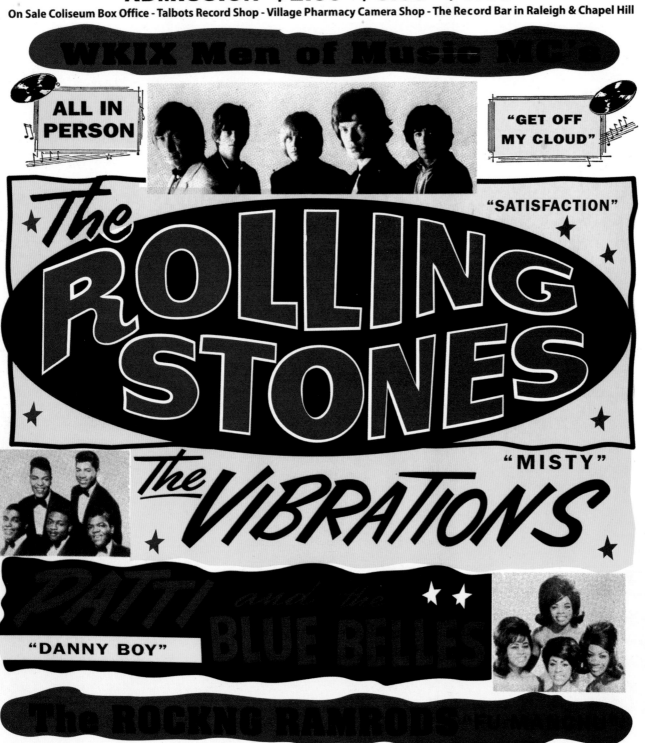

REYNOLDS COLISEUM

WED. NOV. 10

N.C. STATE CAMPUS
RALEIGH

8:00 P.M.

ADMISSION $2.50 - $3.00 - $4.00

On Sale Coliseum Box Office - Talbots Record Shop - Village Pharmacy Camera Shop - The Record Bar in Raleigh & Chapel Hill

WKIX Men of Music MC's

ALL IN PERSON

"GET OFF MY CLOUD"

The **ROLLING STONES**

"SATISFACTION"

The VIBRATIONS

"MISTY"

PATTI and the BLUE BELLES

"DANNY BOY"

The ROCKNG RAMRODS

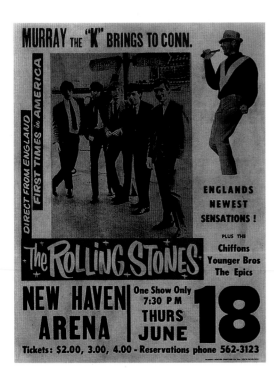

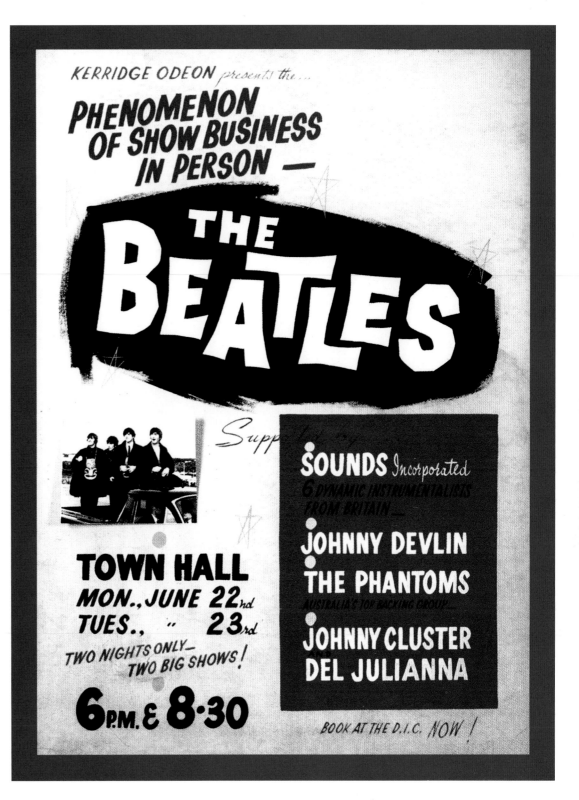

OPPOSITE It is fitting that the Rolling Stones, who drew on US R&B for their early repertoire, should be advertised in 1965 by a poster from Globe, the Baltimore print company responsible for advertising so many early R&B packages. "Satisfaction," their comment on US consumerism, had been recorded in May of that year during an earlier US tour.

TOP LEFT This 1964 two-color poster has been enhanced by yellow paper, which was the background of choice for the Murray Poster Printing Co. of New York City. Murray the K, the self-styled "Fifth Beatle," was a DJ who was influential in encouraging the British Invasion. This was the Stones' first US tour—"a disaster," according to bassist Bill Wyman—with no Top 20 entries yet to help promote it.

BOTTOM LEFT In August of 1964 the "Fab Four" began their second US tour that year. The first, in February, had launched the British Invasion. The support acts included Clarence Frogman Henry and Jackie De Shannon. The Beatles themselves were on for only thirty minutes, during which they raced through eleven of their hits.

ABOVE RIGHT The British Invasion conquered the whole world, not just the United States. This is a lobby card from the first venue of the Beatles' only tour of New Zealand—eleven shows in six days in June of 1964. Local girl Del Julianna pulled out of the tour, but in 1964 Johnny Devlin, "New Zealand's Elvis," produced her recordings of two Barry Gibb songs.

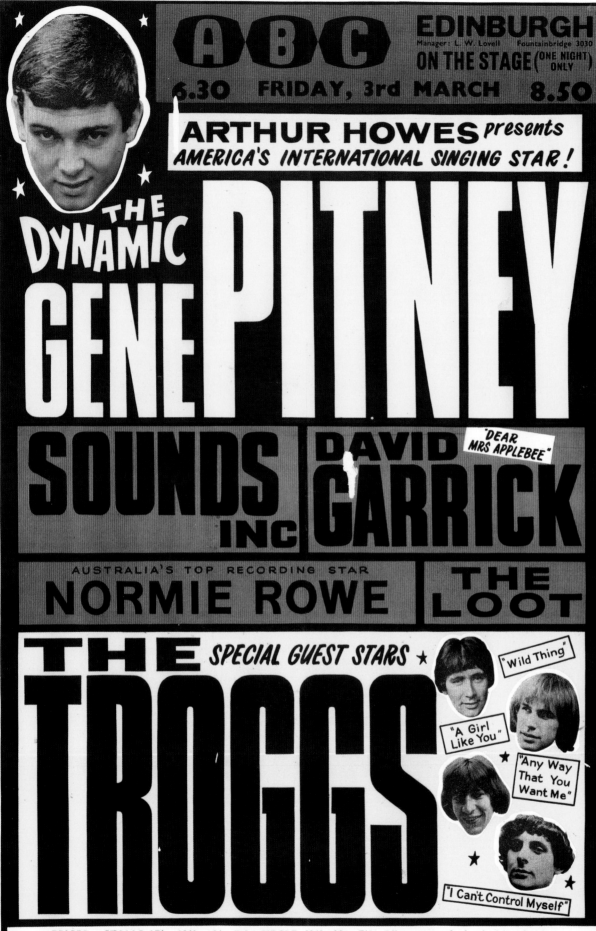

LEFT An international package in Scotland's capital on this bold, colorful 1967 poster by the Electric Modern Printing Company. UK instrumentalists Sounds Inc. had regularly backed visiting US stars since their first break on Gene Vincent's UK tour of 1961. They opened for the Beatles in Shea Stadium and, just before this tour, had appeared on the Fab Four's *Sgt. Pepper* LP.

ABOVE LEFT A two-color handbill from 1965 for one of the British Invasion's finest, the Dave Clark Five, supported by a strong US bill. The Californian venue had opened only a few years earlier as a dinner theater, complete with a revolving circular stage, on which promoters Lewis and Dare staged Broadway touring productions.

ABOVE RIGHT A 1965 mail-order ticket flyer for another attack in the British Invasion, this time led by the Animals. In support, the Headhunters, who had opened for the Beatles' second US tour. The Circle Star's management Lewis and Dare diversified into rock music soon after the opening of their theater-in-the-round. Under new ownership it prospered in the 1970s with Vegas and Motown acts.

ABOVE The prepsychedelic rays of the sun on this 1965 poster are its only concessions to graphic design. For a festival of folk and blues, the lineup shows a strong bias toward the latter and to the emerging mod and R&B sound. The bad weather options described were unnecessary—the day was overcast but with sunny spells.

ABOVE LEFT It was 1966, but the seaside resort of Torquay, on the "English Riviera" in South Devon, still made no concessions to pop culture with this very "square" poster. The addition of a mod fashion show to the bill is an ironic detail; it was the very thing being satirized by the headliners' featured hit, "Dedicated Follower of Fashion."

ABOVE RIGHT A shimmering 1967 poster from UK psychedelic design partnership Hapshash and the Coloured Coat, which comprised Michael English and Nigel Waymouth. The poster advertises the Birmingham rock band the Move (later, with a change of lineup, to become ELO) at the Marquee Club in London, where they performed weekly gigs.

We Are the Mods

The arrival of the Beatles and the British Invasion transformed American rock music almost instantaneously. The poster designs used to promote the very same were rather slower to respond. Posters for early tours by bands such as the Animals, the Kinks, or even the Rolling Stones, were almost identical to the basic boxing and sporting-event styles of the 1950s. At the height of Beatlemania, many promoters found they didn't have to advertise the Beatles at all—shows were sold out the moment tickets went on sale, and for some of their most historic live shows, posters weren't even printed.

For major advances in the sophistication of rock 'n' roll-related design, you had to look back to Britain and, specifically, to the British art schools. In the early '60s, the hands-off, liberal attitudes of British art education spawned a slew of rockers, including John Lennon, Pete Townshend, Ray Davies, and many more. It was the art schools that incubated the idea that rock 'n' roll was not just a musical genre, but part of a whole new youth movement. Music could have links to other means of expression, such as graphic design, photography, fashion, and even political causes such as nuclear disarmament and civil rights, and also tastes in recreational drugs.

Young musicians exchanged records and ideas, and they were called "Mods," after the modernists, a school of thought that had its roots in the coffeehouses of the 1950s' beatnik generation—places where radical ideas of literature and politics were exchanged. These late-night joints became a natural focus for a developing youth culture. In the way that the beatniks had discussed French literature and existentialism, mods now discussed American R&B and Italian movies. In fact, mainland Europe inspired a great deal of mod fashion—similar style statements were being made in France, encouraged by the celebrated magazine *Salut Les Copains*.

The self-consciously stylish mod culture was characterized by a sharp, clean-cut fashion sense (including tailor-made Italian suits) and the adoption of Italian scooters. The music, exemplified by groups such as the Small Faces, the Action, and the Who, was crisp, energetic pop derived from British beat, Jamaican ska, and American soul. When this peculiarly British distillation of European and transatlantic styles reached American shores, its fresh young energy was seized on by a rock-starved nation. The wave of American garage rock, fed by the British Invasion, in turn would influence many of the rock styles that concurrently and subsequently developed—folk, psychedelic, hard rock, and even grunge.

One of the first designs to express this new movement was the poster for the Who's legendary Tuesday night residency at London's Marquee Club, a run of twenty-nine gigs that made the band stars. The promotional campaign mounted by the band and their managers Kit Lambert and Chris Stamp, of which the poster was a part, deliberately set out to make the Who a defining part of being a mod, along with other essential mod accessories, such as the Lambretta, the parka, the Levis, the Fred Perry, and the Raybans. Designer Brian Pikes's famously stark black-and-white Maximum R&B poster—with Pete Townshend in windmill pose, and the "o" in Who turned into a male gender symbol with an added arrow—is now recognized as one of the all-time great rock posters.

As other bands like the Move followed suit, rock 'n' roll took its place beside players from other creative media, such as photographer David Bailey, model Jean Shrimpton, and dancer Rudolph Nureyev. Together, they defined a specific period and ethos, the '60s. This integration of many disciplines foreshadowed the coming psychedelic era when music, graphic design, dance, and even highly innovative light and sound technology, would all combine under the banner of rock.

> "In a sense mods were anti-rock 'n' roll as that form is now defined in the US. They—we—were defining new ways of rebelling, putting Elvis and James Dean behind us."
>
> PETE TOWNSHEND

ABOVE Posing as the quintessential mod band, the Who—left to right: Keith Moon (drums), Roger Daltrey (vocals), John Entwistle (bass), and Pete Townshend (guitar)—through their attitudes as much as through their music, embodied the mod movement's aggressive, youthful energy. Their sound was derived from American rock 'n' roll and R&B, while their look drew on bold British pop art and sharp Continental European fashion.

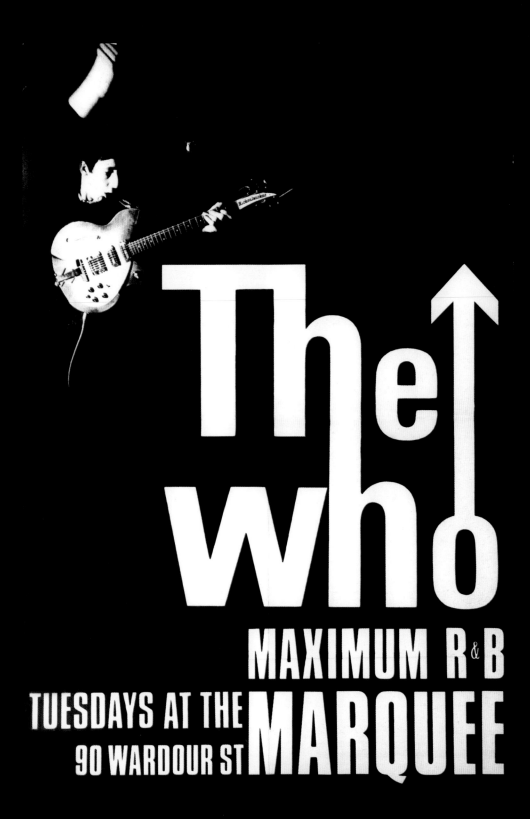

ABOVE The Who's landmark poster by Brian Pike was created for the band's 1964–65 residency at London's Marquee Club. Their manager Kit Lambert came up with the tag Maximum R&B. The bold use of white on black had already been used by the Ricky-Tick Club, but the aggressive image of a live musician was new, and it captured the spirit of the mod era perfectly.

Hear "Sweets for My Sweet"

DON and the GOOD TIMES
FRIDAY, MARCH 18, 8-11 P.M.
Admission $2.25

WEDNESDAY, MARCH 16,	SATURDAY, MARCH 19,	SUNDAY, MARCH 20,
The Twilighters	**The Page Boys**	**Battle of the Bands**
8:00 – 11:00 P. M.	8:00 – 11:00 P. M.	2:00 – 5:30 P. M.
Admission $1.25	Admission $1.25	Admission $1.00

WOODEN SHOE
1210 N. E. 102ND NEAR GATEWAY

DANCE
IN STYLE THE TRASHMEN

Date:

Time:

Place:

GAZZARRI'S
Hollywood A Go Go
319 North La Cienega, L.A.

FEB. 14-19

Closing Feb. 12 TEDDY NEELY FIVE

Dancing – 18 and over
Alcoholic beverages not served to anyone under 21

THE STANDELLS
8 p.m. 'til 2 a.m.—Continuous Entertainment

For Reservations CALL OL 2-9498 Closed Mondays

ABOVE LEFT A typically rough-and-ready garage poster from 1966. The wooden shoe, a nineteenth-century anarchist symbol, gave its name to the popular club in Portland, OR. The Goodtimes' Don Gallucci had been in protogarage band the Kingsmen, playing keyboards on their 1963 hit "Louie Louie." He went on to produce the Stooges' 1970 *Fun House* album.

TOP RIGHT The Trashmen's no-frills 1964 tour-blank flyer exudes humor. The Minneapolis band moved from surf music to garage when the British Invasion arrived. "Surfin' Bird" (their version of the Rivingtons' *Papa-Oom-Mow-Mow*) was a 1963 US No. 4 and, with the support of a Facebook campaign, became a 2010 UK No. 3.

BOTTOM RIGHT Some nice psychedelic floral flourishes distinguish this 1967 garage band flyer. Sunset Strip nightclub Gazzarri's survived from the '60s to the '90s, famously giving early breaks to future rock giants like the Doors and Van Halen. The raw sound of the Standells has since earned them the accolade the "godfathers of punk."

WONE PRESENTS

THE BEACH BOYS

PLUS
"WOOLEY BULLEY"
SAM THE SHAM & THE PHAROAHS
and featured on "SHINDIG" TV
GLENN CAMPBELL
FRI. MAY 21 - 8:30 P.M.
HARA'S SPORTS ARENA
TICKETS: $2.50 - $3.00 - $3.50- $4.00 on sale at Sports Arena Box Office
for information Phone 378-4776

K-poi presents
A MILLION DOLLAR PARTY

...IN PERSON:

THE
★BEACHBOYS ★JAN & DEAN

JIMMY   THE
★CLANTON   ★KINGSMEN

THE   RAY
★RIVINGTONS ★PETERSON

FREDDY   JODY
★CANNON   ★MILLER

JIMMY
★GRIFFIN   ★BRUCE AND TERRY

Direct from London
★PETER & GORDON
HIC ARENA

Fri., July 3 - 7:30 p.m.

Sat., July 4 - 2:00 Matinee
6:30 - 9:00 p.m.

Popular Prices: $2.00 AND $3.00

MEMORIAL GYM. | FRI OCT 23
MIDDLE TENN. STATE COLLEGE
MURFREESBORO   8:00 P. M.

Tickets On Sale: Pigg & Parsons - Student Union Bldg. - McClain & Smith Clothing Store in Lebanon,
& Harvays Central Ticket Office in Nashville   Advance Admission $2.00, At Door $2.50

JOHNNY RIVERS
"MEMPHIS SPECIAL"
STARRING IN PERSON
JOHNNY RIVERS
"MEMPHIS"   "MAYBELLINE"

CHAD AND JEREMY
STEWART "YESTERDAY'S GONE" CLYDE
"A SUMMER SONG"

RONNIE AND THE DAYTONAS
"G. T. O."
★★★★★★★ PLUS SPECIAL GUEST STARS ★★★★★★★
THE VENTURES
"WALK, DON'T RUN '64"

ABOVE LEFT The clean-cut, blue-eyed image of the Beach Boys is reflected in the smiles and crisp verticals of this 1965 poster. Bassist and songwriter Brian Wilson no longer toured with the band following a 1964 anxiety attack; his place was taken by bottom-of-the-bill Glen Campbell, who later played on the band's 1966 masterpiece *Pet Sounds*.

TOP RIGHT These opening dates in Honolulu of the Beach Boys' 1964 Summer Safari Tour came just three days after they had finished recording their *Christmas Album!* The Safari package was much augmented for these Hawaiian parties—only the Kingsmen and Griffin completed the whole grueling tour, which finished four months, sixty-three venues, and some ninety shows later in Worcester, MA.

BOTTOM RIGHT This original Hatch Show Print poster uses distinctive fonts, deep blue and red inks, and a yellow background for a mixed 1964 package tour: LA rock 'n' roll, English folk, hot-rod (surf's meaner cousin), and the Ventures' northwestern instrumental rock. Johnny Rivers, who topped the bill, was outselling Chuck Berry with his versions of Berry's "Memphis" and "Maybelline."

HAROLD LEVENTHAL PRESENTS

"Folk Songs, Country & Blues"

Last Performance in New York
The Great Blues Singer from Houston, Texas
SAM 'LIGHTNIN' HOPKINS

First Performance this Season

THE NEW LOST CITY RAMBLERS
JOHN COHEN   ☆   MIKE SEEGER   ☆   TOM PALEY

CISCO HOUSTON

and introducing ZAREFAH STOREY

SAT. EVE., NOV. 26th 1960 that 8:30 P.M.
at ETHICAL SOCIETY AUDITORIUM 2 West 64th Street
(Corner Central Park West)

all seats $2.25 on Sale at Folklore Center, 110 McDougal Street, New York 12, GR 9-5987, or at Harold Leventhal Mgt. office, 200 West 37th Street, Room 901, JU 6-6553

PART PROCEEDS ENCAMPMENT FOR CITIZEN (SPONSORED BY THE AMERICAN ETHICAL UNION)

BLUES '65
CHUCK BERRY
SKIP JAMES
FIRST WEST COAST APPEARANCE

"BIG MAMA" THORNTON • FRED McDOWELL
CHAMBERS BROS. • LONG GONE MILES

CONCERTS AT 8:00 & 10:30
TICKETS: $2.00 & $3.00
TICKETS AVAILABLE AT THE BOX OFFICE
ALSO THE ASH GROVE & ALL AGENCIES

FEB. 26
SANTA MONICA CIVIC

A CONCERT OF
OLD TIME COUNTRY MUSIC WITH
THE NEW LOST CITY RAMBLERS

AND
THE LEGENDARY KENTUCKY MOUNTAIN BALLADEER AND 5 STRING BANJO VIRTUOSO
COUSIN EMMY
IN HER FIRST AND ONLY BAY AREA APPEARANCES

Tickets at: Sherman Clay, Oakland (444-8575); Breuners Berkeley (843-5583); Campus Records (843-3656); Record City (841-4652); ASUC Box Office (848-4815); Hut T-1 S.F. State; Tresidder Box Office, Stanford (321-2300);. Kepler's Book Shops in Palo Alto and Menlo Park.

PRICES
2.00
2.50
3.50

FRIDAY, APRIL 3 - 8:30	SAT., APRIL 4 - 8:30
GARFIELD JUNIOR HIGH SCHOOL (Rose and Josephine)	PALO ALTO HIGH SCHOOL AUDITORIUM (El Camino at Embarcadero)
BERKELEY	**PALO ALTO**

TOP LEFT Promoter Harold Leventhal was crucial to the success of the postwar folk revival with his support for key figures including Pete Seeger, Woody Guthrie, and Bob Dylan. Leventhal had suffered under McCarthyism, and this event was raising funds for the politically progressive American Ethical Union. The lineup demonstrates the eclectic mix of musical styles heard in coffeehouses at the time.

BOTTOM LEFT A simple but stylish use of typography rescues this one-color, image-free poster for a big-name blues lineup. Ash Grove, one of the ticket outlets for this event, was an influential LA folk and blues club, a cradle of the West Coast folk-rock scene, which included Ry Cooder and the Byrds.

ABOVE RIGHT A determinedly traditional style on this 1959 poster for determinedly traditional music, the New Lost City Ramblers had formed the previous year to emulate the sounds of musicians recorded on old 78 rpm records in the '20s and '30s. They often performed with Cousin Emmy, a popular radio star of the '30s whose career they helped to relaunch.

newport folk festival
july 22-25   1965

food and refreshments

Pete Seeger

A MUSICAL AFTERNOON IN
THE HILLS OF MARIN
for the benefit of
Phil Drath candidate for
congress, first congressional district
SATURDAY , June 4 ..... 2 p.m.
MT. TAMALPAIS THEATER
MT. TAMALPAIS STATE PARK,
Marin County

"mankind must put an end to war or war will put
an end to mankind." John F. Kennedy

admission : general $ 2.50, students
and children $ 1.00, children under
5 free

tickets : san rafael, the record king, 1134 - 4th st.
sausalito, tides book store, 749 bridgeway
petaluma, harmony music store, 43 petaluma
boulevard north
mill valley, greyhound bus station, throckmorton
and miller
santa rosa, apex book store, 29 santa rosa ave.
larkspur, drath for congress headquarters,
1137 magnolia ave.
san francisco, downtown center box office,
325 mason street

produced by mary ann zeller presents

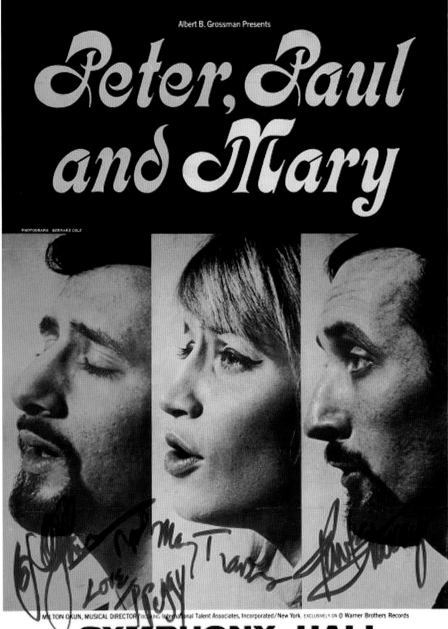

Albert B. Grossman Presents

Peter, Paul and Mary

PHOTOGRAPH BERNARD COLE

MILTON OKUN, MUSICAL DIRECTOR International Talent Associates, Incorporated/New York. EXCLUSIVELY ON Ⓠ Warner Brothers Records

SYMPHONY HALL
(formerly MOSQUE THEATRE) - 1020 Broad St - Newark, N. J.

SATURDAY NOVEMBER 13 at 8:30 PM

All Seats Reserved: $4.50, 4.00, 3.50, 2.75 - On Sale: Box Office
All Bamberger Stores - Newark Park Records - Village Records, So. Orange
Mail Orders to Symphony Hall - Enclose stamped, self-addressed envelope

---

TOP LEFT An evocative hand-drawn
sketch by Jonathan Shahan fills the cover
of the 1965 program of the influential
Newport folk event. The program included
a rambling two-page story by Bob Dylan.
Newport '63 had made him a folk star,
but on the last day of Newport '65, he
alienated some in the folk community by
going electric.

BOTTOM LEFT The jaunty cartoon image for
this 1964 fundraiser for Democrat and
antiwar campaigner Phil Drath concentrates
on Pete Seeger's role as troubadour,
ignoring his frequent clashes with the
American far right since the 1940s.
Seeger, a beacon of the US folk revival,
sang at the inauguration of President
Obama in 2009, just three months short
of the singer's ninetieth birthday.

ABOVE RIGHT This poster is an early
example of a tour blank with the blank
below the performers. Peter, Paul, and
Mary carried forward the '50s folk revival
torch into the '60s. They were brought
together by promoter Albert Grossman
and made their debut in the New York
coffeehouse the Bitter End in 1963,
two years before playing this rather
larger venue.

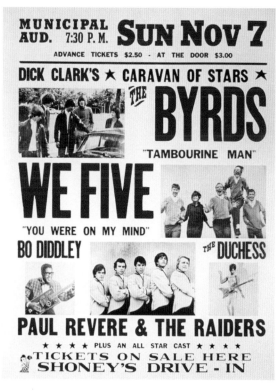

TOP LEFT Dick Clark, host of long-running TV pop show *American Bandstand*, capitalized on its popularity with this folk-rock-flavored live package in 1965. The poster is by Hatch Show Print, one of the first companies to introduce dot-etched photographic plates in its designs in the late '50s. The Duchess gets separate billing, but was really Bo Diddley's glamorous rhythm guitarist.

BOTTOM LEFT Folk City opened in 1960 in the former Gerdes Restaurant in Greenwich Village. Along with the Gaslight Club, it saw the earliest professional engagements of the promising new opening act Bob Dylan in 1961. Veteran blues headliners Lonnie Johnson and Victoria Spivey first played together in the 1920s, and in 1962 Dylan would contribute blues harp to a pair of Spivey albums.

ABOVE RIGHT Eric Von Schmidt's iconic 1965 tour blank for performances by the on- and off-stage partnership of the king and queen of the American Folk Revival. Schmidt was a painter and folk musician from Cambridge, MA, a center of the folk scene, from whom the young Dylan learned many traditional songs, including "House of the Rising Sun."

THE LOVIN' SPOONFUL

Kama Sutra Kama Sutra Kama Sutra Kama Sutra Kama Sutra Kama Sutra

FOREST HILLS TENNIS STADIUM
NEW YORK CITY
JUNE 24 - 1967
WITH SPECIAL APPEARANCE BY
JUDY COLLINS
TICKETS ON SALE AT ALL SINGER CENTERS

PAUL BUTTERFIELD BLUES BAND
JUNE25 TO JULY2

CAFE AU GO-GO

GREENWICH VILLAGE NEW YORK

THE LIVING END PRESENTS
Singer-Songwriter
JONI MITCHELL

OCTOBER 31ST
THROUGH
NOVEMBER 5TH

SHOW STARTS AT 9PM • YOU MUST BE 21
8225 JOHN C. LODGE • 872-4990

TOP LEFT The Lovin' Spoonful was in the US Top 20 with the single "Six O'Clock" in June 1967. But the group in the photo on this poster was not the group at the gig: their Canadian guitarist Zal Yanovsky (front left) had quit, shunned by the rock community for identifying his dealer to avoid deportation after a drug bust in San Francisco in May.

BOTTOM LEFT If ever a band was in the right place at the right time, it was the Butterfield Blues Band. They backed Bob Dylan when he went electric at Newport in 1965, played at Woodstock in 1969, and five days before this residency in the influential New York coffeehouse, Café Au Go Go (psychedelic artist unknown), they had been onstage at the landmark Monterey Pop Festival.

ABOVE RIGHT Detroit's Living End had been a regular venue for local folk duo Chuck and Joni Mitchell. When their marriage failed in May of 1967, Joni moved to New York. Other artists began to record her compositions, and her growing reputation as a singer-songwriter, trumpeted on this poster, earned her a six-night solo run back at the club later that year.

This Land is our Land

While the British mods used slick graphics and promotion to create something close to a parody of 1960s consumer society, American musicians who wanted to have control over their own creativity were moving in a whole different direction. The only real alternative to Beatlemania and the British Invasion was production-line pop like Phil Spector's Wall of Sound and New York's Brill Building, where songwriters like Jerry Goffin and Carole King turned out custom hits. Motown was layering a smooth mohair gloss on old-school R&B and inventing a new highly commercial pop-soul.

The only refuge from a cut-throat music industry was in folk clubs in New York, San Francisco, and campus towns all across the country. Folk venues were the only places where musicians with guitars and without commercial agendas could find a place to play. The US folk scene was a melting pot of eager neophytes and veterans who had sung through the Great Depression of the 1930s, and blues musicians who had been left high and dry by the collapse of the "chitlin'" circuit.

On the East Coast, Greenwich Village was home to a well-established creative subculture. Bob Dylan made his debut in the Village at Gerdes Folk City, and in the wake of the British Invasion new venues sprang up. The short-lived Café au Go Go (1964–69) began as a Village jazz and folk venue but later turned to rock and blues, and staged the first New York concert by the Grateful Dead. Its rival across the street, the Bitter End, was founded in 1961 as a folk club—it is still going strong (some fifty years later) on a diet of blues, folk, jazz, country, soul and, of course, rock. By the 1970s it was held in such high regard that a now-electric Dylan rehearsed and launched his Rolling Thunder Revue there.

On the West Coast, the local folk and surf music scenes were well served by a number of now-legendary clubs. Melrose Avenue in Los Angeles was home to the Ash Grove, a folk club that opened in 1958. Before it closed in 1973 it became a vital meeting point for old and new, a crossroads where trad blues, new rock, West Coast folk, and musicians from the East collided and exchanged musical ideas. From it emerged folk rock, blues, country, and solo performers such as Ry Cooder, Taj Mahal, Linda Ronstadt, Canned Heat, the Chambers Brothers, Chris Hillman, and Jackson Browne. Nearby on Santa Monica Boulevard, Doug Weston's Troubadour folk club became the hub of a new strand of folk rock, staging gigs by Joni Mitchell, James Taylor, Buffalo Springfield, the Eagles and others. Founded in 1957, it still operates today, and one aspect of its program is the promotion of new British bands with, for example, early American appearances by Radiohead and Coldplay.

In San Francisco, Barbara Dane opened her Sugar Hill coffeehouse in 1961. Dane was a folk singer who had crossed over to jazz, and Sugar Hill's strapline was "Home of the Blues." Her husband, folk singer Rolf Cahn, opened his own club a year later in Berkeley, called the Cabal. The Cabal closed in 1965, and the Sugar Hill shut sometime later; but the contribution of both clubs in presenting classic bluesmen to a young audience cannot be overestimated. The fusion of blues, folk, and rock became the West Coast Sound.

The freedom that could be found in the folk clubs was hard won. American folk music had traditionally close ties to activism and the political left. Major icons like Pete Seeger (a Party member) and Woody Guthrie (a committed sympathizer) were unashamedly left-leaning, and many folk artists had been blacklisted during the McCarthy witch-hunts of the 1950s. Political isolation had produced—by necessity—the kind of self-sufficiency that preferred to employ local artists to create their print and promotional material. Although diametrically different in style, both the British mods and

the American folk musicians were discovering that their music was really a part of a broader question of lifestyle.

Some of the folkies, though, might have been horrified to be compared to the likes of the Who. One of the more negative aspects of '60s folk music was its blind bias against rock and electric music. With a bizarre inverted racism, the folkies would tolerate an electric guitar in the hands of a black man in a sharp suit such as Muddy Waters, but if a white boy tried the same trick he'd be ostracized.

The energy generated by the growing scene fueled a major folk revival with Bob Dylan and Joan Baez as its reigning superstars, and Judy Collins and Phil Ochs following in their wake. Members of the Byrds, the Grateful Dead, Jefferson Airplane, and the Buffalo Springfield were all making their bones in folk, but many, led by no less than Dylan himself, were increasingly drawn to electric rock 'n' roll. The outrage caused by Dylan appearing with an electric band at the 1965 Newport Folk Festival also set a course for the psychedelic late '60s, when all things seemed possible.

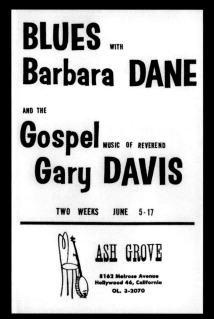

ABOVE LEFT & RIGHT As well as opening and running her own blues and folk club, Sugar Hill, Barbara Dane had been singing at demonstrations for race equality since the '40s, forming natural musical alliances with black blues and jazz singers, including Lightnin' Hopkins and Louis Armstrong. She was a committed opponent of the Vietnam War and in 1966 became the first American musician to tour communist Cuba. In 1970 she set up her own record label to release international protest music. Still singing and protesting, she celebrated her eighty-fifth birthday in 2012 with a coffeehouse performance in Berkeley, CA.

"First of all, I'm a singer, and I've always been a singer. I'm a mom. I'm a producer—well, overall, I'm a resister, I guess . . . something of an explainer, or sometimes a teacher."

BARBARA DANE

UNIQUE CUISINE   COFFEES & DRINKS

Bringing You The Finest in Music & Art

THE NEW ASH GROVE

8162 Melrose Ave.   OL 39193

SCHEDULE OF FEATURED ATTRACTIONS

July 25,26,27   FOLK MUSIC FESTIVAL
                Brownie McGee*Barbara
                Dane*Guy Carawan*Kate
                Hoyt*Bess Hawes*Sam
                Hinton

Aug 1   Guy Carawan*Brownie
                McGee*Kate Hoyt*
                Lynn Gold*Ed Michel

Aug 2   POETRY & JAZZ
                conducted by Lawrence
                Lipton**Featuring
                the Jazz Canto Quertet
                and work of leading
                contemporary poets
(winners of the Ash Grove Poetry Contest
will have their entries read to music.
The final winning entry will be included
in Mr. Lipton's next poetry and jazz
recording. Entries must be submitted
by Aug 1 to the Ash Grove by mail or
in person.)

Aug 3   Guy Carawan*Brownie
                McGee

Aug 8,9   Guy Carawan*Brownie
                McGee*Kate Hoyt

Aug 10   CLASSICAL CONCERT
                Tania Agins-piano
                Fred Katz-cello

THE GALLERY ROOM****OPEN NIGHTLY
Entertainment by guitarist Ed Michel

Benefit Concert!!!

PETE SEEGER

Singing for peace and justice in support of
The Grass Roots Cultural Center

FRI.
FEB. 25

232-5009
RESERVE SEATING
CALIFORNIA THEATRE
Tickets available: Grass Roots, 1947 30th St. at Grape St., San Diego, 92102
and all Ticketron outlets. $8 advance, $9.50 at door 8pm
Join the Grass Roots Sustainers and receive two free tickets.

ABOVE LEFT A crudely copied flyer illustrates the eclectic creative mix served by LA's Ash Grove. Poetry and jazz are sandwiched between folk, blues, and classical music. The club's founder Ed Pearl also staged performances by radical protesters such as Lenny Bruce and Jane Fonda. It was this meeting of different genres that inspired the club's clientele to make new folk and country music for the psychedelic age.

ABOVE RIGHT The Grass Roots Cultural Center was an alternative bookshop in San Diego at the heart of the city's progressive community. It's no surprise that radical folk singer Pete Seeger supported it with this benefit concert. The poster includes a stereotypical image of the Protest Singer—revolutionary cap, microphone, acoustic guitar—which, after all, Seeger helped to create.

3

Psychedelia

1965–1972

The '60s Poster Renaissance

By the mid-1960s, the seismic shift in youth culture and the emergence of a new kind of rock music meant that poster design evolved alongside new tastes and demands. It all peaked in what the media coined the "Summer of Love" in 1967. San Francisco may have been the original epicenter but it quickly went viral, spreading across the country and then going international.

In the wake of Ken Kesey's acid tests, "happenings" had been taking place in the Bay Area. Promoted by the San Francisco music-promotion group Family Dog, the first dance-inspired event was held at the Longshoremen's Hall on Fisherman's Wharf on October 16, 1965. By the standards of what was to come, the handbill—designed by Alton Kelley—was conventional, little more than a handwritten flyer giving the date, time, venue, and bands. Less than a year later, there had been such an explosion that poster design left behind the bounded, the fixed, and all the rules. Psychedelic artwork saw the more staid conventions of op art completely lose their rigidity to flow and melt in a fashion akin to what was going on in the head of an acid tripper. This was also reflected in the way the psychedelic light shows worked in the ballrooms, with the performers and even the audience obscured by amoebic bubbles and other images projected via colored-oil slides.

For the new breed of poster artists, any image was fair game—they stole from any number of sources. Native Americans and the American West of a century before, Egyptology, Zen mandalas, religious iconography, Ringling Bros. and Barnum & Bailey Circus, Japanese woodcuts, hot-rod designs, old Hollywood movies, comic and cartoon characters, even Walt Disney. The end result, informed by the prevalent drug culture right down to the mind-blowing color separation in the lettering, vividly reflected the music that was being played in the ballrooms and clubs they advertised. As the Grateful Dead's drummer Mickey Hart put it, "The posters looked like what we were playing. They were an open call to come and have fun . . . the posters didn't just announce the concerts, they resonated with the style of the times and described visually what the Grateful Dead, Big Brother, Quicksilver, and the Airplane were doing at the Fillmore and the Avalon the following nights."

In order to produce the lettering, images, and colors to maximum psychedelic effect, the pioneer designers also had to experiment with the printing process itself, and even invent modifications to the machinery. To create the rainbow color effects, either by silkscreen or offset lithography, the ink feeders had to be split so the colors could be run together in a single impression to give the effect of multicolored ink.

San Francisco boasted the creative fulcrum of poster pioneers, working flat out to advertise the burgeoning dances and happenings scene as the City by the Bay began to fill up with more and more young Americans looking for the hippie dream. The counterculture spread like wildfire across the country—artists such as Rick Griffin and Victor Moscoso also created posters for the Shrine in Los Angeles—and soon there were ballrooms and longhair haunts in most major cities in North America. In Middle America local scenes had their own clubs and designers. They may have carried certain hallmarks of their Californian counterparts, but these artists added their own idiosyncratic visions to the scene.

> "The '60s posters were where fine art and commercial art met. It was a great time. It meant breaking all the rules."
>
> STANLEY MOUSE

The phenomenal growth of the psychedelic poster mirrored the unprecedented global media frenzy over the hippie phenomenon as a whole. The summer of 1967 saw counterculture icons, including poster designers like Griffin and Wes Wilson, on the cover of *Life* magazine. By the summer's end the businessmen had moved in and hippie paraphernalia was big business. Although there seemed to be an insatiable appetite for posters, by 1972 the poster boom had collapsed. As Airplane drummer Spencer Dryden commented at the time, "The poster thing got ridiculous. You go down on Haight Street and man, people are making posters for the sake of making posters . . . A poster in the first place was made 'cause it was an artistic ad. Now they're putting posters out so they'll be ads again!" Perhaps, ultimately, it was simply down to wall space. People had collected enough. And the music business, recognizing the part posters had played in the promotion of the music, resolved to make the phenomenon continue and killed the demand.

As aspects of the counterculture were absorbed into the mainstream, many of the poster pioneers continued to produce outstanding work in a different context. Alton Kelley and Stanley Mouse adapted their styles to keep pace with the changing rock scenes of the '70s, '80s, and beyond. Griffin and Greg Irons, now both deceased, diversified and for a while worked in the medium of comic books. Nigel Waymouth pursued a career as a painter and much-sought-after portraitist, while psychedelic-poster king Wes Wilson severed his ties with the scene and moved to the rural peace of the Ozarks.

OPPOSITE The area around the junction of the Haight and Ashbury Streets in San Francisco, near the eastern entrance to the Golden Gate Park, was the public epicenter of the hippie movement. The down-at-heel district offered cheap housing for individuals who flocked from all over the US in search of the hippie dream.

TOP LEFT As the Summer of Love unfolded in San Francisco, the Grateful Dead carried the West Coast sound eastward. Daniel Fennell designed the poster for the Dead's first New York appearance—a classic piece of 1967 psychedelia with its obscure lettering and color-clashing collage of images.

BOTTOM LEFT Designed by Stanley Mouse in 1966, the images of Winnie the Pooh and Piglet are based on the drawings of E.H. Shepard, the English artist and book illustrator known for his work for Kenneth Grahame and A. A. Milne. Pooh and Piglet are used to advertise this congress for peace at Mt. Tamalpais Outdoor Theater.

ABOVE RIGHT Classic 1967 artwork from Hapshash using their trademark silver, black and white, and printed by Osiris Agency to advertise the debut single by Tomorrow, a quartet that featured singer Keith West (of *A Teenage Opera* fame) and lead guitarist Steve Howe (later of Yes). The band was a mainstay of UFO and the underground scene.

ABOVE LEFT The third Isle of Wight Festival took place at East Afton Farm on August 26–30 and was promoted by Fiery Creations. Designed by David Fairbrother-Roe, who also produced the artwork for previous festivals, the 1970 event boasted the starriest bill to date. The festival marked the last live UK appearance by Jimi Hendrix, and was marred by sections of the audience who wanted it to be a free event.

TOP RIGHT The second Isle of Wight Festival on August 29–31, 1969, heralded Bob Dylan's first live public performance in three years. David Fairbrother-Roe came up with the design, which was used not only for the posters but also the program and tickets. The artwork shows the era's love of classic Hollywood, here adapting images from the 1933 Merian C. Cooper and Ernest B. Schoedsack feature film, *King Kong*.

BOTTOM RIGHT Cartoonist Edward Barker worked extensively on the UK's first underground newspaper, *International Times* (*IT*) and seldom branched out into poster design. And yet his Phun City Festival poster (Barker was the festival's co-organizer), held on the south coast of England in the summer of 1970, shows his mischievous sense of humor is present in the central image of the Robert Crumb-like dancing man.

TOP LEFT By 1969, the psychedelic poster boom in the UK was over and even collectives like Hapshash were exploring new avenues of creativity. This poster for a commercial pop festival in the Midlands suggests that two years after its peak, the new art boom was not only over but marketing was once again looking at tried-and-trusted styles from the late '50s and early '60s to advertise live music events.

BOTTOM LEFT As the world cashed in on flower-power paraphernalia, standards quickly dropped. This poster, designed and printed by EBM Studios for a pop concert at the Royal Albert Hall, suggests that everyone wanted a slice of the paisley pie—it is a rather half-hearted mix of the establishment (a photo of the Victorian venue) jazzed up with some colored psychedelic lettering and Day-Glo shapes to give it a "trippy" effect.

ABOVE RIGHT In the immediate aftermath of the psychedelic explosion, the British music scene underwent a blues boom and the accompanying marketing reverted to a more basic style of presentation more in line with poster artwork of the early '60s. This poster uses a central image that is pure "psychedelic Aubrey Beardsley" in the tradition of Hapshash and the Coloured

Coat (although not designed by them), while advertising a central London gig by two no-nonsense blues boomers, Fleetwood Mac and one-man band Duster Bennett, both acts signed to Blue Horizon Records.

ABOVE LEFT Though formed in Holland, the Fool collective did most of its work in swinging London, most famously painting the façade on the Fab Four's Baker Street Apple Boutique. Founding member Simon Posthuma would later say that their "mission" was to introduce "bright colors in a grey world of pinstriped suits and homburgs under a dreary sky." This poster for the Apple Boutique perfectly realized the collective's mission statement.

TOP RIGHT This is a beautifully intricate, idealized and highly romanticized drawing of Dylan in 1967, created by Fool founder Marijke Koger, in red ink on a yellow background. The effect is warm and charming, and phantasmagorical, with its nymphs and fairies creating a feeling redolent of Arthur Rackham; and it is one that rather belies the cutting-edge modernism of its subject.

BOTTOM RIGHT The follow-up to the 1968 Newport Pop Festival had to be moved to a new location in Northridge, CA, at Devonshire Downs, following complaints from locals at the original Orange County venue. The poster—designed by Bob Masse—boasted a potent bill of top rock, soul, and blues musicians. It's worth noting how, by 1969, rock posters were generally using less visually mind-blowing ways to get their message across. As the star performer, Hendrix's image dominates the design and the guitarist was paid $50,000 for his appearance, the total cost of the 1968 event the year previously.

OPPOSITE Based on a photograph taken by noted rock photographer Linda Eastman (later McCartney), Martin Sharp's swirling image of guitarist Jimi Hendrix is one of his most enduring. It was later used as the front cover for both the first-ever anthology of rock posters, *Get On Down*, and Richard Neville's memoir, *Hippie Hippie Shake*.

LEFT Designed by Hapshash and the Coloured Coat and produced by Joe Boyd's Osiris Poster Company for the underground avant-garde Soft Machine, in 1967. One of the pioneering aspects of Hapshash was their frequent use of expensive silver and gold inks. The silver creates a fine backdrop for the art nouveau-style imagery, while the bold red lettering makes perfect use of curve and line.

ABOVE LEFT Michael English and Nigel Waymouth secured their first job together designing posters for the UFO (Unlimited Freak Out) Club in London, in December 1966. The club's co-founders, Joe Boyd and John Hopkins, believed that this creative combination "would result in something special." Initially calling themselves Cosmic Colours, they changed their name to Hapshash and the Coloured Coat in March '67.

Critic George Melly described their work as "a rubbery synthesis of Disney and Mabel Lucy Atwell taken to the edge of illegibility."

TOP RIGHT One of Hapshash's most celebrated posters, advertising a Jimi Hendrix Experience show at the Fillmore, San Francisco, in 1967, the designers cast the guitarist as a Native American chief with a bow and arrow in one hand and peace pipe in the other (Hendrix was half Cherokee). Using otherworldly blues, oranges, and reds, the poster reinforces its aboriginal connections with an elk skull in the bottom left-hand corner.

BOTTOM RIGHT Here Hapshash and the Coloured Coat wrap an image of singer Arthur Brown, self-proclaimed "God of Hell Fire," into a dragon and serpents' lair. Not content to infuse it with foreboding psychedelic hues and colors, the pair also threw in classic images they absorbed growing up. The poster manages to achieve maximum color effect without sacrificing harmony or balance.

70 71 **ABOVE LEFT** A gorgeous, cosmic poster by Hapshash and the Coloured Coat advertising the Pink Floyd appearance at London's UFO Club in the summer of 1967. At the time the band, led by a still-functioning Syd Barrett, were at the top of their game and were darlings of the underground; that did not stop them enjoying pop hits in the national charts with the likes of "See Emily Play."

TOP RIGHT Not long after Martin Sharp arrived from Australia to help set up the UK version of *Oz* magazine, he met guitarist Eric Clapton at the Pheasantry in Chelsea. This chance encounter led to a long and fruitful association with Clapton and his band, Cream. Published by Peter Ledeboer's company Big O in 1967, this poster reveals Sharp's love of the collage technique.

BOTTOM RIGHT Produced for the *International Times'* benefit concert at the Alexandra Palace in south London in April 1967, this silkscreen print was designed by Mike McInnerney, the publication's art editor. "I never tired of watching people float around during these events," he said, "occasionally blowing bubbles, totally self absorbed." The poster was produced using two printings, and as the print process progressed, the inks were changed at the bottom and top of the poster and blended with one pull of the squeegee, thereby making each poster unique.

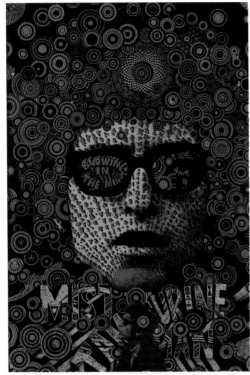

TOP LEFT When the Summer of Love hit, Bob Dylan was recuperating near Woodstock in upstate New York after his near-fatal motorcycle crash. Dylan kept his distance, and his albums from that era reflect a strong back-to-roots feel that was at odds with the prevailing hippie ethos. Here, Martin Sharp gives Dylan a work-over in celebration of his pot-inspired classic, "Tambourine Man."

BOTTOM LEFT Inspired by the Donovan hit song "Sunshine Superman," this poster typifies Sharp's approach. The expatriate Australian pioneered litho printing using silver and gold foil boards, which he uses here in the area around the central photo of the singer. Sharp would take the silver foil technique to its logical conclusion on Cream's *Wheels of Fire* sleeve.

ABOVE RIGHT Unlike his contemporaries working the UK underground scene, some of Martin Sharp's best late-'60s art had a crazed, kinetic edge, as evidenced in this 1967 advert for the UFO club. The wavy lines, love hearts, and surrealistic dismembered guitar player on a silver foil background perfectly capture the energy of headliners Dantalian's Chariot, a band that boasted what many believe was the greatest lightshow of the era.

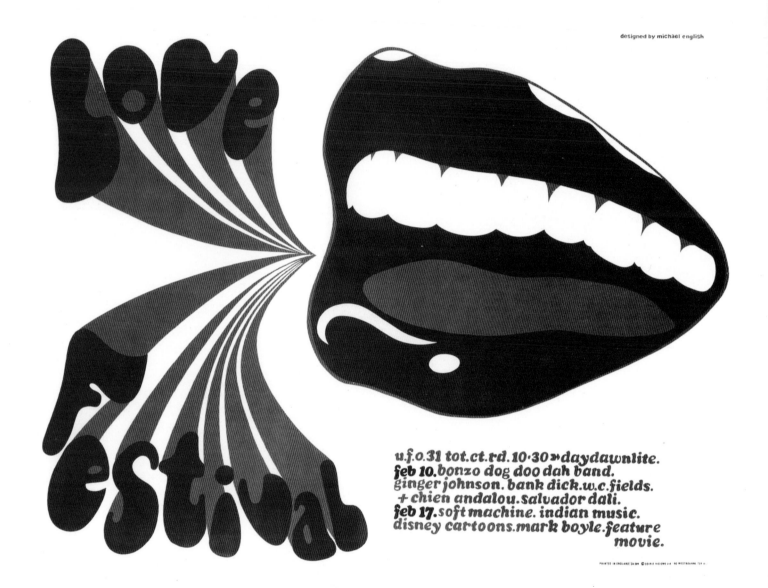

designed by michael english

u.f.o.31 tot.ct.rd.10·30»daydawnlite.
feb 10.bonzo dog doo dah band.
ginger johnson. bank dick.w.c.fields.
+ chien andalou.salvador dali.
feb 17.soft machine. indian music.
disney cartoons.mark boyle.feature
                                movie.

PRINTED IN ENGLAND/24.5M © OSIRIS VISIONS LTD. R2 WESTBOURNE TER H.

ABOVE This 1967 poster by Michael English, advertising upcoming gigs at the UFO Club by the Bonzos and the Soft Machine—as part of the Love Festival— was inspired by Man Ray's painting *Observatory Time*. The silkscreen poster sports a pair of giant sensual Day-Glo pink lips with gleaming white teeth and tendrils blossoming into big fat letters.

ABOVE LEFT David Wills of Oz Publications Ink had studied at the fabled Twickenham College of Art in the early '60s alongside graphic artist Barney Bubbles. In 1968 the pair had collaborated on the *Oz* issue twelve, *Tax Dodge Special*. This poster was designed for a benefit gig to raise funds for the *Oz School Kids' Issue* obscenity trial. The repressive climate that came in its wake forced Wills to quit the UK for California.

TOP RIGHT This comparatively orthodox-looking poster, designed for American satirical band the Mothers of Invention, features core artwork by Cal Schenkel (who designed the band's LP cover), with Michael English adding the lettering and reclining nude. In 1969, following the flop of their musical endeavors, English and Waymouth dissolved their partnership, and English would go on to explore hyper-real art.

BOTTOM RIGHT From 1966 onward, Gary Grimshaw was principal poster artist for Detroit's ballroom, the Grande. Produced for an inspired double bill of Sun Ra and MC5 at the Community Arts Auditorium in Detroit, the poster employs concentric lines around the central image (a head and shoulders shot of the great Sun Ra himself) to create a spatial, cosmic feel that perfectly captures the flavor of the evening's music.

The Psychedelic Ballrooms

In 1965 America was in the full throes of experiencing the Beatles and the rest of the British Invasion bands. The music-promotion group the Family Dog started out as a loose aggregation of nascent hippies intent on bringing rock 'n' roll dances to the Bay Area. These early Dog collective members included Ellen Harmon, Alton Kelley, Jack Towle, and Luria Castell. The latter, a native of San Francisco and former political activist, had a vision that ran along the lines of "San Francisco can be the American Liverpool." The group's first show that October, at the Longshoreman's Hall—entitled "A tribute to Dr. Strange" and featuring the Jefferson Airplane, Great Society, and the Charlatans—was the first gathering of the tribes, and a huge success.

Chet Helms subsequently stepped in as the Family Dog's main organizer and, from January 1966, Helms was running dances at San Francisco's California Hall and the Open Theater. Meanwhile Bill Graham was hiring the Fillmore Auditorium in the city for similar functions.

Helms and his Family Dog finally found their spiritual home at the Avalon, an old dancehall on the corner of Sutter and Van Ness at 1268 Sutter Street. The Avalon was known for its eclectic bills showcasing not only local but also big names of the era as well as community and political events. To promote his dances and shows, Helms gathered around him the cream of poster artists. As well as the so-called Big Five—Wes Wilson, Alton Kelley, Stanley Mouse, Rick Griffin, and Victor Moscoso—he employed other talented designers, such as Robert Fried and Bob Schnepf.

Indeed, Helms was the archetypal hippie, a philanthropist who was not in it for the money. One inevitable consequence of this hippie state of mind was that Helms often experienced financial problems, and he finally quit the full-time promotion business in the early 1970s. By contrast, Bill Graham, who ran the Fillmore, was always viewed as a hard-headed businessman. Graham first hired the Fillmore for a benefit gig in late 1965 and saw the possibilities of using the venue for dances and concerts.

The original "Fillmore" was situated in the city's black-populated district, on Fillmore Street and Geary, and Graham began promoting eclectic bills that were similar to those promoted by Helms, although the Family Dog was always regarded as having a much more laid-back atmosphere. After a show on July 4, 1968, featuring Creedence Clearwater Revival, Graham took over the larger Carousel Ballroom (located at 10 South Van Ness Avenue), which had recently been used by local bands (including the Grateful Dead) to put on shows. Rechristening the auditorium the Fillmore West, Graham continued to promote there until 1971.

Graham opened the Fillmore East in 1968 as an East Coast equivalent of his fabled San Francisco venue. Located on Second Avenue near East 6th Street in the East Village, New York City, the building had been both a Yiddish theater and a movie house. The venue started promoting music in 1967, and Graham opened its doors for the first time on March 8, 1968, with a show by Big Brother & the Holding Company. Graham decided to shut his Fillmore operations on June 27, 1971.

Constructed in 1928 at 8952 Grand River Avenue in Detroit, the Grande was initially a multipurpose building that included retail outlets on its first floor and a ballroom on the second. In 1966 it was acquired by local teacher and DJ Russ Gibb, who'd just returned from San Francisco where he'd witnessed the early days of the Fillmore. Teaming up with local activist and band manager John Sinclair, the two soon made the Grande Ballroom the Midwestern equivalent of the Avalon and its counterparts.

Sadly, the Grande closed its doors in 1972 and has rarely been used since. By the early '70s, rock audiences were getting far bigger than the ballrooms could handle—massive outdoor festivals became the norm, and rock moved into the sports stadiums. The era of the psychedelic ballroom and its poster culture had come to an end.

> "These posters are so much more than just historical documents or promotional tools for our business; they are art, as the music itself is art, and in many cases they are very fine, high art."
>
> BILL GRAHAM (FROM *THE ART OF ROCK* BY PAUL GRUSHKIN)

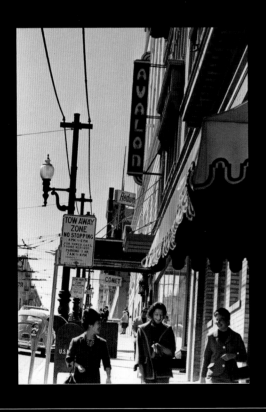

ABOVE LEFT The Avalon Ballroom, located at 1268 Sutter Street, San Francisco, was home to Chet Helms's Family Dog. Between April 1966 and November 1968, the Family Dog produced promotional handbills and posters for the Avalon that are now regarded as original pieces of art in their own right. The work was originated by all of the top designers, including Alton Kelley, Stanley Mouse, Rick Griffin, Victor Moscoso, and Wes Wilson.

ABOVE RIGHT A classic Rick Griffin artwork, with the artist at the peak of his powers employing a visceral bleeding heart and almost illegible, eye-burning lettering to advertise this Family Dog concert. The program featured Quicksilver Messenger Service and Kaleidoscope at the Avalon Ballroom, from January 12 to 14, 1968.

ABOVE LEFT Known as "The Seed," this was the granddaddy of the San Francisco poster art explosion. Designed by Charlatans' band members George Hunter and Mike Ferguson in 1965, it harks back to a Victoriana feel of frontier days. Because the group was late in starting their residency at the Red Dog Saloon, two versions of the poster exist with different dates from June '65.

TOP RIGHT Less colorful than his late-'60s work, this poster for Zappa and Alice Cooper at Cal State Fullerton on November 8, 1972, retains Griffin's predilection for the visceral, using a number of Viking-helmeted, sword-wielding eyeballs to maximum effect. Cooper, who was about to become a huge international act, had been produced by Zappa for his label Straight Records.

BOTTOM RIGHT This pharaonic-style image with the "Steal Your Face" logo on the headphones and its reference to the Egyptian *Book of the Dead* is in perfect keeping with the band's ethos. Griffin worked with the Grateful Dead until his death in 1991 but he produced this 1984 poster independently; few examples remain, as the band's management took most of the copies from him outside the show at Berkeley Community Theater.

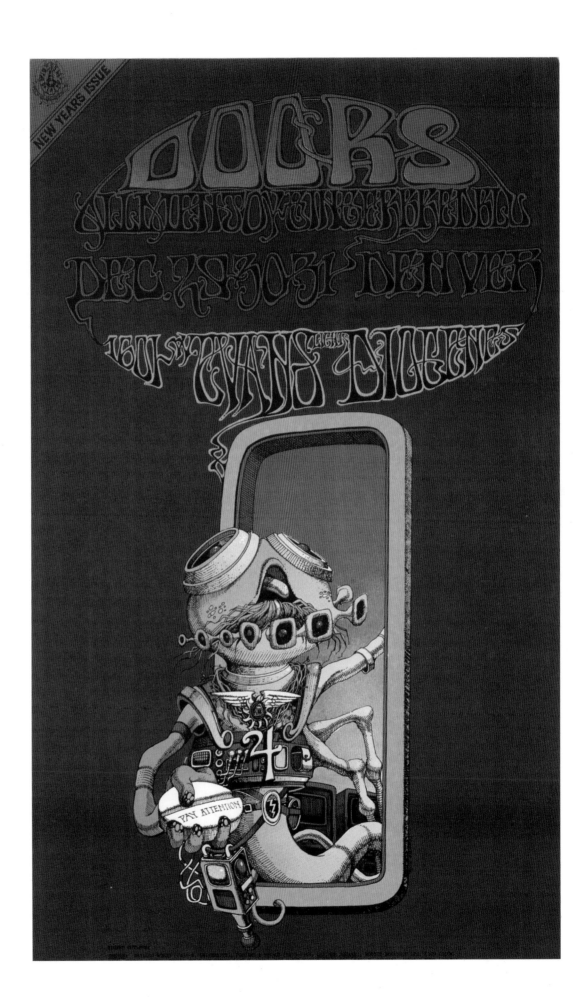

TOP LEFT This clever concept by Victor Moscoso is one of a series produced for his Neon Rose Company. Moscoso realized that he and his fellow poster pioneers would see little financial reward for their labors for Family Dog and Bill Graham, so he decided to create and distribute his own series of posters for shows at the Matrix Club. This bold and highly stylistic design was created for the Chambers Brothers in March 1967.

BOTTOM LEFT The Matrix Club was one of the first places in San Francisco to nurture the burgeoning psychedelic rock sound. Leidenthal, who created a number of posters for the venue in 1967, produced a red ink drawing of the Cheshire Cat for a concert by Big Brother. Earlier Matrix posters and handbills included both two-color and black-and-white designs.

ABOVE RIGHT A truly iconic design—an early collaboration by Alton Kelley and Stanley Mouse—that later became a recurring motif in the Grateful Dead's iconography. The poster for the band's appearance at the Avalon Ballroom in 1966 was influenced by Edmund J. Sullivan's illustrations for the *Rubaiyat of Omar Khayyam*.

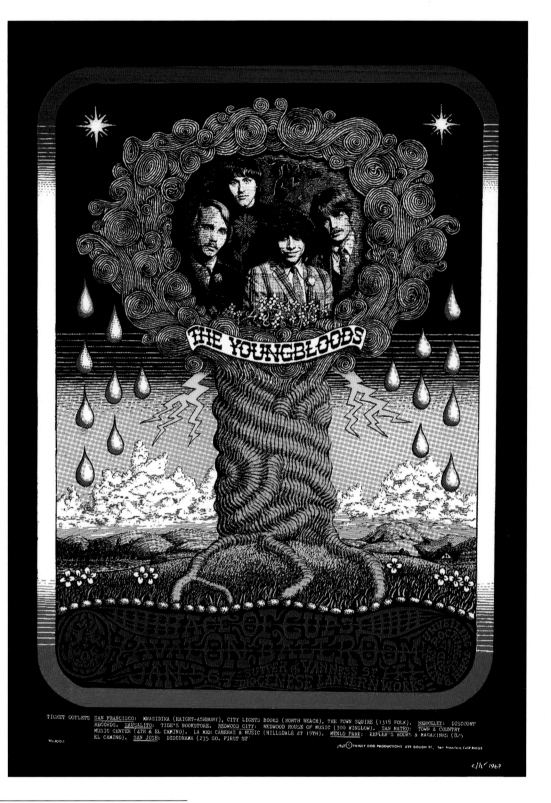

TOP LEFT Designed by Wes Wilson in 1966 (the title "Tribal Stomp" and the photograph was suggested by Family Dog promoter Chet Helms), the poster's influential lettering style already shows a degree of sophistication. This poster was the first of many to incorporate Native Americans as the central image.

BOTTOM LEFT In this early work for the Avalon by Wes Wilson, the Family Dog logo—a top-hatted, cigarette-smoking Native American with the motto, "May the baby Jesus shut your mouth, and open your mind"—is used as the central image against a backdrop of the colors of the American flag.

ABOVE RIGHT This is a rare example of a poster designed by the painter Charles Laurens Heald in 1968. The artist moved to the Bay Area in the mid-'60s and began to paint full-time. The headlining act, the Youngbloods—a drawing of the band members is in the "cloud tree"—moved to the West Coast from New York, and had one of the big hits of the Summer of Love, the anthemic "Get Together."

LEFT Bob Fried was a commercial artist who relocated to San Francisco from New York. Inspired by the burgeoning poster explosion and encouraged by Victor Moscoso, Fried began to produce his own posters. This 1968 artwork illustrates his driving principal—to keep the design simple so as to convey a feeling of dimensional space, similar to that experienced during an acid trip.

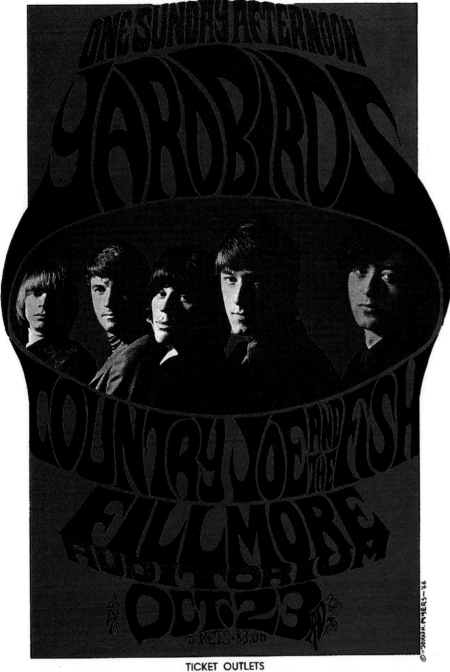

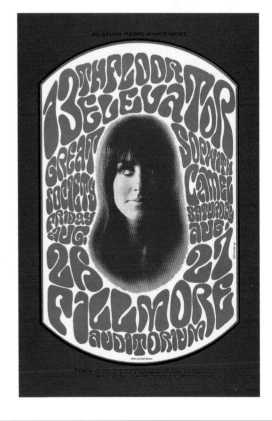

ABOVE LEFT Hailing from New York City, John H. Myers worked on various posters and handbills as well as on buttons and bumper stickers for shows at the Matrix, Avalon, and Fillmore in '66 and '67. The Yardbirds were hugely popular in the US; the photograph in this 1966 design includes the short-lived classic twin-guitar lineup of Jeff Beck and Jimmy Page.

TOP RIGHT A fine example of Wes Wilson's brilliance with lettering—he fills up the whole frame, creating shapes out of words. Given Wilson's lack of formal training, the lettering, which is inspired by art nouveau typefaces and draftsmanship, is superb.

BOTTOM RIGHT Although not the headline act, this poster makes intriguing use of a photo made by Herb Greene of the attractive Grace Slick, the Great Society's lead singer, and later star of Jefferson Airplane. The 13th Floor Elevators, LSD-inspired rock pioneers from Austin, TX, featuring lead singer Roky Erickson, were regular visitors to both the Fillmore and Avalon ballrooms.

ABOVE LEFT When Bill Graham's main designer Wes Wilson quit in May 1967, he called upon other artists, including his wife Bonnie MacLean, to deal with the demanding weekly schedule of shows. In the early days, MacLean's job was to collect tickets, pass out handbills, and count receipts. Suddenly, from drawing lists of current band lineups and coming attractions on a chalkboard at the top of the Fillmore's stairs, she was thrust into the spotlight—a role she was admirably up to fulfilling, as her poster design for the Jim Kweskin Jug Band attests.

TOP RIGHT Though largely untrained in graphic design, Bonnie MacLean created some memorable posters for the Fillmore, including this example for Paul Butterfield and Cream, which employs an ornate, medieval-gothic style, and exudes the spirituality of the '60s counterculture.

BOTTOM RIGHT MacLean followed in the psychedelic traditions established by Wes Wilson, but she started to add her own distinctive touches, such as Native American totem poles and Nehru jackets. Her recurring motif, as evidenced in this poster for the Yardbirds and the Doors, was the human face, with expressions ranging from the beatific, as illustrated here, to those of hypnotic intensity.

BILL GRAHAM PRESENTS IN SAN FRANCISCO

RIGHT Wes Wilson's style had been copied by so many artists that when a dispute over remuneration with Bill Graham caused him to quit, his replacements provoked barely a ripple. This design, advertising bluesman Otis Rush, is classic Wilson, with its exaggerated lettering, pastel colorways, and wavy lines—a superb evocation of Wilson's desire to produce art for an audience that was "tuned into the psychedelic experience."

ABOVE LEFT A poster by Nicholas Kouninos that commemorates the first gig in San Francisco by one of the Summer of Love's biggest bands, Procol Harum, in November 1967. Leader Gary Brooker would later credit the Fillmore with "the absolute making of our whole style." A mythological lion and griffin, which allude to the band's British roots, are woven into Kouninos's vertical design.

ABOVE RIGHT Produced in postcard format only, this work by Bonnie Green, who created a number of designs for the Grande Ballroom during this period, employs highly colored images in the vein of art produced by Holland's The Fool. The "postcard" was promoting Kensington Market, Pacific Gas & Electric, Renaissance Faire, and MC5 at the Grande on October 18, 1968.

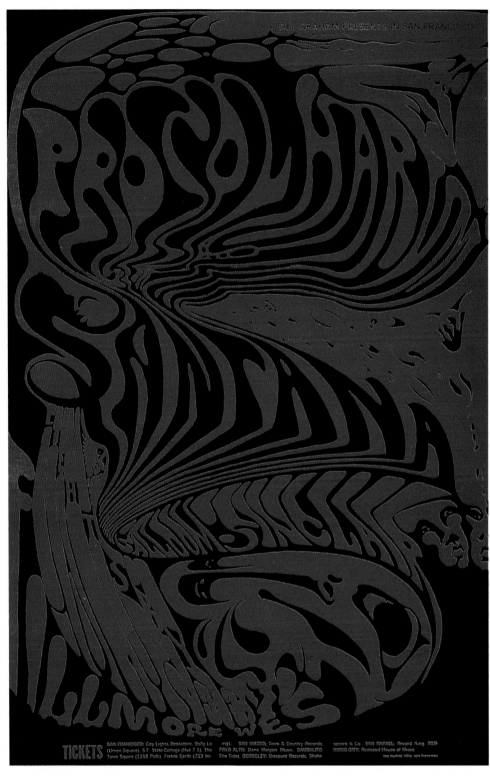

TOP LEFT Designed by cartoonist Bernard "Hap" Kliban, this was a benefit show for New Stage and Straight Theater, with Moby Grape, Big Brother and the Holding Company, Country Joe and the Fish, and the Sparrow, at Avalon Ballroom on March 5, 1967. The Straight, situated in the very heart of the hippie district, was a former cinema that members of the hip community were successfully converting into an Avalon/Fillmore-style venue.

BOTTOM LEFT Situated to the north of San Francisco, at Sausalito, the Ark was a popular destination for bands that had been playing the city's ballrooms earlier in the evening. Moby Grape had a close association with the club, using it both as a rehearsal space and for live gigs. Many of the Ark posters were regarded as crude and were ignored by collectors of the era. This is arguably one of the best.

ABOVE RIGHT Lee Conklin produced a prolific body of work for the Fillmore West. Between 1968 and 1969 he created thirty-one posters. His aim was to translate the hallucinatory journey of the drug experience on to paper, and he frequently worked while coming down from an acid trip. His designs incorporated morphing grotesque images, as might be envisioned under the influence of LSD, to fill every part of the page.

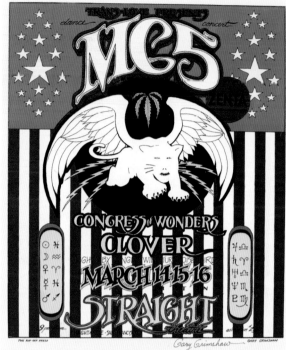

ABOVE LEFT After Bill Graham moved his operation to new premises, San Francisco's very own sons the Flamin' Groovies took over the original venue on Geary Boulevard and promoted some shows there in 1970, hence the title the New Old Fillmore. This fine-looking poster by Mark T. Behrens advertises an evening of no-nonsense rock 'n' roll from two like-minded bands.

TOP RIGHT A superbly ironic use of the Stars and Stripes to herald three nights in San Francisco by the fiercest anti-establishment, politically radical band of the late '60s, Detroit's MC5. Gary Grimshaw employs imagery including the ubiquitous marijuana leaf, astrological signs, and the central winged cat signifying the MC5's strong affiliation with the White Panther Party, founded by manager John Sinclair.

BOTTOM RIGHT In the wake of his success with the Grande, promoter Russ Gibb cast his net farther afield and staged the First Annual Rock & Roll Revival at the Michigan State Fairgrounds in May 1969. Grimshaw's poster reveals a stunning lineup of Midwest acts and stars from beyond, such as Dr. John (from New Orleans) and Johnny Winter (Texas). Marred by bad weather, the event still drew between 25,000 and 30,000 fans.

OPPOSITE Celebrating Abraham Lincoln's 158th birthday with a zany, cartoonlike Abe wearing a Paisley-patterned top hat, this event poster by an unknown artist featured a great bill headlined by the Mojo Men—one of the first psychedelic groups produced by Sly Stone for DJ and scene-maker Tom Donahue's Autumn label. Note that Love, later to emerge as one of the most influential bands of the era, are featured lower on the bill.

Sparta Advertising Club
San Jose, California

BIG ABE'S BIRTHDAY PARTY • SANTA CLARA COUNTY FAIRGROUNDS • SATURDAY, FEBRUARY 11, 1967 • 8:30 P.M. • $2.50

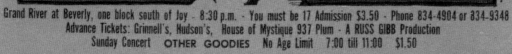

OPPOSITE, TOP RIGHT Due to the restricted budgets, many of the Grande shows were advertised in postcard format—including this one for the Jeff Beck Group in 1968. "Within a year I got to the point where I could make the posters look the way I wanted them," commented Grimshaw. "I found it hardest to deal with the multiple colors; one of my key tasks was learning mechanical separations and how to obtain effects with film overlays."

OPPOSITE, BOTTOM RIGHT The human skull and demon on a dark purple background creates the perfect sinister twilight ambience for three shows headlined by Detroit bad boys the Amboy Dukes in 1968. Led by guitarist Ted Nugent, whose *Journey to the Center of the Mind* album was a psychedelic favorite, this image was produced by Donnie Dope in postcard format only.

TOP LEFT By the middle of 1968, Gary Grimshaw was so busy with designing promotional materials for the Grande, running its lightshow, and other political activities, that additional help was required. Carl Lundgren was a more than able deputy, as this design for shows by James Cotton and the MC5 proves.

BOTTOM LEFT By late 1967, Grimshaw was at the top of his game, adeptly dealing with the Grande's tight artwork, printing deadlines, and coming up with matchless designs on a weekly basis. Using a photograph of singer Ed Sanders as the central image, this poster for the Fugs' shows is no exception. The Grande and its attendant culture had a fierce political edge, so New York anarchists the Fugs would have felt at home there.

ABOVE RIGHT Using an image of a seagull in full flight, this early poster by Grimshaw (the first he created for the Grande) was produced in 1966. Over the next few years he would become more technically proficient, and his work increasingly sophisticated and politicized. His art would help make the Grande arguably the most loved and greatest psychedelic ballroom outside of San Francisco.

ABOVE LEFT Austin, TX, was a liberal oasis in a right-wing state, and had a thriving longhair scene that revolved around its premier venue, the Vulcan Gas Company. Though later known to millions around the world for his Fabulous Furry Freak Brothers comics, Gilbert Shelton was a mainstay of the scene and designed a number of posters for the Vulcan, including this one featuring Austin's top groups, the Conqueroo and Shiva's Head Band.

TOP RIGHT Though unable to match the creative hub of nearby Detroit, the Chicago psychedelic scene contributed some fascinating poster art later in the period, often drawn by Daniel Clyne, who created this example for a Grateful Dead show at the Windy City's fabled Aragon Ballroom, in 1970.

BOTTOM RIGHT When Grimshaw was driven underground by the authorities on obscenity charges, Lundgren came into his own at the Grande, producing designs for shows by the likes of Jefferson Airplane and Pink Floyd. Lundgren had an early interest in fantasy art and illustration, especially the work of Frank Frazetta. His style may have been more florid than Grimshaw's, but it was always elegantly rendered, as in this design for Spooky Tooth's billing in 1968.

ABOVE LEFT The poster for what became the most famous rock festival in history, Woodstock, defined a new era. Due to a change of location, a highly ornate prototype by David Byrd had to dropped, to be replaced by the iconic guitar neck and white dove of peace designed by Arnold Skolnick. The image reveals the bucolic feel that was seeping into music, design, and the hippie consciousness as the decade ended.

TOP RIGHT John Van Hamersveld emerged from the early '60s LA surf culture. He formed Pinnacle Productions and, inspired by what was happening up the coast, started working on concerts in LA, notably at the Shrine Auditorium, where Hendrix, Electric Flag, and Soft Machine formed the lineup in February 1968. He eventually gravitated to creating sleeve artwork for bands such as the Beatles, Rolling Stones, and Jefferson Airplane.

BOTTOM RIGHT Van Hamersveld's second poster—for Jefferson Airplane and Charlie Musselwhite at the Shrine Auditorium in 1968—makes exceptional use of colored Native American beading to create a powerful, psychedelic mosaic effect. Over the next forty years, the artist was one of the most widely used in rock 'n' roll circles, designing record sleeves for the Stones, Kiss, Blondie, and the 2005 Cream reunion shows.

Family Dog & Hapshash

Two of the most distinctive rock poster series were published by San Francisco's Family Dog and London's Hapshash and the Coloured Coat. Though united by the counterculture, the use of mind-enhancing drugs, and the promotion of the new psychedelic rock, these two entities were worlds apart, not just geographically but also stylistically.

By early 1966 San Francisco ballroom culture was in full swing. The cheapest way of advertising the shows was to fly-post—unlike advertising in newspapers, fly-posting was a cheap and effective method and it cost nothing. The demand for posters was soon high.

Wes Wilson, a former student at San Francisco State University, was working at a small press—Contact Printing—in the city, but had no formal training as a graphic designer. His boss, Bob Carr, was in touch with the San Francisco jazz and beat poetry scenes, and through these connections jobs from the new entrepreneurs soon started to flow in. Wilson was soon creating artwork for Chet Helms at the Family Dog on a regular basis.

While Helms tended to give Wilson themes to work on, over at the Fillmore Bill Graham was also employing the designer; however, Graham allowed Wes complete artistic freedom. Thus it was no surprise that Wilson eventually quit the Family Dog and went to work for Graham full-time in June of 1966. Wilson's replacement was Alton Kelley, who'd arrived in the Bay Area from the East Coast at around the same time. Kelley loved motorcycles and cars—he had studied industrial design, but had little formal drafting and art training. He'd arrived in San Francisco and landed the job with Helms but soon realized it was beyond him. Fortuitously, he had already met his future partner-in-crime the previous summer on Pine Street—Stanley "Mouse" Miller. Raised in Detroit, Mouse also had a fixation with automobile culture and had cut his teeth designing for the hot-rod circuit.

It was while working for Family Dog that Kelley's and Mouse's work really blossomed. Kelley had a talent for plundering and adopting imagery and styles from all kinds of sources. Mouse excelled at composition and lettering. Kelley often came up with the ideas that Mouse, with his drafting skills, would then execute. The now-legendary *Zig-Zag Man* poster for a show at the Avalon in June of '66 was a breakthrough, capturing the attention of Bill Graham.

Kelley and Mouse also occasionally collaborated with another member of the Dog team, Rick Griffin. Griffin was a product of SoCal surf culture, and had worked as a designer for *Surfer* magazine until he joined a traveling band of artist-musicians, the Jook Savages. The group ended up playing in San Francisco in 1965, where they presented the Jook Savage Art Show at the Psychedelic Shop on Haight Street. Griffin's poster for this event drew so much attention to him as an artist that he moved to designing posters full time.

Helms and Graham both used Griffin, and he designed some two-dozen posters for the Family Dog and Fillmore over a two-year period. His black-and-white line work was the foundation for his graphic brilliance, but he soon embraced the challenge of color, which the lithographic printing technology placed at his disposal.

Completing what became known as the "Big Five" was Victor Moscoso. Born in Spain, Moscoso differed from his contemporaries in that he was academically trained and had worked as an instructor at the San Francisco Art Institute before being seduced by the psychedelic scene when he started going to the Avalon. Moscoso's style brought innovation to the Family Dog art collective. His intense visual style came about by manipulating color and form to create optical effects.

Hapshash and the Coloured Coat was London's equivalent of the Haight-Ashbury poster collective. As soon as the first club, the UFO Club,

started, posters were needed to advertise it and were a far less expensive option than taking out ads in the regular press.

The poster for the first show at the club, entitled *Night Tripper*, was designed by a former Ealing College of Art graduate, Michael English. A fan of the pop art painters, English was involved in the "Swinging London" scene, selling items like Union Jack sunglasses to the boutiques on Carnaby Street. English also contributed to the first underground paper, *International Times*. Nigel Waymouth had no formal training as a designer. He was an economic history graduate who had studied at several London art colleges. Like English, he gravitated to the pre-underground swingin' London scene, opening a boutique in Chelsea with his girlfriend Sheila Cohen and friend John Pearse, a Savile Row-trained tailor. The Granny Takes a Trip store opened at 488 Kings Road in February of 1966 and soon attracted interest from English rock royalty like the Beatles and Cream. Waymouth regularly painted swirling murals on the front of the building.

Producer Joe Boyd introduced Waymouth to English at the UFO and suggested they pair up to create posters for the club and other happenings in the capital. The duo's first collaboration was a poster called *UFO Festival*, which sported a pair of giant Day-Glo pink lips inspired by Man Ray's painting *Observatory Time*. Assuming the name of Hapshash and the Coloured Coat (a weird hybrid of drug terminology and the Egyptian *Book of the Dead*), Waymouth and English gave color and vision to the British Summer of Love, designing posters for the clubs UFO and its successor Middle Earth, and for new bands such as Pink Floyd, Soft Machine, the Move, and Tomorrow. Drawing on artists as disparate as William Blake, Max Ernst, and Hieronymus Bosch, Hapshash developed a style that the singer and critic George Melly would describe as "nouveau art nouveau." There was also a lightness of touch that made their work more dreamlike. The posters were produced by Osiris Visions, which, like its American counterparts, spotted that there was a market hungry for them.

As in the United States, the bubble quickly burst and, after being involved in the recording of two Hapshash-related LPs, Waymouth and English went their separate ways. The value of their work remains high: in 2008 an original Hendrix Fillmore poster was valued by Bonhams for $125,000!

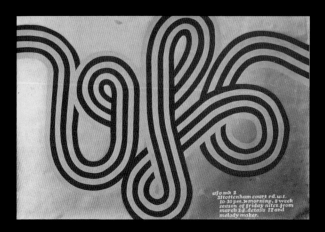

LEFT Known as "Toothpaste," this is an early example of Hapshash's design work. It features red and pink neon cursive lettering that spells UFO, as if it were squeezed from a tube of toothpaste on to a gold background, to advertise upcoming shows at UFO—London's first psychedelic club—in spring 1967.

TOP LEFT Chet Helms and his company, the Family Dog, pioneered the psychedelic poster art revolution and turned the Avalon into one of San Francisco's most-loved ballrooms of the era. Unlike his rival, Bill Graham, Chet was a down-to-earth figure and was less interested in money—and more focused on throwing a great party. He might never have earned a fortune, but as an ideas man the San Francisco scene would have been poorer without him.

BOTTOM LEFT A 1967 poster by Victor Moscoso that features his trademark layers of color—mixing green, cyan, and red over a picture of a young woman's staring eyes to advertise early shows in San Francisco by LA's the Doors; here, playing at Avalon Ballroom, March 3 and 4, 1967. The support act, Sparrow, later changed their name and had great success as Steppenwolf.

ABOVE RIGHT An early example of Hapshash's psychedelic style, with bulbous lettering that uses a central image of two dancing '50s rockers. The Purple Gang were a psychedelic jug band from Manchester, and English designed this piece to advertise their first single on Transatlantic Records. The song, produced by Joe Boyd, was inspired by the boutique of the same name that Nigel Waymouth opened at 488 King's Road in London's fashionable Chelsea district.

4

Mainstream, Prog Rock & Metal

1969–1975

Psychedelic '70s

By the end of the 1960s, popular music was becoming the dominant cultural form in the Western world. And rock had become the dominant form of popular music—"rock" in the wider sense, that is, embracing rock-jazz, fusion, and other genre crossovers. Rock started to be taken seriously as an important creative and commercial force, and rock poster designers also acquired a new self-awareness. They saw themselves as artists, part of a graphic art tradition. Some, such as West-Coasters Stanley Mouse and Alton Kelley, borrowed from the poster styles of earlier ages and from comics; others, like Joe Petagno in his work for Motörhead, from sci-fi imagery.

Print technology was improving all the time, and richer, more detailed full-color imagery was now possible. Typography developed as a separate discipline and the number of display fonts increased rapidly. This allowed graphic artists to concentrate on pure, text-free images, and specialist designers and studios emerged.

One such studio was Hipgnosis, founded in London by Peter Christopherson, Aubrey Powell, and Storm Thorgerson in 1968. Best known for their Pink Floyd album covers, these artists came to represent the '70s antithesis of psychedelic design (despite launching their career with the quintessentially psychedelic artwork of Pink Floyd's *A Saucerful of Secrets* LP, which was released in 1968). Hipgnosis developed a clean-lined, sharply focused graphic and photographic house style, often using humorous, surreally literal, or sexual interpretations of album titles as a stepping-off point.

Hipgnosis was closely associated with the mainstream rock of the mid-'70s. Rock's audience was outgrowing the theaters and dancehalls that used to house it; for the biggest stars, only vast sports arenas were large enough to accommodate their fans. The music that worked best in such places, stadium rock, was often a stripped-down, crowd-pleasing style— with simpler, bolder posters to match.

Other strands of rock also emerged, however. Progressive rock was the label given to a school of music that developed from the extended improvisation of keyboard-driven bands such as Procol Harem and Yes, who focused on instrumental virtuosity and more complex composition; not surprisingly, the artwork for such bands' posters and album covers often sought to reflect these "higher" musical aspirations.

The real world was considered too ordinary for such inventive music, which was promoted with images of magical, fantastical characters and landscapes. In the United Kingdom one artist, Roger Dean, epitomized this approach more than any other. Dean's dreamlike scenery and mythical beasts are instantly recognizable and became synonymous with progressive rock. Recognizability was a key element of the artwork for many strands of '70s rock, and this was a time when a group's image was almost more important than its music. This was, after all, the period that also gave us glam rock and David Bowie.

Increasingly, a single artist or studio found themselves responsible for producing all of the visual output of a rock performer (for example, Dean's long-term relationship with Yes, and Hipgnosis's work for the English art rock

> "I like to mess with reality . . . to bend reality. Some of my works beg the question of is it real or not?"
>
> STORM THORGERSON, HIPGNOSIS

band 10cc), and a single powerful image was used across a whole range of media platforms in order to maximize the image's impact. Album covers, T-shirts, buttons—the concert poster lost a little of its unique function and became just one element of an overarching marketing strategy. But as rock stars began to feed the demand from fans for merchandise bearing their image, the poster made the transition from being simply a way of providing advance notice of a live event, to becoming a souvenir of it afterward. During the course of the '70s, the rock poster had less and less to do with the actual process of touring and became a product in its own right.

Rock's progress from counterculture voice to mainstream institution didn't please everyone. Some groups and fans reacted to the wealth and fame of arena rock's new superstar elite with a back-to-basics approach to their music: with raw rock 'n' roll, played in intimate venues to small audiences in the tradition of garage rock bands. In the UK, this '70s movement was known as pub rock. It was, by definition, a low-key reaction to stadium rock, but it gave rise to the musical whirlwind that would temporarily stop the stadium rock juggernaut in its tracks—punk!

One band that uniquely straddled a plethora of styles, from psychedelic to heavy metal to punk, was the group of space rockers Hawkwind. Emerging from the light shows and hippie happenings of the '60s, Hawkwind carved out their own enduring rock niche with a big, dirty, hallucinogenic wall of sound, which was promoted in the '70s by the art of brilliant graphic artist Barney Bubbles.

Bubbles (whose real name was Colin Fulcher) came to rock music after training in industrial design and product packaging. He cut his designer teeth on imaginatively packaged records, including pub-rock band Brinsley Schwarz's eponymous debut LP, the die-cut sleeve for Hawkwind's *In Search of Space*, and the lavishly accessorized *Glastonbury Fayre* triple album (which featured Brinsley Schwarz, the Grateful Dead, Hawkwind, and others). His early poster work for Hawkwind in the '70s owes a debt to traditional graphic art through a series of strikingly retro images. Bubbles found his own style—geometric, visually literate, and full of humor—in his later work for punk and new-wave stars such as Elvis Costello and Ian Dury.

Thus Bubbles, like Hawkwind, was a survivor across many phases of rock fashion. But the new wave that they both embraced swept many of their contemporaries away. When punk rock kicked in, rock music—and the posters that promoted it—would never be quite the same again.

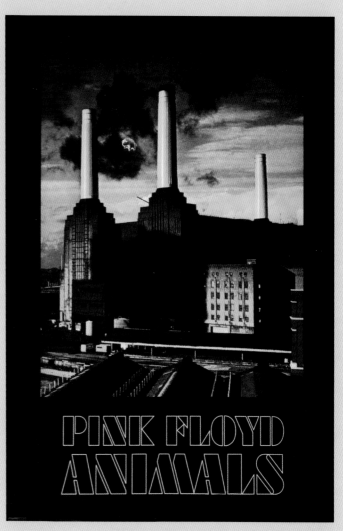

TOP LEFT Mason, Gilmour, Waters and Wright photographed in 1973: the lineup of Pink Floyd, which took the band from underground clubs in London to sell-out stadium tours around the world. Pink Floyd's love of theatricality—from their early light shows to the monumental stage set of *The Wall*—was important in their successful transition to large arenas.

BOTTOM LEFT A 1973 souvenir poster by Barney Bubbles. The rough edges of Hawkwind's psychedelic rock gave them, and their designer, street cred at a time when other mainstream '70s acts were being seen as obsolete dinosaurs; Bubbles' association with the band gained him access to UK new-wave clients such as Ian Dury and Elvis Costello toward the end of the decade.

ABOVE RIGHT The original idea for Pink Floyd's 1977 *Animals* cover came from Roger Waters, and was executed by the band's long-time visual collaborators Aubrey Powell and Storm Thorgerson of Hipgnosis. Bad weather on the second day of photography caused the thirty-foot inflatable pig (nicknamed Algie) to escape from its moorings over Battersea Power Station in London, disrupting air traffic.

ABOVE LEFT Yes had recorded but not yet released their breakthrough album *Fragile* at the time of the gig advertised on this 1971 tour-blank poster. The LP would be the band's first to use the artwork of Roger Dean; but, in the meantime, the band's tour posters continued to use the original logo by Haig Adishian (superimposed here on an art deco scene) from their 1969 debut.

TOP RIGHT This two-color Jethro Tull tour blank for a 1970 tour, promoted by the Chrysalis Agency (named for its founders *Chris* Wright and Terry *Ellis*), captures the essence of the live Jethro Tull experience—the image of flamboyant frontman Ian Anderson on a black background mimicking Brian Pike's Maximum R&B design for the Who's publicity material in 1964.

BOTTOM RIGHT A 1971 souvenir poster for English prog-rock band Van Der Graaf Generator. The surreal landscape is typical of the work of artist Paul Whitehead, who also designed the covers of early Genesis LPs. Whitehead later created the Mad Hatter logo for Genesis and Van Der Graaf Generator's record company Charisma (which was founded by VDGG's manager Tony Stratton-Smith).

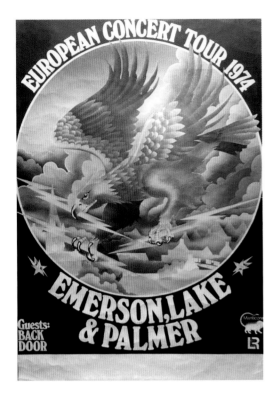

TOP LEFT A tour blank (artist unknown) printed by Blue Egg Publishing for ELP's 1974 world tour. The band's seventy-three performances included two American legs and spawned the triple live album *Welcome Back My Friends to the Show that Never Ends*. The contrast between the stadium-filling prog-rock trio and unknown pub-jazz trio Back Door, ELP's support on the European dates, must have been intriguing, to say the least.

BOTTOM LEFT A 1971 tour blank (artist unknown) for Scottish psychedelic folksters (and Woodstock veterans) the Incredible String Band, here touring their first all-electric LP *Liquid Acrobat As Regards the Air*. The poster was produced by Ranelagh Press, a specialist book printer of some 200 years' standing; Hipgnosis had used the same printer, based in north London, for the studio's early Pink Floyd posters.

ABOVE RIGHT Austin, TX, artist Jim Franklin's regular inclusion of armadillos in his artwork inspired the name of a new club, Armadillo World Headquarters, for which this 1971 poster was created. Following the closure of the flagship rock company the Vulcan Gas Company, Armadillo World HQ opened in 1970 and became an important venue for showcasing rock in the early '70s.

ABOVE LEFT This 1998 limited-edition reprint of an original 1970 Bath Festival poster, signed by the festival's promoter Freddie Bannister, shows the extent to which rock was becoming aware of its own collectable past. The lineup of the 1970 west-of-England festival rivaled that of the Isle of Wight later the same year, although bad weather and poor organization limited its impact at the time.

TOP RIGHT Promoter Bill Graham helped to usher in the stadium age when he closed his legendary Fillmore venues in New York and San Francisco to concentrate on larger, more profitable ventures. The lettering on this 1972 handbill featuring a young Bruce Springsteen was created by Randy Tuten, Bill Graham's in-house designer during the '70s.

BOTTOM RIGHT Deep Purple's Friday night gig in an Edinburgh cinema had to wait until after the main feature had been shown, judging from the start time on this 1970 monochrome flyer. The band were nearing the end of a punishing tour schedule—no fewer than 127 gigs in eleven months, with new members Ian Gillan and Roger Glover—and were about to record their classic *In Rock* LP.

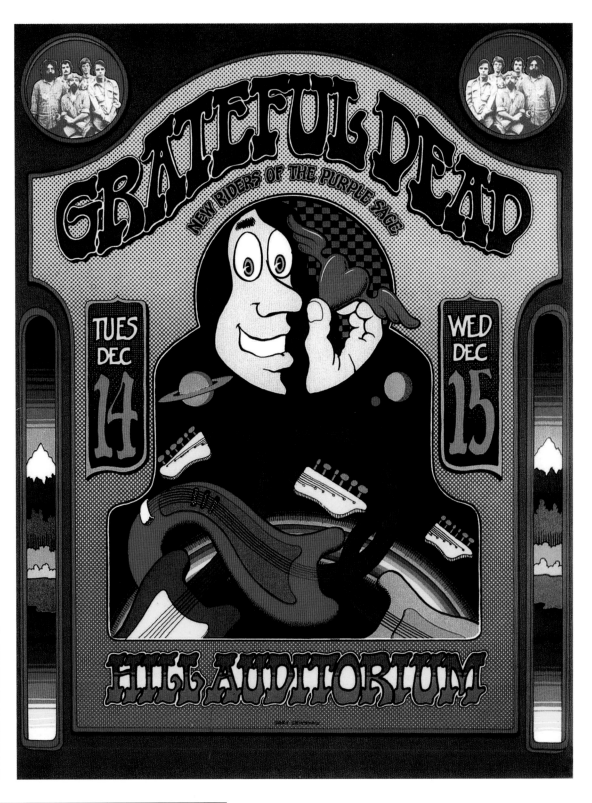

TOP LEFT A program for the second south London Crystal Palace Garden Party—the first, headlined by Pink Floyd in May 1971, had been blighted by heavy rain. For the second garden party, in July, an inexperienced Elton John and his backing musicians Dee Murray and Nigel Olsson struggled to entertain the crowd; but better weather and show-stealing sets from Gallagher, Fairport, and Yes ensured the event's survival until 1975.

BOTTOM LEFT War's fusion of political activism and easy funk helped to bring the West Coast sound into the '70s. The Concord Pavilion, designed by architects Frank Gehry and Peter Walker, had opened in Concord, MA, a year before this 1976 gig; its open-air amphitheater was constructed to satisfy the demands of promoters for venues with a greater paying-audience capacity than the traditional theaters.

ABOVE RIGHT Grimshaw is best known through his posters for Detroit's Grande Ballroom and Detroit band the MC5. After the Grande closed in 1970, he continued to design posters for concert promoters in Detroit and Ann Arbor. When the Grateful Dead and New Riders of the Purple Sage performed at Ann Arbor's Hill Auditorium, MI, on December 14 and 15, 1971, Grimshaw was commissioned to design the poster by the promoters UAC/Daystar.

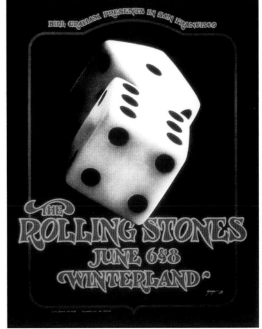

OPPOSITE This was one of four posters designed for the Rolling Stones by Royal College of Art graduate John Pasche. In keeping with the retro style that was a hallmark of much of early '70s rock imagery, the illustration was inspired by travel posters of the '30s, particularly those created in France by the Ukrainian-born designer Adolphe Mouron Cassandre.

ABOVE LEFT By the time John Pasche created his second Stones tour poster, the artist had also been commissioned to design the iconic tongue-and-lips logo for the band's new record label. Pasche, a painstaking airbrush artist, was inspired by his initial meeting with Mick Jagger; he recalled: "The first thing you were aware of was the size of his lips and mouth."

TOP RIGHT Bill Graham gave artist David Singer the honor of producing the final poster for his Fillmore West venue before it closed in 1971, a year before the San Francisco Winterland gigs advertised in this poster. Here, Singer makes a visual joke with rolling bones (slang for dice)—"Tumbling Dice" was the lead single from the Stones' 1972 album *Exile On Main Street*.

BOTTOM RIGHT This movie and soundtrack promotion for *Rainbow Bridge*—the 1972 documovie featuring Jimi Hendrix in concert on the island of Maui, Hawaii—was created by Rod Dyer, a commercial graphic artist who later designed the logo for TV's Disney Channel, and who still works in the entertainment industry today. The sparse, angular design seems at odds with the meditative images, rounded lettering, and psychedelic ethos of the event it promotes.

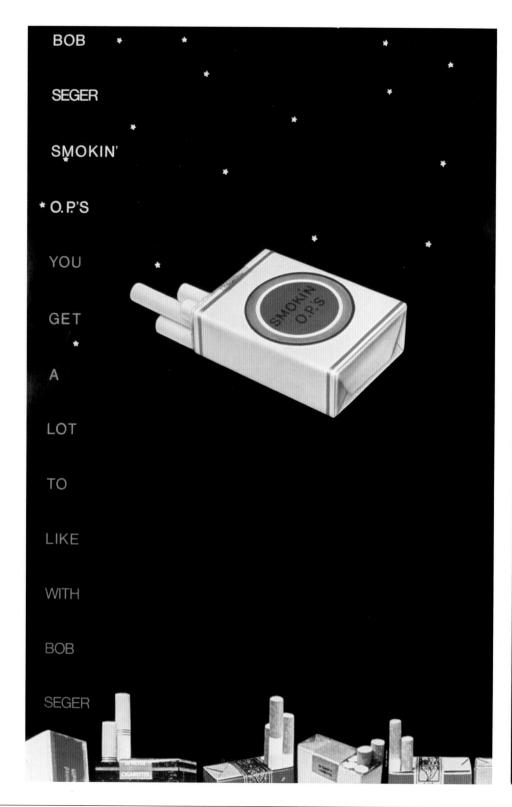

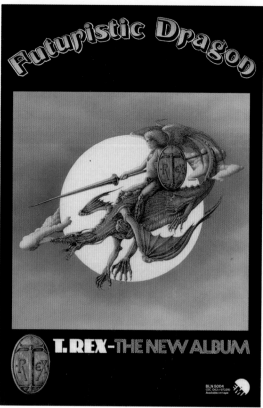

ABOVE LEFT The cover for Bob Seger's 1972 album, imitating a pack of Lucky Strikes, was one of eight designed for Seger by his road manager Thomas Weschler. The album was a collection of cover versions; "smoking O.P.'s" meant smoking other people's cigarettes, rather than buying your own. The promotional poster by Rod Dyer develops Weschler's theme by borrowing Marlboro's slogan, "You Get a Lot to Like."

TOP RIGHT Dr. Hook singer Dennis Locorriere remembers this 1972 support slot for Van Morrison as the moment Dr. Hook stepped up a gear. The triangular poster—created, fittingly enough, for Triangle Productions—was an effective gimmick, although it imposed severe limitations of layout and design on the poster artist, Pat Ryan of the Peanut Gallery collective in Fairfax, CA.

BOTTOM RIGHT Promotional poster for T. Rex's UK-only 1976 LP, with artwork by George Underwood, who had previously designed the cover of the band's first LP in 1968, *My People Were Fair and Had Sky in their Hair*. Underwood played in early '60s bands with his lifelong friend David Bowie, and he designed the singer's *Hunky Dory* and *Ziggy Stardust* covers.

ABOVE LEFT Thomas Morris was a prolific West Coast designer of rock posters from 1968 to 1990 through his Jellyroll Press and Sharpshooter Studios. Morris produced numerous posters for Gold Rush Productions in the early '70s, including this 1973 poster for a Boz Scaggs event. The "texture" of the photography in the poster helps to disguise the fact that its design is limited to two colors for the budget-conscious promoters.

ABOVE RIGHT Designer Dennis Loren typically worked with rich colors, mirror images, and detailed illustrations developed from photographs. This 1972 poster is a classic example. Supporting West Coast old hand Steve Miller at this gig was English band Trapeze, whose lineup included future Deep Purple bass player Glenn Hughes.

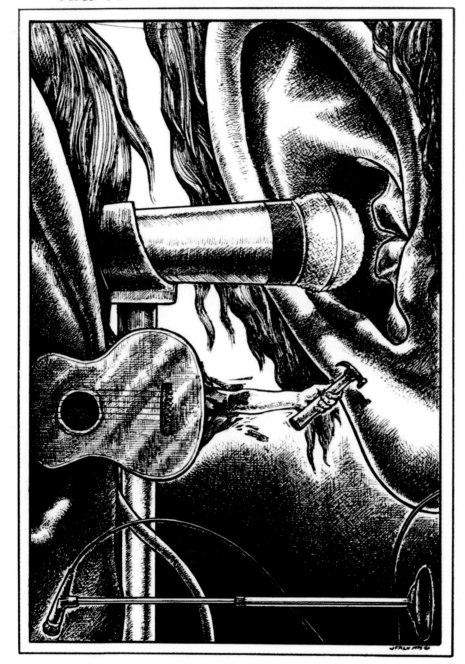

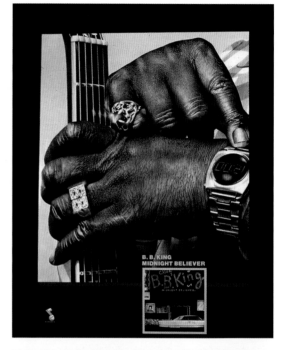

ABOVE LEFT Armadillo World HQ regular Jim Franklin uses graphic imagery to show us just how loud Bruce Springsteen is going to be at these 1974 gigs in Austin, TX. Springsteen, struggling to cross from critical to popular acclaim, was about to begin the fourteen-month recording marathon of his breakthrough album *Born To Run*.

TOP RIGHT In contrast to his earlier, sparser designs, blues fan Rod Dyer uses an image rich in detail—the wrinkled fingers, the bling, the strings and frets, the hour—on this 1978 promotional poster. *Midnight Believer* was the first of two collaborations by bluesman B.B. King with jazzmen the Crusaders. Both returned him to the Top 30 singles and album charts.

BOTTOM RIGHT The distinctive fine penmanship of Mark T. Behrens first appeared on West Coast posters in 1969. This 1972 lineup included one of the last performances of Osceola (named after an eighteenth-century Seminole Native American leader), veterans of Chet Helms' Family Dog and also regulars at fundraisers for Native American causes.

TOP LEFT Bold graphic Britishness compensates for the cluttered, rub-down lettering on this 1975 original full-color poster (cheaper run-ons were two color only) designed by Martine Grainey for Peter Grainey Graphics. The husband and wife team worked regularly for promoter Mel Bush in the mid-'70s; much of their work is now printed in limited editions for the growing market in rock memorabilia.

TOP RIGHT The 1969 Isle of Wight Festival's souvenir program was an exuberantly colorful art-deco affair. By contrast, the surprisingly stark poster focuses entirely on the event's big selling point—the first gig by Dylan in three years since his near-fatal motorcycle accident. Only two weeks earlier, Dylan had turned down a spot at Woodstock.

ABOVE The gatefold cover of Alice Cooper's 1974 collection, drawn by leading draftsman Drew Struzan, is here used as a promotional poster. The following year, Struzan designed the artwork for the singer's solo debut, *Welcome to my Nightmare*, but soon moved into movies—he designed the posters of all the *Star Wars*, *Back to the Future* and *Indiana Jones* episodes.

TOP LEFT Flyer by Paul Whitehead, who also designed the covers for Genesis albums *Trespass*, *Nursery Cryme*, and their new release *Foxtrot*, which this 1972 tour was promoting. Genesis and String Driven Thing were labelmates at Charisma, the record company owned by promoter Tony Stratton-Smith. The flyer was printed by the London firm Blue Egg Publishing.

BOTTOM LEFT A 1978 design by David Costa of Wherefore Art, which now designs printwork for major artists, including Michael Jackson and Beatles packages. Promoter Freddie Bannister cut his teeth on the Bath Festivals of 1969 and 1970. This event saw the first Starship performance without Grace Slick, who had flown home early after an argument with guitarist Paul Kantner.

ABOVE RIGHT Silver foil poster from 1969, hand-screenprinted by Pete Sinfield, King Crimson's lyricist. The design was conceived by Barry Godber, who also created the image of "21st Century Schizoid Man" on the band's first album cover, *In the Court of the Crimson King*. The album cover was Godber's only cover art, and he died only a few months after its 1969 release, aged just twenty-four.

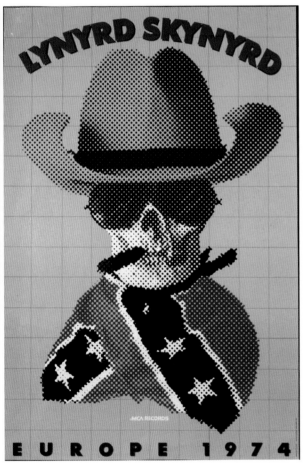

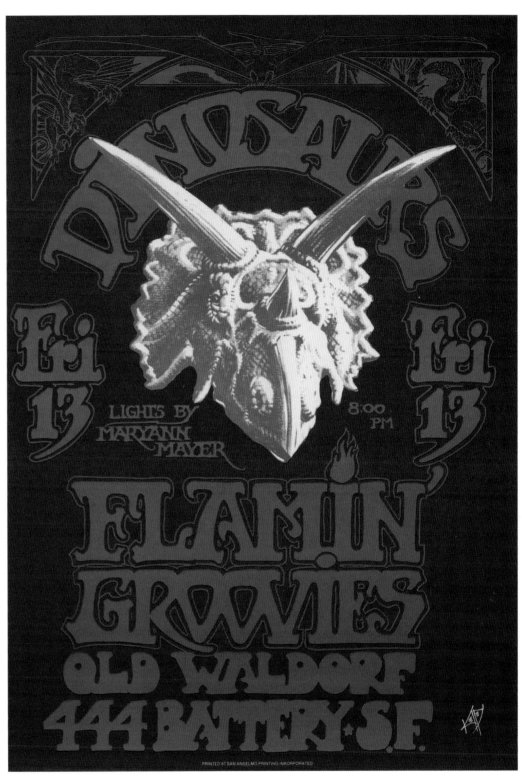

TOP LEFT This 1970 poster was created by Dezign Design and printed by Ranelagh Press, a long-established printworks that began to diversify into underground music posters in the late '60s. The Roundhouse, a hub for London's hippie counterculture, hosted its Pop Proms as a counterblast to the long-running annual proms (promenades) of classical music in the city's Albert Hall concert venue.

BOTTOM LEFT Lynyrd Skynyrd's three-week tour of Europe in November 1974 was the first time the band had played outside of the US, and the tour's success prompted a return trip in October of the following year. This poster, created by designer Rod Dyer, spells out the band's Southern States identity for its new-found transatlantic audience.

ABOVE RIGHT Designed in 1982, this is a later work by one of the kings of the psychedelic poster, Alton Kelley. Kelley was an appropriately West Coast choice for the Dinosaurs, formed in the same year this poster was created. A part-time group, the Dinosaurs comprised former members of Country Joe and the Fish, Big Brother and the Holding Company, Quicksilver Messenger Service, Jefferson Airplane, and the Grateful Dead.

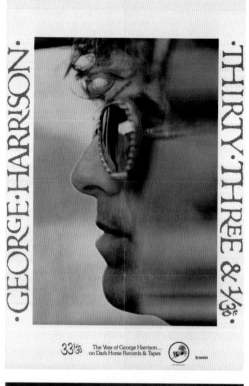

ABOVE LEFT The poster promoting David Bowie's 1972 LP, *The Rise and Fall of Ziggy Stardust and the Spiders From Mars*, was cropped directly from the front cover artwork. The black-and-white photo by Brian Ward, shot on a cold, wet night on Heddon Street in central London, was hand-colored by Terry Pastor. Pastor chose turquoise for Bowie's jumpsuit, as it stood out well against the other colors.

TOP RIGHT Promotional poster for Harrison's 1976 album, released in the wake of his infamous *He's So Fine* versus *My Sweet Lord* copyright infringement troubles. The photo was made by Bob Cato, a Quaker, pacifist, and long-serving album designer at Columbia and United Artists. The hand-drawn lettering by Mike Manoogian neatly incorporates the *om* symbol, reflecting Harrison's belief in Hinduism.

BOTTOM RIGHT Roxy Music's stylish cover designs sustained a remarkable consistency of vision under the art direction of singer Brian Ferry and his old friend from art-school days, Nick de Ville. In 1974 the cover of their fourth album featured two German fans—whom Ferry met while on holiday in Portugal— photographed by Eric Boman. It was censored in the United States.

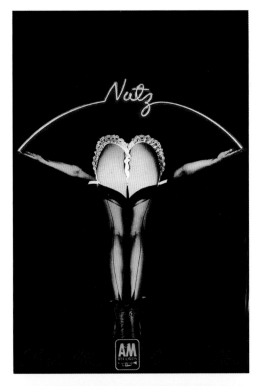

TOP LEFT Sex has always been a selling point on posters, whatever the era or prevailing social conventions. Liverpool pub-rockers Nutz are now largely forgotten, but their 1974 debut LP, containing the track "As Far as the Eye Can See," was promoted with this visually arresting image by designer Geoff Halpin of his wife Linda.

TOP RIGHT The artwork of albums by the Scorpions regularly courted controversy. The original, humorously suggestive covers of 1979's *Lovedrive*, and 1980's *Animal Magnetism* were designed by Storm Thorgerson. Certain US outlets insisted that the risqué image on Lovedrive be replaced with a safer design, on which this poster-program for the 1980 Animal Magnetism Tour was also based.

ABOVE This 1975 promotional poster was for the first solo album by guitarist Steve Howe of Yes. By this time, the elaborate music of prog-rockers Yes and the organic forms of designer Roger Dean had become inseparable in the public eye. The cushion-like forms seen here are a development of the "landscape seating" which Dean installed in the renowned London jazz club, Ronnie Scott's.

Futurescapes

Three artists are responsible for some of the strongest images associated with the progressive rock movement of the late 1960s and early 1970s: Stanley Mouse and Alton Kelley in the United States, and Roger Dean in the United Kingdom.

While his contemporary Barney Bubbles came to album art through packaging design, Dean's roots were in furniture. His sea urchin-inspired design for a chair led to a commission for seating in Ronnie Scott's eponymous London jazz club. There, he created an upholstered landscape for patrons to sit on, which brought him to the attention of the music industry. One of his earliest rock commissions, in 1972, was the label logo for the young Richard Branson's new record label, Virgin.

The creatures and imaginary landscapes on which Dean based his furniture became the subject of colorful, hyper-realistic paintings. They graced scores of UK prog rock album covers for Uriah Heep, Greenslade, and others. Resolutely free of straight lines, they owe much to the landscapes of classical Chinese art, and to Dean's own delight in natural organic and inorganic forms. He is particularly associated with classic prog rockers Yes. The fragile floating world he has developed over decades working on their album covers is an evolving creation of remarkable consistency.

In the US, prog rock and the artwork that promoted it had its roots in the counterculture of the 1960s. Stanley Mouse and Alton Kelley had learned their craft on the West Coast scene, making hundreds of posters for Bill Graham and Chet Helms. Their designs promoted many of prog rock's forefathers—Big Brother and the Holding Company, Quicksilver Messenger Service, and others. Although Stanley Mouse had a useful background in custom hot-rod decoration, Alton Kelley had little previous experience of graphic art before designing posters for the Family Dog.

They were strongly influenced by the advertising posters of the art nouveau period, in particular the work of Alphonse Mucha and Edmund Sullivan. A Sullivan image of a skeleton was the basis of their most famous work, originally produced for a 1966 concert by the Grateful Dead at San Francisco's Avalon Ballroom. Their poster of a dancing skeleton with a wreath and crown of roses was eventually adopted as a recurring motif by the band. Kelley and Mouse went on to design several iconic album sleeves for the Dead, including *American Beauty* and *Workingman's Dead*.

In 1967 Kelley and Mouse took part in an art show called the Joint Show at the Moore Gallery in San Fancisco, with Rick Griffin, Wes Wilson, and Victor Moscoso. The press dubbed the poster artists "the Big Five." Kelley and Mouse continued to work together throughout the 1970s and 1980s, notably on the covers of all of Journey's album releases. Kelley died in 2008, three months after their last collaboration—the cover of the program for that year's Rock and Roll Hall of Fame induction ceremony.

LEFT Kelley (left) and Mouse first met in San Francisco, CA, in 1965. Their friendship and fruitful art partnership lasted until Kelley's death in 2008. They successfully updated their dreamlike '60s style for the '70s with album cover designs for the Steve Miller Band, Journey, and the Grateful Dead, their work becoming comparable to Roger Dean's.

ABOVE English artist Roger Dean designed his first LP cover in 1968, but it wasn't until his work on two albums by Osibisa in 1971 that he was adopted by the prog rock movement. In 1972 alone, Dean's landscapes appeared on twelve releases. Since his first work for Yes in 1971, he has produced over forty covers for the band and its offshoots.

"When I was doing my first album covers I had very little competition . . . I was allowed to learn my craft in public."

ROGER DEAN

ABOVE LEFT Roger Dean's cover for Greenslade's eponymous debut album in 1973, adapted for a promotional poster. It is typical of Dean's fantastical creatures and scenery, which became synonymous with UK progressive rock of the mid-'70s. Dean only designed Greenslade's first two covers; but the logo and the four-armed figure, the band's visual identity, reappeared on many later releases.

ABOVE RIGHT At the birth of stadium rock, Alton Kelley and Stanley Mouse were already veterans of the psychedelic '60s, as their artwork for this 1976 retrospective celebration of the Summer of Love proves. In the '70s their style became bolder and less abstract—and more suited to the arena-filling sounds of the time.

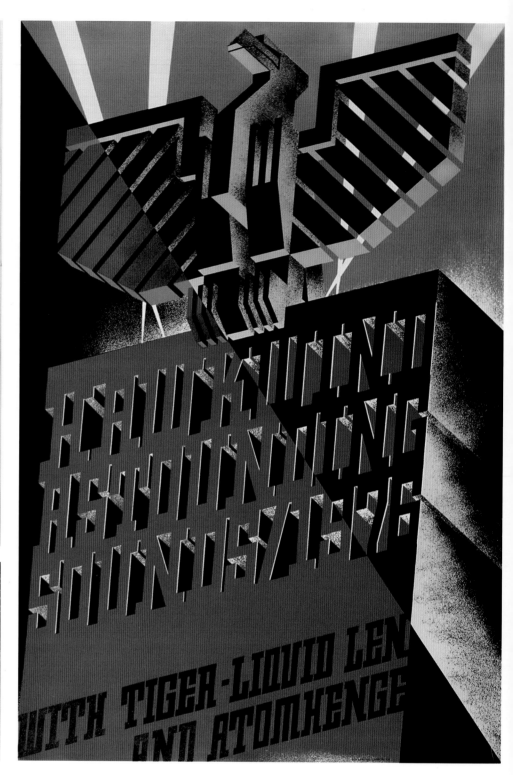

TOP LEFT A highly decorative 1974 tour blank combining art nouveau with '60s psychedelia—its designer, the artist Barney Bubbles, was strongly influenced by both. The central figure was inspired by an 1899 Moët & Chandon champagne ad by Alphonse Mucha, while the influence of Bubbles's trip to the West Coast in 1968, at the height of the psychedelic era, is underlined by the inclusion of the words Love and Peace.

BOTTOM LEFT This poster for a 1976 compilation album—Hawkwind's last for their old record label United Artists— owes much to Cassandre, France's leading commercial graphic artist of the '30s. Barney Bubbles enjoyed a long working relationship with Hawkwind, and it was one of the last to which he openly put his name; from 1976 he preferred to work anonymously.

ABOVE RIGHT A 1976 tour poster in support of Hawkwind's first album, *Astounding Sounds, Amazing Music*, for their new label Charisma. Barney Bubbles' fascination with retro sources of inspiration continued with this nod to between-the-wars fascism—a deliberately ironic image for a band defiantly rooted in counterculture.

RIGHT *Face the Music*, from 1975, was the first cover on which the Electric Light Orchestra used their initials. Mick Haggerty neatly solved the problem of a long name versus an unfamiliar acronym by combining both in the poster's metallic-styled lettering. Haggerty, a protégé of Rod Dyer, went on to design iconic album covers in the '80s and '90s, including Bowie's *Let's Dance* and the Police's *Ghost in the Machine*.

BILL GRAHAM PRESENTS

THE
WHO
&

THE
GRATEFUL
DEAD

OCTOBER 9-10 OAKLAND STADIUM

LEFT Philip Garris already had album sleeves for the Grateful Dead's 1975 *Blues for Allah* and their guitarist Bob Weir's 1976 solo *Kingfish* to his credit, when Bill Graham commissioned this poster for their 1976 double bill. Images of death, and an open-winged owl with its whoo-hoo call, are visually witty references to the bands' names.

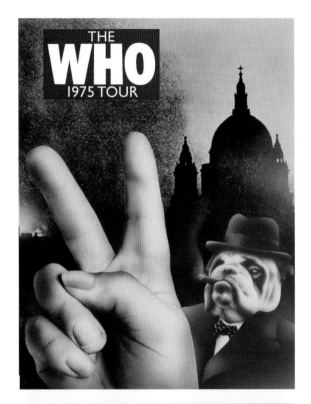

QUADROPHENIA

Double Album 2657613 Distributed by Polydor Also Available on Cassette. C3526001 8 Track 3876101.

Artwork © 1973 Track Records/Photography Graham Hughes.

TOP LEFT John Pasche airbrushed this two-color poster for a 1975 tour in support of *The Who by Numbers*, the band's first release since *Quadrophenia*. Pasche's dark wartime imagery is much closer to the LP's somber tone than the album cover itself, which was a join-the-dots cartoon by bass-player John Entwistle. In the same year, Pasche produced artwork for Scottish teenyboppers the Bay City Rollers.

BOTTOM LEFT Poster for a ten-day UK tour in 1973 by the Who, promoting their current album *Quadrophenia*. The band and tour are somewhat overshadowed by the bold graphics of the design. The complex studio sound of the new material proved difficult for the straightforward guitar–bass–drums lineup to recreate live, even with backing tapes.

ABOVE RIGHT Promotional poster for the Who's 1973 rock opera *Quadrophenia*. The image is from the same photo sessions that produced the double album's cover—designed and photographed by Roger Daltrey's cousin, Graham Hughes— albeit from a different view. With the exception of Keith Moon's, the faces of the band members reflected in the wing mirrors of the scooter were shot at the time, rather than added later.

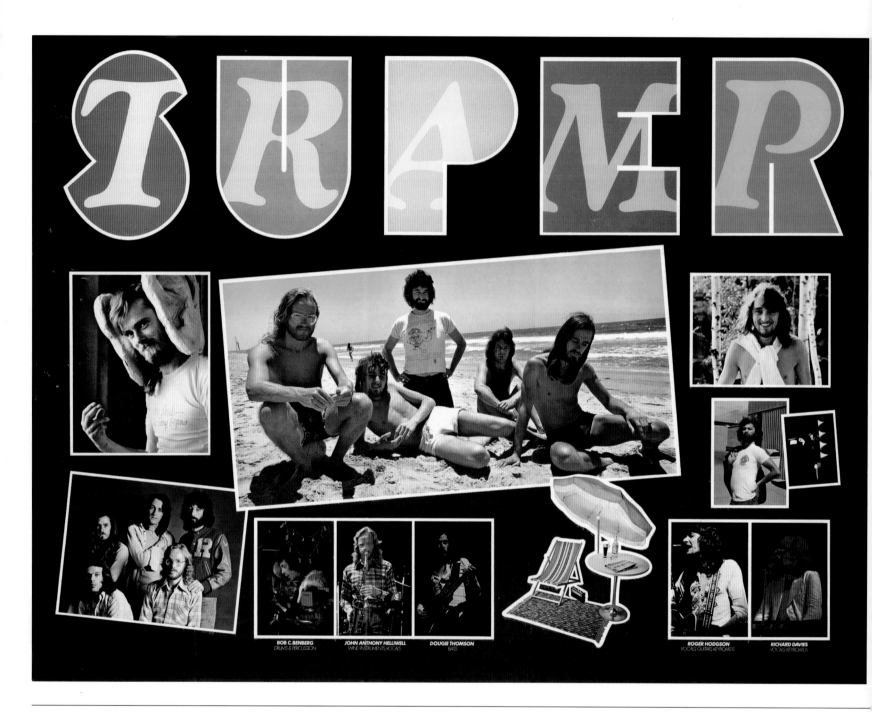

ABOVE Fold-out poster-program for Supertramp's 1975 tour in support of *Crisis? What Crisis?*, the follow-up to their breakthrough album *Crime of the Century*. It incorporates elements of the album cover design by Paul Wakefield, Dick Ward, and Fabio Nicoli (A&M's Art Director), with group-member biographies and images on the reverse.

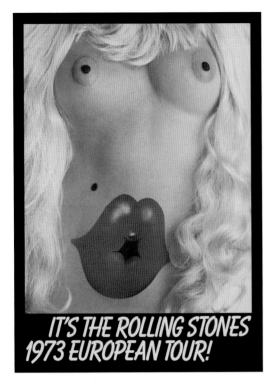

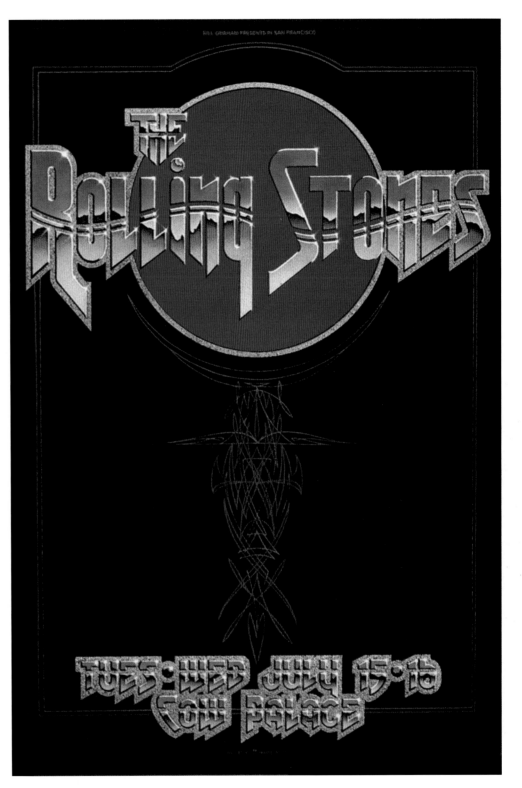

TOP LEFT The Stones' 1973 European tour played a mixture of large halls and medium-sized arenas, mirroring the transition to larger venues which many bands and promoters were making at the time. John Pasche's less-than-subtle photographic souvenir poster marked a departure from the retro travel images of his earlier work for the band.

BOTTOM LEFT Promotional poster for the Rolling Stones' 1974 LP *It's Only Rock'n'Roll*, with artwork by Belgian illustrator Guy Peellaert. Peellaert had published *Rock Dreams*, his book of imagined rock portraits, a year earlier. Its success led to commissions from the Stones, and from David Bowie, for whose album *Diamond Dogs* Peellaert also designed the cover.

ABOVE RIGHT The poster for the Stones' 1975 North American tour, their first with Ronnie Wood, featured a swooping eagle with a jet engine on each wing. But individual venues often printed their own designs; for the San Francisco gigs at the Cow Palace, Bill Graham commissioned the maestros of poster art to create this design: Stanley Mouse, Alton Kelley, Randy Tuten, and Crazy Arab.

ABOVE LEFT Jim Fitzpatrick created this 1976 promotional poster for Irish rockers Thin Lizzy. The band had recorded their sixth studio album, *Jailbreak*, after a breakthrough UK tour in 1975 supporting British boogie band Status Quo. The poster capitalizes on Lizzy's new reputation as an exciting live act by incorporating performance photos of each member.

TOP RIGHT Alice Cooper's second solo album, *Goes to Hell*, gave him a 1976 hit with "I Never Cry," a confessional ballad about the singer's alcoholism. Unfortunately, Cooper's ill health led to the cancelation of the supporting tour. Rod Dyer designed this tour blank for the event, incorporating his artwork for the album's cover.

BOTTOM RIGHT Irish artist Jim Fitzpatrick was an obvious choice for Thin Lizzy. His Celtic-inspired artwork graces almost all of the band's albums, including their 1973 LP *Vagabonds of the Western World* (a nod to Irish playwright J.M. Synge's *Playboy of the Western World*).

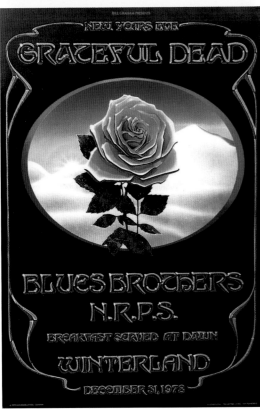

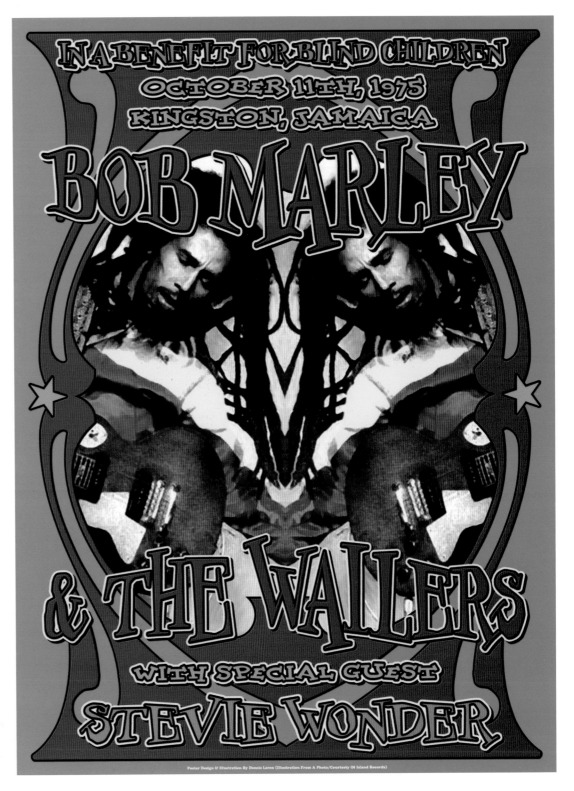

TOP LEFT Randy Tuten added graphics to David Singer's collage from the cover of the just-released *Festival*. Under Bill Graham's management, Carlos Santana returned from the jazzier reaches of *Caravanserai* to a more commercial form of Latin funk. *Festival* was followed the same year by the live/studio double *Moonflower*, Santana's first Top 10 album since 1972 (and last until 1999).

BOTTOM LEFT Icy blues set the tone for a sad milestone, the closing concert at San Francisco's Winterland Ballroom. Who better to mark the end of an era than the Grateful Dead (who released their five-hour set as a four-CD set twenty-five years later); and who better to publicize it than the poster artists of their generation, Stanley Mouse and Alton Kelley?

ABOVE RIGHT Another example of Dennis Loren's striking use of bold color and mirror image. This 1975 benefit for the Jamaican Institute for the Blind featured the first and last reformation of the original Wailers lineup after their split in 1973. Wonder and Marley closed the concert by jamming together on the former's "Superstition" and the latter's "I Shot the Sheriff."

122 123 **ABOVE LEFT** A dark, threatening image by Randy Tuten and William Bostedt for what proved to be the last two Led Zeppelin gigs in the US. Backstage violence during the first gig almost resulted in the cancelation of the second. Then the latter was overshadowed by news of the death of singer Robert Plant's young son; the remaining dates on the tour were immediately canceled.

ABOVE RIGHT Poster for the 1976 cinema release of the mixture of live footage and fantasy sequences that was *The Song Remains the Same*. The central image shows the disused cinema in which the band rehearsed for their 1973 US tour, during which the movie's concert performances were filmed at Madison Square Garden. A recreated Madison Square stage was constructed in the UK in 1974 to shoot the closeups.

ABOVE Martine Grainey's design is an inimical take on the rock poster as railway timetable. In 1975 Led Zeppelin were at the very pinnacle of the rock mountain, with the release of their double album *Physical Graffiti* (hence the name of the steam engine in the poster). Earl's Court was at that time the biggest venue in the UK, and the three-night run was eventually extended to five.

FREDERICK BANNISTER PRESENTS PINK FLOYD THE STEVE MILLER BAND CAPTAIN BEEFHEART ROY HARPER AND LINDA LEWIS AT KNEBWORTH JULY 5th 1975

ALL ROADS LEAD TO KNEBWORTH · PINK FLOYD · 1975

OPPOSITE TOP Signed by the promoter, this poster is a 1999 limited-edition reprint of the original for Freddie Bannister's second Knebworth Festival, staged in 1975. The poster was designed by Storm Thorgerson of Hipgnosis, the studio closely associated with the headliners Pink Floyd. Bannister also circulated a one-color, white-on-black, text-only poster listing the performers in a form that was easier to read from a distance.

OPPOSITE BOTTOM For the 2010 exhibition Storm Thorgerson: Right But Wrong, Thorgerson found a typically quirky way to illustrate the body of work that he and Hipgnosis had contributed to Pink Floyd's visual image—this is one of a series of photographs titled *Back Catalogue*, displaying six of his instantly recognizable Floyd album cover designs.

ABOVE LEFT A 1977 poster for one of Bill Graham's major concerts held at Oakland Coliseum, CA, designed by in-house artists Randy Tuten and William Bostedt. The huge, inflated pig-balloon was a feature of Pink Floyd's performances on the band's six-month tour promoting the album *Animals*, which contained the song "Pigs (Three Different Ones)."

ABOVE RIGHT Another product of Pink Floyd's long relationship with designer Storm Thorgerson of Hipgnosis, this poster promotes the band's 1995 live release *P.U.L.S.E* with a three-dimensional development of the album cover's graphic artwork. Ten pairs of these "Pulse Eyes" were produced, making them among the most collectable prog rock artifacts ever.

126 127 **ABOVE LEFT** Graphic artist Mick Haggerty adapted his original album cover design for this 1979 promotional poster. Here, a pastiche of a breakfast diner menu card is developed from the original photographic image on the sleeve. LA-based, English-born Haggerty's love of kitsch Americana would lead to similar work at A&M Records with Supertramp's labelmates the Go-Go's, on their 1982 album *Vacation*.

TOP RIGHT This poster was created for the sixty-seventh gig of the 107-date US tour in promotion of the 1975 album that had turned the band into superstars, the eponymous *Fleetwood Mac*. The poster artwork is a relatively straightforward exercise in color and typography, with no hand-drawn elements. Michigan Palace was an old cinema that was later used by Eminem for scenes in his *8 Mile* movie.

BOTTOM RIGHT A deco-inspired poster by Randy Tuten and William Bostedt (aka Daddy Bread) for Fleetwood Mac's concert at Oakland Stadium, CA, in 1977. This performance was part of the Mac's eighteen-month world tour in support of their new album *Rumours*.

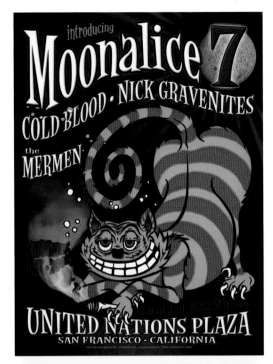

TOP LEFT Although Moonalice—a band made up of veterans of the West Coast scene—debuted as recently as 2007, the style of this poster, designed by Chris Shaw, references the heyday of '60s poster design. Moonalice commission a different poster (under Shaw's art direction) for every gig they play—well over 350 to date—and give away copies to the audience at the end.

BOTTOM LEFT Designed by promoter and Austin, TX, legend Bill Narum, this poster was for a very Texan gig in 1979. Rising Texan bluesman Stevie Ray Vaughan plays second fiddle to the brother of ZZ Top bassist Dusty Hill. Narum drew posters for Austin's famous Armadillo World HQ club, and designed all the covers for Dusty's band from *Tres Hombres* to *Degüello*.

ABOVE RIGHT The fictional whale Moby Dick can be seen in the soup in this vibrant 1977 Halloween poster for Moby Grape. Artist Jim Phillips emerged from the Santa Cruz surf community in the early '60s and still designs skateboards, surfboards, and snowboards today. Moby Grape, the legendary band from the '60s West Coast scene, split in 1971 but have reformed periodically ever since.

The Birth of the Stadium Show

Rock music's growth in status and social significance during the 1960s was reflected in the size of its audience. Attendance at performances by the most popular rock groups was outgrowing the clubs and ballrooms that had so far served the genre. Theaters were no longer big enough, as the Beatles had demonstrated at New York's Shea Stadium in 1965. Huge audiences generated huge revenues, and the biggest rock bands of the day now looked for auditoriums that were large enough to accommodate them.

Pop festivals were one answer. In 1969 Woodstock was not the first, but it did mark a turning point, a coming of age for rock 'n' roll. On the one hand it was the climax of the radical musical and social explorations of the '60s, a celebration of the freewheeling hippie spirit. On the other it was a demonstration of the demand and the commercial potential of live rock music, attracting half a million people and spawning five LPs of live recordings and a general-release movie. What rock band wouldn't want to play to such a large audience, or receive the ticket sales and spin-off income from it? The biggest rock stars of the day—the Rolling Stones and Led Zeppelin, for example, neither of which had been on the Woodstock bill—now began to exploit the capacity of sports arenas. Stadium rock was born and, at the first stadium concerts, stars such as Bob Dylan and the Who played to crowds in excess of 20,000.

It wasn't just the venues that were larger than before. Performances on such stages became theatrically more dramatic, in their efforts to reach the farthest members of the vast audience. The Who's Roger Daltrey (just five feet six inches tall) enlarged his onstage presence with big hair, platform boots, and tasseled stage clothes—and by swinging his microphone around his head in wide circles.

Other types of technical support also grew to keep pace with these larger-than-life onstage antics. In the bands' attempts to grab the audience's attention and keep them entertained, lightshows and pyrotechnics became (literally) flashier—brighter, more colorful, faster changing. And, of course, larger auditoriums demanded more powerful sound systems. Much of the music, like the performances, became less subtle; rock got louder and heavier in its efforts to communicate with the crowds. New heavy-metal acts such as Black Sabbath and Grand Funk Railroad distilled the virtuosity of '60s hard-rock pioneers like Jimi Hendrix into the music's essential components: simple riffs and high volume.

Posters of the day reflected this pumped-up, blunter form of rock. After the shimmering uncertainty of the psychedelic age, images were bolder, cartoonlike, or (more and more frequently) photographic. Often designed initially for an album cover, the same artwork was used on posters promoting not only the album but also the supporting tour, and, eventually, on the merchandise sold during the tour—the buttons, T-shirts, buckles, pins, and coffee mugs from which a now-commercialized rock industry derived so much of its income.

A central item in that range of merchandise was the souvenir poster. In the early '70s rock posters became desirable works of art in their own right and not merely vehicles for promoting live performances. In fact, as major events were promoted less frequently on billboards and telegraph poles than by advertisements in print and broadcast media, a new design industry arose that produced rock posters solely for the decoration of students' bedroom walls. Hipgnosis's poster included in Pink Floyd's *Dark Side of the Moon* was an oft-seen staple.

Not all stadium rock was heavy or simplistic, of course, and in the decades following the '70s several bands rose to the challenge of restoring some subtlety to the music they played in stadiums. U2, for example, developed a grandstanding, anthemic sound that was far removed from their intimate pub and punk-rock roots. The complexity and length of some rock music, from the expansive jams of the Grateful Dead to the orchestrated prog rock of Genesis, filled arenas with music of detail rather than of simplicity.

The 1980s stadium bands were arena rock acts like Foreigner, Kiss, and Bon Jovi. As rock fashion changed once again, they in turn gave way to the biggest of the indie bands: Nirvana, R.E.M., and Coldplay. By then, the commercial value of arena rock had been so conclusively proven by ticket and merchandise income that others wanted in on the act. A stadium tour can now attract significant big-name sponsorship from clothing, food, and drink manufacturers; tours by stadium-rock veterans the Rolling Stones have been supported by industrial and financial giants such as Budweiser, Volkswagen, and American Express. The Stones have raised some eyebrows with their willingness to accommodate corporate entertainment suites and retail outlets within the stadiums in which they perform. We've come a long way since Woodstock, it seems, and it's no longer "only rock 'n' roll."

OPPOSITE The Beatles in Shea Stadium at the start of their second US tour of 1965. The prototype for all stadium gigs, this event demonstrated the possibility and profitability of arena rock. The tour spurred new developments in stage lighting and amplification—at Shea, even the Beatles couldn't hear themselves play, despite using custom-made 100-watt Vox amps.

ABOVE LEFT David Singer's poster for a notorious episode of stadium rock excess from 1973. When the Who's Keith Moon passed out during the set, on a mixture of brandy and tranquilisers, Pete Townshend jokingly asked the audience if anyone could play drums. Nineteen-year-old fan Scot Halpin volunteered, and played for the last three songs of the evening.

ABOVE RIGHT Rare posters are valuable items of memorabilia. The wild reputation of the band and its fans caused the local authorities to cancel the Stones' plan to play two Welsh castles in one day during their 1973 European tour. All but a few copies of the poster, a combination of whimsical dragon fantasy and leering Jagger tongue, by artist K. Burness, were withdrawn and destroyed.

5

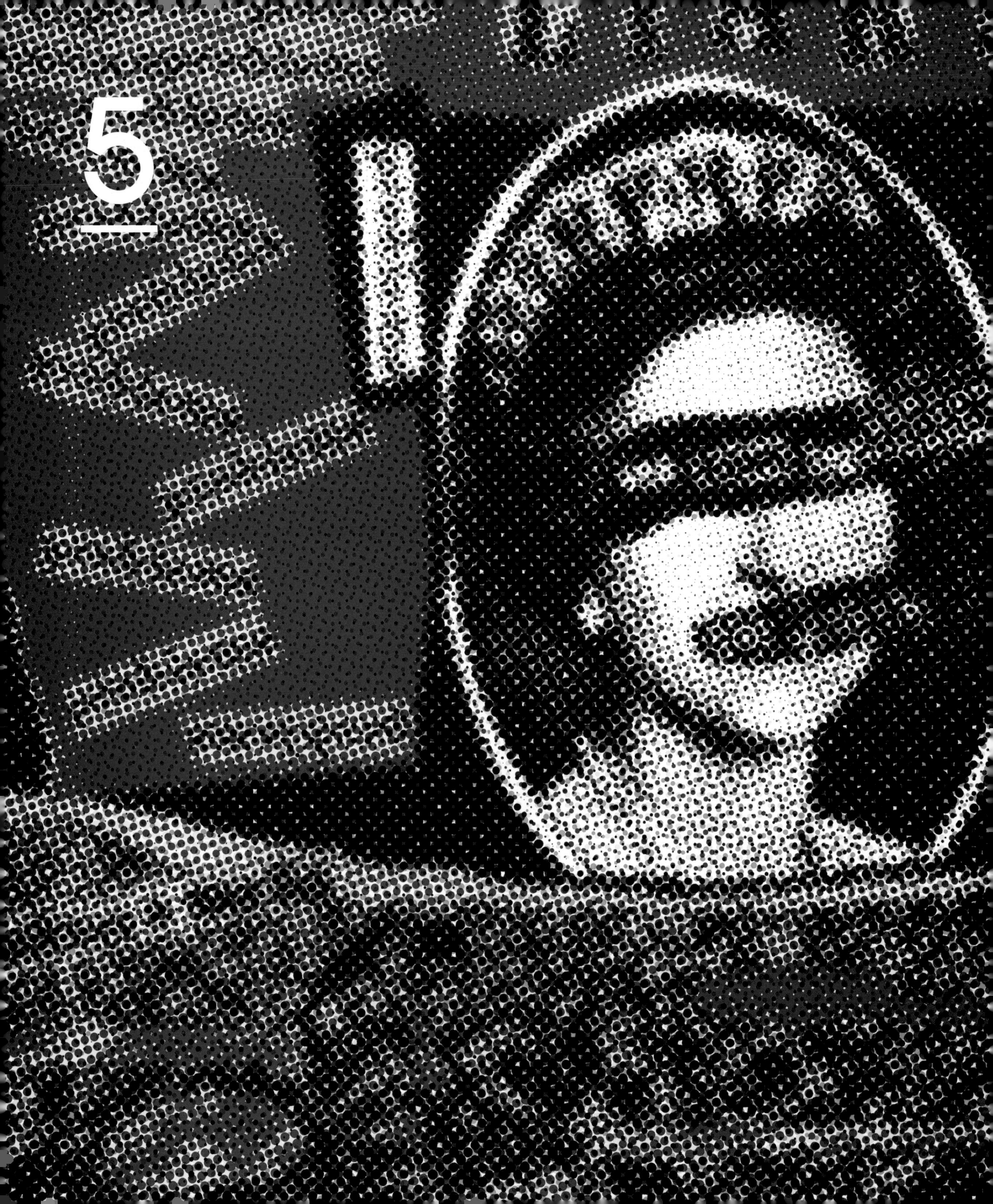

Punk & New Wave

1976–1986

The Blitzkrieg Bop

Punk was a reaction to the status quo and a rejection of the increasingly corporate direction that rock music was taking. Slick production values, grandiose stage sets, jet-set lifestyles, and superstar status further distanced the new breed of late '60s and early '70s "rock stars" from the audiences that subsidized their excesses. Rock 'n' roll was getting a bit stale in its old age.

That is not to say that there wasn't already a reaction to corporate excess before punk came along to kick over the statues. Since its earliest days, rock music's inherent sense of rebellion had been hard to contain, and protopunk antecedents within the US late hippie underground and the pub rock circuit in London helped germinate the seed that was to become "punk." The incendiary performances of the MC5 and Stooges in Detroit, Alice Cooper's shock rock flamboyance, the Velvet Underground's lyrical flirtation with prostitution, sexual deviancy, and drug addiction—all contributed to a critical mass just waiting for a catalyst.

New York's Greenwich Village provided a suitably liberal environment for the New York Dolls to develop their chops and try out their makeup. Glam rock had seen rock musicians flirting with androgyny, with Marc Bolan, Lou Reed, and David Bowie playing games with gender roles and representations, but the Dolls combined cross-dressing with outright confrontation before imploding spectacularly in 1975.

From 1974, New York's then crime- and poverty-ravaged Bowery District provided the backdrop to the birth of a distinct scene based around Hilly Kristal's CBGB club. *PUNK* magazine was on hand to lend the new zeitgeist a name, and within the next eighteen months, virtually the entire US punk vanguard of Patti Smith, the Ramones, Television, Talking Heads, Blondie, and the Heartbreakers (formed from the ashes of the New York Dolls by guitarist Johnny Thunders and drummer Jerry Nolan) would find a home, and an audience, through the growing reputation of the club.

In London, Malcolm McLaren and Vivienne Westwood began to develop a punk aesthetic from their base in the King's Road, Chelsea, in West London. Their shop—initially established in 1971 as Let It Rock but soon changing to Too Fast to Live, Too Young to Die, and subsequently to Sex in the spring of 1974—became a hub for the developing UK punk scene, though few realized at the time what impact it would have over the following years. Along with collaborator Bernie Rhodes, McLaren and Westwood developed a range of clothing that drew on sex and bondage wear combined with distilled situationist and anarchist slogans, with a clear intention to shock and outrage. McLaren had visited New York during the previous year, and had been involved in managing the New York Dolls as their career nose-dived, and he felt that an accommodation between his fashion ideas and back-to-basics rock music could drive a wedge into the complacency of contemporary popular culture.

The Sex Pistols, formed from a group of teenagers who hung around the Sex boutique, were to fulfill McLaren's wishes, though the employment of lead singer and spokesman Johnny Rotten (John Lydon)—an individual with a mind of his own—led to far more spectacular and less containable results than he had originally bargained for. A former associate of McLaren's, graphic designer Jamie Reid, was brought in to turn the Pistols' rage into visual form on record

covers, posters, and flyers. Drawing on his background in the subversive graphics linked to the situationist-inspired King Mob and the radical political magazine *Suburban Press*, Reid drew on collage, ransom note typography, fluorescent colors, and particularly hard-hitting imagery that set out to subvert traditional power relationships. The impending Silver Jubilee of the British monarch Queen Elizabeth II in 1977 provided a bigger public platform to rally against, and the ensuing media storm and backlash against the group helped fan the flames faster than anyone involved could have hoped.

Many others were waiting in the wings. The Clash, Buzzcocks, and the Damned were at the forefront of the UK punk explosion, each group adopting a distinct set of visual conventions that drew from, but did not merely replicate, Reid's punk aesthetic. Buzzcocks collaborated with designer Malcolm Garrett to develop a visual style that drew on modernist codes and typographic traditions, set within a contemporary framework. The Damned and the Clash relied more heavily on the image of the group themselves—a more consistent link with rock music's traditional modes of representation, though given a twist through harder-edged photography and a breaking of the typographic rule book.

New wave, a term initially seen as interchangeable with punk, saw the establishment of stronger links between the music industry and its antagonistic young offspring, together with a greater financial investment as its commercial viability became more apparent. Barney Bubbles, a designer who had started out producing light shows for British underground "happenings" and contributed to *Oz* magazine, helped lead a sophisticated new visual approach that would dominate popular culture over the following decade. His designs for Ian Dury, Elvis Costello, and Nick Lowe were playful and graphically powerful at the same time.

Younger designers also came to prominence during the punk era. Peter Saville, a former contemporary of Malcolm Garrett at Manchester Polytechnic, developed a similarly sophisticated graphic style that owed a lot to modernism and the past, but was equally in the "now." In the United States, Winston Smith—collaborating with singer Jello Biafra—began to move the agitational styles developed by Jamie Reid forward in new and more confrontational directions through his work for Dead Kennedys. Hardcore was developing as an independent musical offspring of punk as the clock turned to the 1980s, and Raymond Pettibon's visceral and surreal illustrations of the underbelly of modern consumer culture led the way to the establishment of a new visual aesthetic that the mainstream would find particularly difficult to co-opt.

Contemporary punk styles—visual and musical—vary enormously. Though punk and new wave have long since become recognized elements of the rock music canon, and to a certain extent no longer hold outsider status (the Ramones, the Clash, and the Sex Pistols have all been inducted into the Rock and Roll Hall of Fame, though the latter did at least refuse to attend the ceremony), a worldwide punk and hardcore underground remains, still kicking back against authority and delighting in nonconformity.

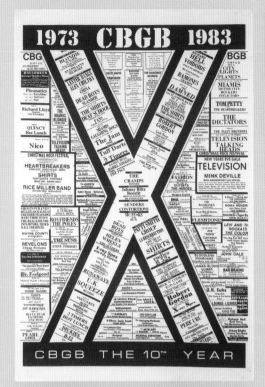

TOP LEFT Poster celebrating the 10th Anniversary of CBGB, 1973–1983, featuring a collage of past concert listings at the venue that proved instrumental in the development of punk. The venue at 315 Bowery in the Lower East Side provided a base for early gigs by Television, the Ramones, Patti Smith, Blondie, and Talking Heads.

BOTTOM LEFT Detroit's MC5—an abbreviation of Motor City Five—featured guitarists Wayne Kramer and Fred Smith and vocalist Rob Tyner. Their explosive live shows quickly built a sizeable local following as they led the Detroit rock scene through a renaissance, alongside the Stooges, from nearby Ann Arbor.

ABOVE RIGHT John Lydon (aka Johnny Rotten) and Sex Pistols manager Malcolm McLaren leaving a West London police station, July 1977.

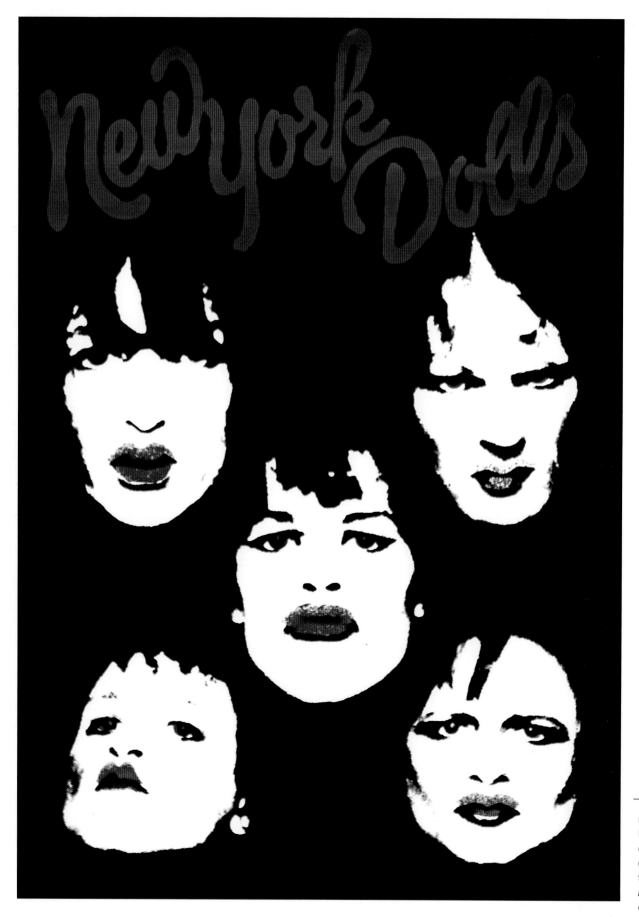

LEFT While the design of this New York Dolls group portrait carries a link to certain rock traditions—black-and-white close-cropped portraiture in the style of the Beatles' *With the Beatles* (*Meet the Beatles* in the US) album cover—the use of pink lipstick on each group member, mirrored by the lipstick-pink typography, signifies a questioning of traditional gender boundaries.

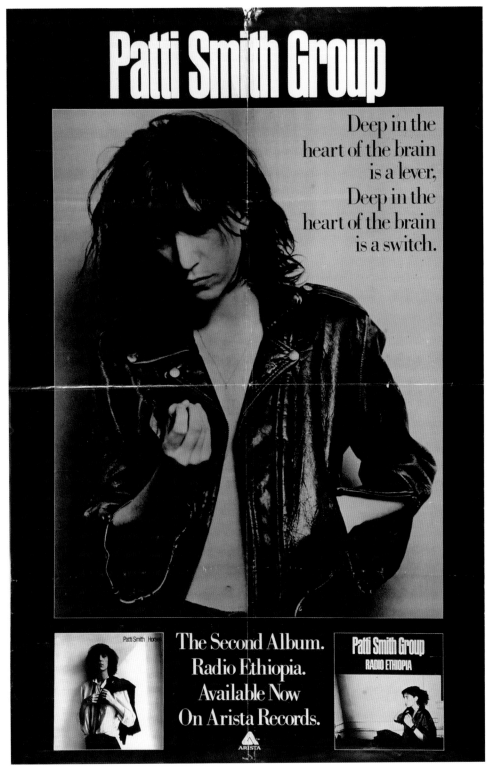

TOP LEFT The Iggy and the Stooges live album *Metallic KO* was released by Marc Zermati's influential Skydog label in 1976. The album was recorded in Detroit, MI, on February 9, 1974, at the group's final show, and features a riotous performance in the face of a hostile audience. The poster image here reflects some of that provocative antagonism.

BOTTOM LEFT This Mercury Records promotional poster of the New York Dolls was created for their eponymous debut album, released in July 1973. Gender roles and the notion of masculinity are once more questioned through provocative group photography by fashion photographer Toshi.

ABOVE RIGHT The first two albums by the Patti Smith Group, *Horses* and *Radio Ethiopia*, were released by Arista Records in November 1975 and October 1976, respectively. Smith's androgynous image is emphasized in the album cover photos by Robert Mapplethorpe (*Horses*) and Judy Linn (*Radio Ethiopia*), and in this strong central portrait by Lynn Goldsmith.

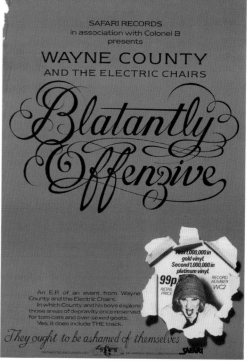

ABOVE LEFT Poster promoting the debut album by Richard Hell and the Voidoids, *Blank Generation*, released by Sire Records in October 1977, and their accompanying UK tour with the Clash. Hell had been a key member of New York protopunk groups the Neon Boys, Television, and the Heartbreakers.

TOP RIGHT Barry Jones designed this poster publicizing Wayne County at the Roxy Club in London, on March 4, 1977. Club founder and co-manager Jones employed his art-school-honed skills to produce collage posters advertising shows at the venue by using a color photocopier—a very rare (and expensive) form of new technology at the time.

BOTTOM RIGHT The "Blatantly Offensive" EP by Wayne County and the Electric Chairs (released by Safari Records in the UK in 1978) promoted by this poster included the notorious song "Fuck Off," first released as a single in 1977. County had been a key figure in the New York protopunk scene based around Max's Kansas City Club in the early '70s, before relocating to London in 1977.

**ALBUM SUICIDE BY SUICIDE / BRON 508
SINGLE CHEREE BY SUICIDE / BRO 57**

ABOVE LEFT Suitably bloodstained typography adorns this December 1977 poster for the eponymous debut album by Suicide, a New York electronic-music duo comprising Martin Rev and Alan Vega. Suicide had formed in 1970, but it wasn't until 1977 that Rev and Vega committed material to vinyl. Timothy Jackson and Alan Vega designed the poster, and Michael Robinson made the photo.

TOP RIGHT This November 1977 poster advertising the Ramones' album *Rocket to Russia* follows visual conventions similar to their debut album release, with the group (photographed by their manager Danny Fields) in coarse, high-contrast black-and-white against a brick wall, although the inclusion of a second color marks a higher level of investment and production.

BOTTOM RIGHT Blondie was at Mabuhay Gardens in San Francisco for a two-night residency in March 1977. This was during Blondie's first US tour, and the group was supported at both gigs by local heroes Crime. The venue, nicknamed the "Fab Mab," was fast becoming the premier venue for punk rock in San Francisco.

LEFT The Sex Pistols were to play at Derby King's Hall in the UK on December 4, 1976, for the second date on the Anarchy in the UK Tour. Following a media backlash against the group, however, dates were canceled, including this one. The bands on the tour—the Sex Pistols, Heartbreakers, the Damned, and the Clash—were asked to perform privately at the venue to local councillors before the planned concert, but refused.

TOP The image for this November 1976 poster advertising the Sex Pistols' debut single, "Anarchy in the UK," was created from a torn eight by four inches souvenir flag adorned with ransom note titles, bulldog clips, and safety pins. Jamie Reid designed the poster, and the photography was by Ray Stevenson.

BOTTOM LEFT This Sex Pistols promotional poster, *Pretty Vacant*, was designed by Jamie Reid and appropriates the image of two buses from US West Coast situationist group Point-Blank!, who themselves produced publications stating, "no copyrite, reproduce at will."

BOTTOM RIGHT Another poster by Jamie Reid, this time advertising the Sex Pistols at Mr. George's in Coventry, UK on December 17, 1977. The Never Mind the Bans Tour refers to both a series of canceled gigs during that year, and to the title of the group's debut album, *Never Mind the Bollocks*.

ABOVE LEFT Jamie Reid designed this November 1977 poster for the Sex Pistols' *Never Mind the Bollocks* album. Its provocative title ("bollocks" is popular slang for "testicles") led to a court appearance on obscenity charges for Virgin Records boss Richard Branson. The charges were successfully defended, but the case did little to calm the controversy surrounding the group.

TOP RIGHT For the cover of the Sex Pistols' fourth single, "Holidays in the Sun," and this October 1977 promotional poster, Jamie Reid borrowed from a tourist brochure promoting holidays in Belgium, adapting the dialog in the cartoon strip to reflect the song's lyrics. Virgin Records faced legal action from the copyright owners of the original advertisement and were forced to withdraw the sleeve.

BOTTOM RIGHT This collage poster designed by Jamie Reid was included with the first edition of the Sex Pistols' album *Never Mind the Bollocks*, and has individual illustrations for each song.

TOP Promotional poster for the Sex Pistols *Great Rock 'n' Roll Swindle* album. By the time the movie of the same name was released in 1980, the group had split up and bassist Sid Vicious had died from a heroin overdose while on remand for the murder of his girlfriend, Nancy Spungen.

BOTTOM RIGHT Sex Pistols, *God Save the Queen* poster, May 1977. Probably the most iconic example of punk art, Reid's graphic collage appropriated an official photo of the British monarch by Cecil Beaton, adding torn strips across the eyes and mouth and crudely rendered "ransom note" typography.

ON EPIC RECORDS AND TAPES

TOP Pictured is the banner poster for the US release of the Clash's eponymous debut album. The album did not secure a US issue until some time after the group's second album, *Give 'Em Enough Rope*, had attracted interest stateside, and this poster includes photos of the band during different phases of its development.

BOTTOM LEFT This March 1977 poster was created for the debut single by the Clash, "White Riot," and features an image of the group in posed "arrest" positions photographed by Caroline Coon.

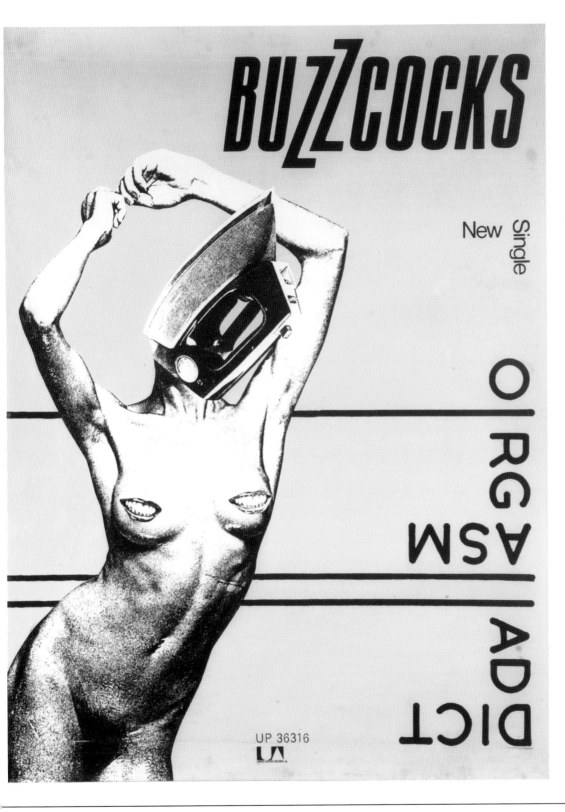

OPPOSITE, BOTTOM RIGHT The Clash, *Cut the Crap*, November 1985. The final release by the Clash—by which time, guitarist and key songwriter Mick Jones had quit and the group was in disarray. The poster attempts to mirror the concept of the album as a back-to-basics and hard-hitting punk rock record, but the record itself was let down by poor production and received little critical or commercial success.

ABOVE LEFT Promotional poster for Buzzcocks' second single, "Orgasm Addict," their major label debut, released on United Artists in October 1977. The poster incorporates the sleeve illustration by Linder Sterling and typography by Malcolm Garrett, although the grid was reworked (without the designer's consent) by United Artists' in-house design department.

TOP RIGHT Buzzcocks' single "What Do I Get?" was released in January 1978. Drawing on the simple geometric angles of the single sleeve designed by Malcolm Garrett, the poster creates an intriguing puzzle for the viewer to solve.

BOTTOM RIGHT Buzzcocks' debut album, *Another Music in a Different Kitchen*, was released on the United Artists label in March 1978. The poster—designed by Malcolm Garrett—mirrors the album cover art. Initial copies of the album came with a specially designed silver carrier bag labeled "Product."

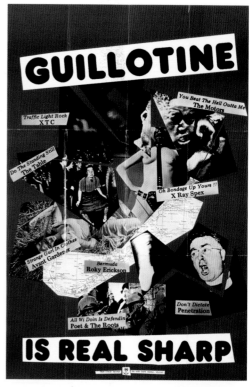

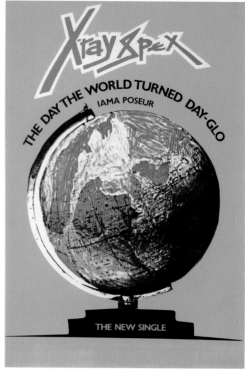

ABOVE LEFT X-Ray Spex *Oh Bondage, Up Yours!* poster was based on the picture sleeve for the group's debut single on Virgin Records in October 1977. The central image of singer Poly Styrene was shot at the Roxy Club in London, and was color-photocopied to increase its tonal depth. The poster was designed by Poly Styrene, with typography created by Sophia Horgan.

TOP RIGHT This promotional poster was for *Guillotine*, a compilation album released by Virgin Records in February 1978 to showcase the company's new wave catalog. The album included tracks by Penetration, XTC, X-Ray Spex, the Motors, and others, and was pressed on an unusual ten-inch format. The poster collage bears no relation to the album artwork, but it does reflect a suitably eclectic visual approach.

BOTTOM RIGHT This poster for X-Ray Spex's *The Day the World Turned Day-Glo*, from March 1978, was designed by singer Poly Styrene. The globe photograph, made by Falcon Stuart, was colored-in using felt tip pens and color-photocopied, with additional hand-rendered typography by Sophia Horgan.

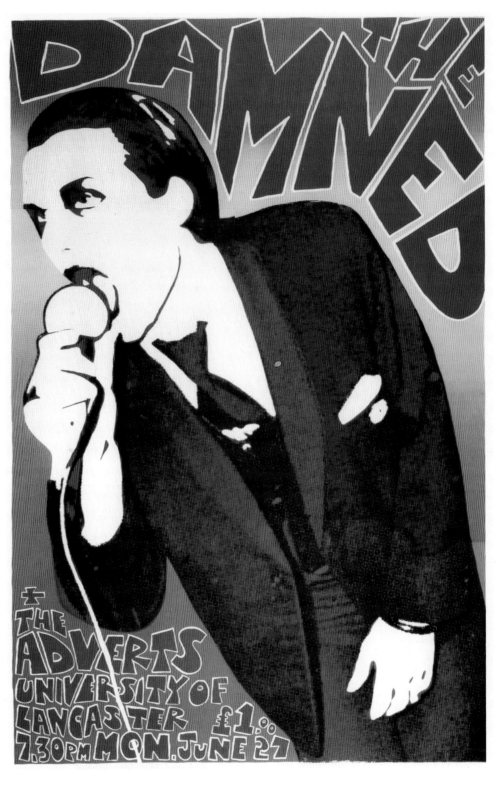

ABOVE LEFT The Damned, 5th Anniversary gig at the Lyceum, London, July 5, 1981. Resembling a fan's scrapbook, the collage artwork for the poster utilizes photos, press cuttings, ephemera, and graphic material gathered for the group over the previous five years.

ABOVE RIGHT A screenprinted poster promoting a gig by the Damned and the Adverts at the University of Lancaster on June 27, 1977. Colleges up and down the country promoted gigs by up-and-coming punk groups, and posters were often designed in-house by students—with a resulting tendency not to follow style guidelines or art direction by the record label, or official group identity.

DIY Design

Punk opened many doors to individuals and groups wanting to establish themselves through music, fashion, movies, print, and the whole range of visual arts, yet perhaps its most telling legacy was in empowering individuals. Two leading advocates—Jamie Reid and Raymond Pettibon—inspired a generation to "do it themselves."

The sense of empowerment was fueled by a range of different sources, however, ranging from the direct call-to-arms of the early DIY (or "do-it-yourself") pioneers in the UK to the blindingly simple fact that the basic directness of punk's aesthetic inspired others to think that (if it's so easy), maybe they could have a go, too. The eponymous debut album by the Ramones failed to set the world alight in terms of commercial or critical acceptance, but its inherent musical properties—three chords and surplus energy—proved to others that rock 'n' roll need not be an exclusive club.

Early press reports on the punk phenomenon had emphasized the technical incompetence of the musicians concerned, many of whom wore their lack of musical sophistication as something of a badge of honor. The phrase "anyone can do it" then became something of a punk credo, a critical inversion of what could be seen as a negative aspect of punk's "everyman," everyday "ordinariness," generating a sense of inclusion, rather than a derogatory exclusion from popular culture.

Graphically, punk's aggression and subversive aesthetic played out in similarly dynamic ways. Since "anyone" could now make a form of rock music, it followed that "anyone" could release a record, create a record cover, or produce a poster. The instantaneous, devil-may-care attitude of punk's musical primary movers was reflected in the graphic styles that accompanied their output. At the vanguard in the UK, Jamie Reid set the standard through his work with the Sex Pistols. Drawing on traditions of protest graphics, particularly the Dada- and surrealism-inspired situationist movement of the '60s and elements of the late hippie underground in the US and UK, Reid developed an armory of graphic tools and techniques designed to shock and disturb.

The situationist strategy of *détournement* provided Reid with a template with which to subvert the power of hierarchical images. The Silver Jubilee celebrations of 1977 saw the UK adorned with union flags and images of Queen Elizabeth II, now celebrating twenty-five years on the throne, with her forelock-tugging public (apparently) keen to come to the party. The authority of such imagery was crying out for some radical re-appropriation, and Reid

duly obliged—taking the official photographic portrait of Her Majesty the Queen by Cecil Beaton and intervening directly with the image, through the use of safety pins, swastikas, and ransom-note type. Such effrontery had rarely been seen before (or at least not within a pop-music context), and the public and media backlash was swift and severe, which in turn only supplied more fuel for Reid and his punk contemporaries to continue to stoke the fire.

In a similar way to the empowering nature of "simple" punk music spawning a generation of copyists and inspired amateurs alike, Reid's direct graphic interventions inspired a host of followers to take up their scalpels and marker pens. An undercurrent of much of Reid's work—that the populist media surrounding you is your canvas; go steal, parody, pastiche, and piss-take—was the spur to action. However, much like the Ramones template, where those seeking to emulate the group's sound discovered that it takes more than a rudimentary knowledge of the form to come anywhere close, these new designers frequently discovered that Reid's methodology was underpinned by both technique and skill. This punk thing was harder than it looked, as well as sounded.

In the US, hardcore—a movement derived directly from punk, but inspired by a new intensity and political vision—gave rise to a vast underground network of gigs, record and tape releases, and 'zines, setting out to build its own world away from the music industry altogether. The driving aesthetic here was the flyer, a simple printed or photocopied sheet of paper with a hard-hitting and visually direct message.

The designer most associated with West Coast hardcore during this time was Raymond Pettibon (real name Raymond Ginn), who rose to prominence through his work for his brother Greg's band, Black Flag. Pettibon originally played bass for the band, but eventually stepped aside to concentrate solely on visual work. One of his first innovations was the "four-bar logo," which would become the core graphic identity for Black Flag, and is still a potent symbol of the early hardcore scene. Pettibon followed this with a series of often disturbing and sometimes violent and anti-authoritarian India ink cartoonlike drawings that adorned the covers of Black Flag record releases,

"There was so much spontaneity. Me and Malcolm knew each other really well and we just got on and did what we did. It was an attitude . . . the thing I did appreciate from the Pistols was the attitude."

JAMIE REID

as well as hundreds of flyers for gigs by the band. Like Reid before him, Pettibon was much emulated and copied. As pioneering punk artists, both provided inspiration for others to create their own visual aesthetic, which sometimes resulted in a new direction for punk graphic design, while equally sometimes falling flat on its face. However, as with all do-it-yourself punk output, the act of creation is often more important than the product created, and Reid and Pettibon should be celebrated not only for their own incredible skill and artistry, but also for empowering others to "have a go" themselves.

OPPOSITE LEFT Photographic portrait of Jamie Reid, circa 1990.

OPPOSITE RIGHT Raymond Pettibon at the Ruskin Theater, Santa Monica, CA, on January 30, 2011, for an event hosted by Art Los Angeles Contemporary, a West Coast international contemporary art fair.

ABOVE LEFT Flyer designed by Raymond Pettibon promoting a gig by Black Flag with Dead Kennedys at the Mabuhay Gardens, San Francisco, on October 10, 1979—a lineup that featured two of the

ABOVE RIGHT Sex Pistols "God Save The Queen" promotional poster, May 1977, by Jamie Reid. Reid produced several different variations of this poster design, which was based around an image taken

148 149 **ABOVE LEFT** This poster was designed by Jamie Reid to promote the debut single by Dead Kennedys, "California Über Alles." The swastika was used by early punks as a shock symbol. Here, it takes on a more literal meaning, linking the song's title—a barbed reinterpretation of a Nazi slogan—with the lyrical observation that "Zen Fascism" had replaced the hippie ideals following the Summer of Love.

TOP RIGHT Publicizing Crime, the Dils, and UXA, plus a Sex Pistols video showing at the Mabuhay Gardens in San Francisco on December 18, 1977, this poster was designed in typically hard-hitting graphic style by photographer and group associate James Stark.

BOTTOM RIGHT A Los Angeles 1977 tour blank—using an iconic image designed by Gary Panter—for the Screamers, who were to become retrospectively fêted as major influences on West Coast punk and hardcore long after their demise, despite never having a record released during their short lifetime.

ABOVE LEFT A two-color poster for legendary LA punk innovators the X, playing at the Numbers club in Houston, TX, on November 1982. Here, the group's simple but effective name allows for its use as a graphic device, forming a grid for portraits of each member of the band.

ABOVE RIGHT This hardcore flyer for a show by Black Flag, UXA, Adolescents, and Screws at Baces Hall on October 24, 1980, in Los Angeles was based on an illustration by Raymond Pettibon, who also created the iconic Black Flag logo. Pettibon's hard-hitting and surreal images of a dystopian American society were hugely influential within the hardcore scene.

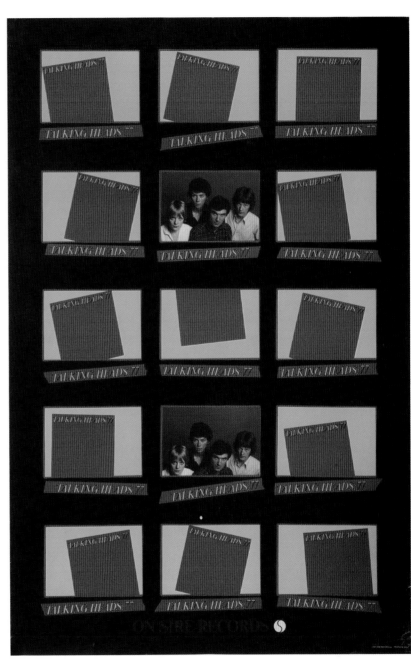

OPPOSITE, TOP LEFT This Stiff Records promotional poster for Elvis Costello's debut album, *My Aim Is True*, in July 1977, was designed by Barney Bubbles, with photography by Keith Morris. Costello was presented as a kind of modern-day alternative Buddy Holly.

OPPOSITE, BOTTOM LEFT Elvis Costello, *Get Happy!* promotional poster, February 1980. Costello's trademark spectacles make another appearance on this typically playful abstract collage by Bubbles, which uses simple graphic elements to construct an image of a light bulb doubling as a portrait of the singer.

OPPOSITE, RIGHT This second poster variation for Costello's *Get Happy!* campaign, once again designed by Barney Bubbles, this time uses purely typographic elements and a play on key words in the song titles from the album.

ABOVE LEFT The Jam, *Sound Affects*, November 1980. The poster reflects the album cover design, itself a pastiche of the artwork used on the *Sound Effects* records produced by the BBC (British Broadcasting Corporation) in the '60s.

ABOVE RIGHT *Talking Heads '77*, October 1977. The typographic simplicity of the album cover (designed by David Byrne and Jerry Harrison, with photography by Mick Rock) is repeated on the poster, though with playful variations of cropping and framing to give the overall design a dynamic impact. The angular layout also dramatizes the choice of italicized type on the original cover.

ABOVE LEFT Theatre of Hate's *Do You Believe in the Westworld?* promotional poster, created in January 1982, was designed by C. More Tone (Chris Morton), former in-house designer at Stiff Records. The simple two-color design uses strong angles for visual impact.

ABOVE RIGHT Eastern Front hardcore punk festival, Berkeley, CA, July 1981. The lineup for this two-day festival included scene leaders from North American hardcore, such as D.O.A., Flipper, T.S.O.L., and the Fix, together with UK postpunk/dub group the Slits. Based on a photo of a Japanese kamikaze pilot, the poster is suitably bold and provocative.

OUTLAW PRESENTS

THE SELECTER

PLUS SUPPORT

FRIDAY
13th MARCH 7·30 pm

ALL TICKETS £3.00 FROM BOX OFFICE & USUAL AGENTS.

LIVERPOOL ROYAL COURT

Publicity & Display Ltd., Godalming, Surrey.

ABOVE The Selecter, Liverpool Royal Court, March 13, 1981. Having started out as part of the Two Tone stable of artists, sharing the debut single release on that label with the Specials, the Selecter enjoyed a high level of success before disbanding in the spring of 1981. The gloved hand references the first album cover of '60s band the Music Machine.

RIGHT The Selecter, Mo-Dettes, and the Beat at the Electric Ballroom, London, October 13, 1979. Created at the height of the ska revival in the UK, this gig poster incorporates the Two Tone label identity designed by Jerry Dammers from the Specials: the fictional character Walt Jabsco in a black suit, white shirt, black tie, and "pork pie" hat.

STRAIGHT MUSIC PRESENTS

THE SELECTER

THE MO-DETTES
THE BEAT

ELECTRIC BALLROOM
184 CAMDEN HIGH ST. NW1 (NEAREST TUBE CAMDEN TOWN)

SATURDAY 13th OCTOBER at 7·30

TICKETS £2.00 (INC VAT) ADVANCE ELECTRIC BALLROOM BOX OFFICE TEL. 485 9006
LONDON THEATRE BOOKINGS, SHAFTESBURY AVE., TEL. 439 3371. PREMIER BOX OFFICE, TEL. 240 2245.
OR ROCK ON RECORDS, 3 KENTISH TOWN RD., NW1. TEL. 485 5088.

ABOVE LEFT This poster showing Gang of Four, 3 Swimmers, and Little Bears from Bangkok, at the Showbox in Seattle, WA, on July 10, 1981, was designed by Art Chantry. Chantry had moved to Seattle in 1978 and began designing posters for the local punk community. This gig featured the highly charged, political postpunk UK band the Gang of Four as headliners.

TOP RIGHT Squeeze, "Cool for Cats" promotional poster, March 1979. The combination of simple graphic elements and playful typography is reminiscent of '50s movie and pop music graphics, in keeping with the single's title, which was itself taken from a '50s TV show.

BOTTOM RIGHT Psychedelic Furs "We Love You" poster, October 1979, designed by Richard Butler, vocalist with the group. The Psychedelic Furs were to achieve international prominence through the use of their 1981 single "Pretty in Pink" as a Hollywood movie title in 1986, with the group subsequently re-recording the song for the soundtrack.

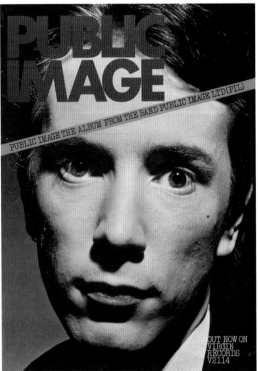

ABOVE LEFT Public Image Limited (PiL) "Memories" promotional poster, October 1979. The single was taken from their forthcoming album *Metal Box*, which incorporated innovative packaging as a set of three twelve-inch discs contained in a round metal canister.

TOP RIGHT Public Image Limited debut album poster, December 1978. The album cover concept by Terry Jones and Dennis Morris, reflected in the poster design, was to present a totally fresh corporate image for the new group, in the style of high-end fashion magazines.

BOTTOM RIGHT Public Image promotional poster, 1979. The self-titled debut single by John Lydon's new group, following the Sex Pistols' split in February 1978, was packaged in a wraparound newspaper sleeve. This poster follows the same theme, though the additional overprint of the PiL logo indicates that it was produced during the following year, as the group developed a consistent graphic identity.

ABOVE LEFT For their fourth album, the Clash took inspiration from the Frente Sandinista de Liberación Nacional, or FSLN, a left-wing political group that took control of Nicaragua in Central America and established a revolutionary government in 1979. The poster draws on the imagery and graphic styles associated with the revolution.

TOP RIGHT Siouxsie & the Banshees, *The Scream*, November 1978. The album cover included a photo of swimmers underwater that was shot by Paul Wakefield. A similarly claustrophobic feeling relating to water is communicated through this promotional poster, which was art directed by Jill Mumford.

BOTTOM RIGHT Siouxsie & the Banshees, *Once Upon a Time*, December 1981; the first compilation album release of Banshees material. A focus on images of lead vocalist Siouxsie Sioux had by this time come to dominate the group's visual identity. The poster was designed by Stylorouge, at that point a new graphic design agency recently formed by creative director Rob O'Connor.

RIGHT Promotional poster for the Plasmatics gig at the Hammersmith Odeon, London, August 8, 1980. The group's outrageous stage performances included smashing TV sets, chainsawing guitars, and blowing up cars. All of which led the band into direct conflict with the local governing body, the GLC; the gig was canceled by its fire inspectors, who deemed it to be a health and safety risk.

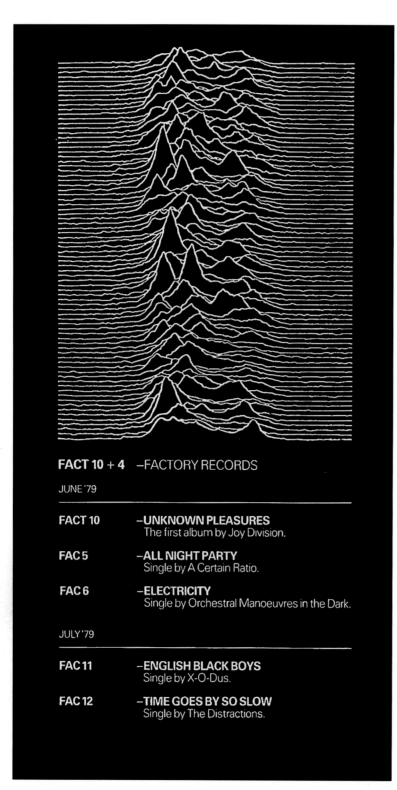

FACT 10 + 4 —FACTORY RECORDS

JUNE '79

FACT 10 —**UNKNOWN PLEASURES**
The first album by Joy Division.

FAC 5 —**ALL NIGHT PARTY**
Single by A Certain Ratio.

FAC 6 —**ELECTRICITY**
Single by Orchestral Manoeuvres in the Dark.

JULY '79

FAC 11 —**ENGLISH BLACK BOYS**
Single by X-O-Dus.

FAC 12 —**TIME GOES BY SO SLOW**
Single by The Distractions.

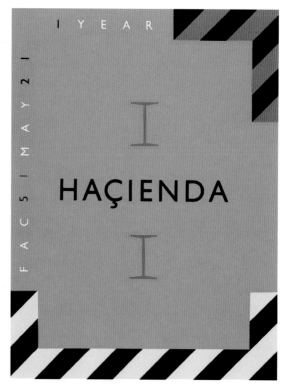

I YEAR

FAC 51 MAY 21

HAÇIENDA

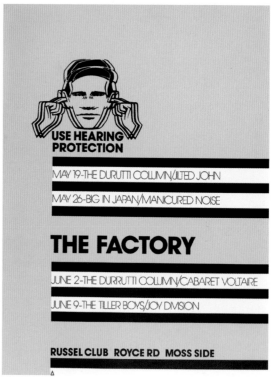

USE HEARING PROTECTION

MAY 19-THE DURUTTI COLUMN/JILTED JOHN

MAY 26-BIG IN JAPAN/MANICURED NOISE

THE FACTORY

JUNE 2-THE DURRUTTI COLUMN/CABARET VOLTAIRE

JUNE 9-THE TILLER BOYS/JOY DIVISION

RUSSEL CLUB   ROYCE RD   MOSS SIDE

ABOVE, LEFT Factory Records promotional poster FACT 10 + 4, designed by Peter Saville, June 1979. The title simply refers to the catalog number of Joy Division's debut album, *Unknown Pleasures*, and four further releases by the label. Factory famously attributed catalog numbers to all their "products," including FAC 51, the Haçienda nightclub.

ABOVE, TOP RIGHT FAC 51, the Haçienda nightclub's first anniversary, May 21, 1983, designed by Peter Saville. Elements of the graphic design, including the yellow and black stripes, reflect the visual style of the club's decor (created by interior designer Ben Kelly), which drew its inspiration from industrial architecture.

ABOVE, BOTTOM RIGHT The Factory, club promotional poster designed by Peter Saville, May 1978. The poster was assigned the catalog number FAC 1 as the first "product" from the company set up by local entrepreneur and TV presenter Tony Wilson. Factory would establish a record label six months later, but at this stage the company's focus was on promoting local gigs in Manchester.

ABOVE Promotional poster for the debut album by the Slits, *Cut*, released by Island Records in September 1979. With strong photography by Pennie Smith, the three main members of the group—Ari Upp, Viv Albertine, and Tessa Pollitt—are shown covered in mud and wearing just loincloths. The same image was used for the album cover, gaining the band much publicity in the process.

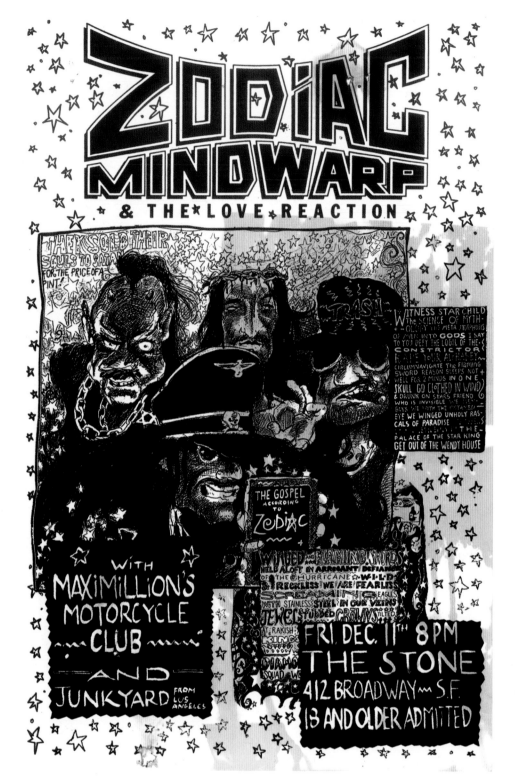

160 161 **ABOVE LEFT** Poster advertising Zodiac Mindwarp & the Love Reaction with Maximillion's Motorcycle Club and Junkyard at the Stone in San Francisco, CA, on December 11, 1987.

ABOVE RIGHT Texas Love In, featuring the Big Boys, the Dicks, Really Red, Butthole Surfers, and Recipients, at the A.L.A. Club in Austin, TX, on January 16, 1982. The poster, designed by Big Boys singer Randy "Biscuit" Turner, shows a classic lineup of Texan hardcore punk.

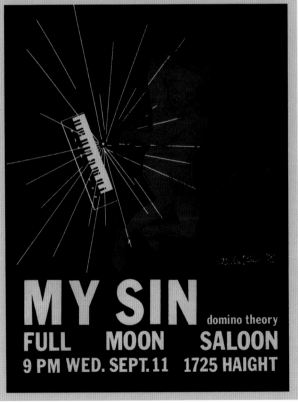

ABOVE LEFT This Butthole Surfers, Houston and Dallas poster, from December 1989, was designed by Frank Kozik. Originally working as a poster designer for punk groups in Austin, TX, Kozik was to revolutionize rock poster design over the following decade following his relocation to San Francisco.

TOP RIGHT The Replacements, Flying Color, and the Catheads at the Fillmore, San Francisco, CA, May 3, 1986.

BOTTOM RIGHT This poster for My Sin, at the Full Moon Saloon in San Francisco, September 11, 1985, was designed by Michael Hall. My Sin was actually a stage name for one-man electronic dark wave performer Stan Fairbanks.

The Blank Generation

New York City has long supported a thriving arts scene, but as the late '60s segued into the early '70s, it hosted a series of events that were to be influential far beyond the city limits. During the early part of the decade, New York's art and music innovators had frequented a few small clubs in the city. The Mercer Arts Center and Max's Kansas City had provided a home for the Velvet Underground, New York Dolls, and Wayne County to throw rock's rule book out of the window and start over again, and a sense of impending change permeated the East Coast music scene. It was to take an opportune combination of events for the next step in the narrative to unfurl—together with a key locus around which a new scene could coalesce. A small, seemingly inconsequential club called CBGB was to become that place.

The band Television, formed in New York in 1973 by aspiring poets Richard Hell and Tom Verlaine, pioneered the way. Looking for a venue to present their new musical vision to the waiting world, they came across Hilly Kristal's CBGB club at 315 Bowery in the Lower East Side, a run-down bar in an area long since fallen into decline. Kristal had originally intended the bar to feature country, bluegrass, and blues music (hence the acronym CBGB), along with poetry readings and other performance art events, but he agreed to let the pair play a residency at the club with their band. Television established a cult following over the next few months and was soon followed through the same doors by other new and aspiring groups, including the Ramones, the Patti Smith Group, the Fast, Blondie, and Talking Heads. John Holstrom, Ged Dunn, and Legs McNeil's *PUNK* magazine gave the new movement a name.

If there was a shared vision within this quite dissimilar collection of misfits, it was that rock could be re-envisioned: pared down and stripped back to its essential elements. For Television and Talking Heads, that meant literally deconstructing the musical structure and reassembling it into a more direct and visceral form. Patti Smith developed a similarly iconoclastic approach to language itself, building her solo spoken-word performances into a rock framework with the help of guitarist Lenny Kaye. For the Ramones, this new shift toward an aesthetic minimalism manifested itself as a series of short, sharp bursts of high-speed energy and volume, dispensing with guitar solos and many other long-held staples of rock music structure, while Blondie drew musical inspiration from earlier forms of rock 'n' roll and the directness of classic pop.

The visual aesthetic of this developing scene mirrored its musical return to fundamental principles. Graphics were simple, clean, and unadorned with excess decoration. The purity of the message defined the form—dress codes, typographic styles, even reproduction values were distilled to their most basic elements. This sense of pared-down clarity and directness paved the way for a punk and new wave explosion on both sides of the Atlantic, and signified a cultural shift that was to change rock music forever.

ABOVE LEFT Portrait of Hilly Kristal, CBGB proprietor, January 2002.

ABOVE RIGHT Television on stage at CBGB, 1975. The band, formed by school friends Richard Meyers (aka Richard Hell) and Tom Verlaine, alongside lead guitarist Richard Lloyd and drummer Billy Ficca, helped to build the early New York punk scene before internal rivalry led to an acrimonious final split in 1978.

"I think by 1974 glam rock had run its course and you could see the new directions bands were going in. I think the Little Hippodrome show where Television opened for the New York Dolls reflected it best—you could see and hear that something new was going on. After the show, someone told me about CBGB, and she made it sound like the most exciting place on Earth."

JOHN HOLMSTROM, *PUNK* MAGAZINE

ABOVE Movie still from *Burning Down the House: The Story of CBGB*, a documentary appraisal of the iconic venue directed by Mandy Stein, released in 2009.

6

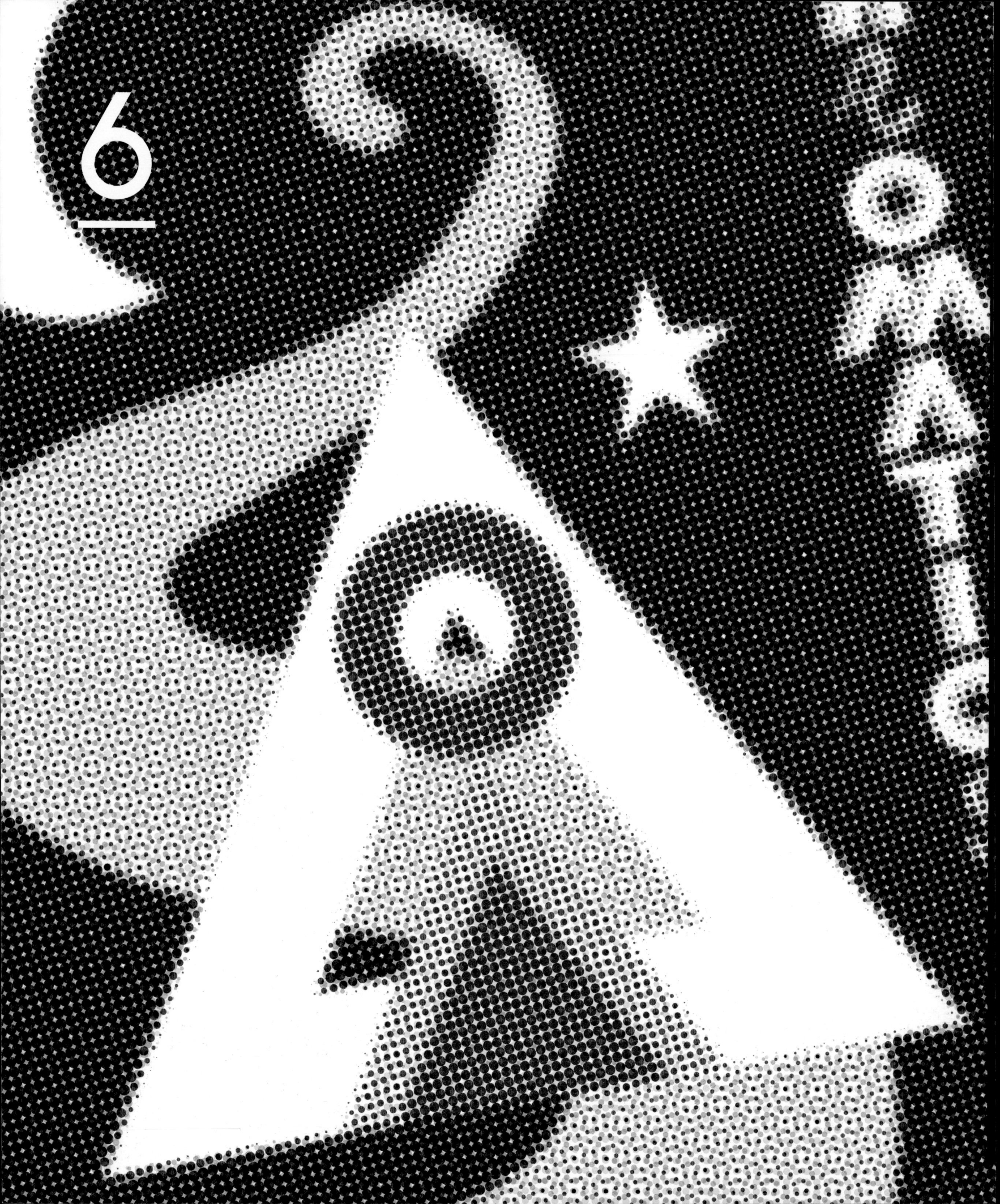

Hip-Hop
& Dance

1982–2010

Born in the USA

Nominally streets apart, house and hip-hop are in so many ways close cousins. Overwhelmingly black at its outset, hip-hop gave a voice to Bronx communities that had been abandoned after ill-conceived road-building projects. House music, largely black and gay, was a raw response by Chicagoans to the death of disco. DJ Frankie Knuckles bluntly described it as "disco's revenge." These days, they are among the world's most successful music genre franchises.

Hip-hop's look was sealed a long time before the first MC had boasted into a mic. Although there was little connection between hip-hop and graffiti in its early years, by the early '80s, it was considered part of a sacred quartet that also included breakdancing, DJ'ing, and MC'ing. It informed and creatively guided much of the early rap scene, which was either based on the inflated bubble lettering pioneered by graffiti artist Phase 2 (which the artist described as "softies"), or looked as though it had been produced with Letraset and copious supplies of coffee on mom's kitchen table (and not a million miles away from the old boxing bill posters).

The graffiti style of lettering, distended and cartoonlike, seemed to suit the personality of the music perfectly, with its larger-than-life MCs' party incantations and DJs whose look was entirely modeled on the pimp-daddy himself, Rick James. Hip-hop's look helped its music. "When writers started treating graffiti as art, it opened things up for rap to be treated as legitimate music by music writers," claims former *NME* (*New Musical Express* magazine) writer Richard Grabel. "And people also started writing about breakdancing. So the three prongs of black youth culture at the time—rap, graffiti, and breakdancing—started getting covered a lot more in the mainstream press." It came together beautifully at Kool Lady Blue's now infamous parties at the Roxy in the early '80s, where she brought graffiti artists like Phase 2 onto the bill with performers such as Afrika Bambaataa, Rocksteady Crew, and Fearless Four.

House style was never as codified as rap. While house music may have germinated in Chicago, IL, where a lively and vibrant postdisco scene had incubated under the watchful eyes of city heroes Frankie Knuckles and Ron Hardy, it was in the UK that the combustible addition of the drug ecstasy gave house music its passport to travel the globe.

Acid house's design aesthetic was jumbled and unfocussed compared with the spray-painted delineation of hip-hop, but there existed an incredibly creative climate that drew inspiration from wildly disparate fields, ranging from punk rock (of which there were surprisingly numerous parallels) to the first Summer Of Love in San Francisco—and even as far as Roger Dean, the go-to progressive rock designer of the early '70s.

Punk rock, the seeming antithesis of acid house, provided the inspiration for so much. First, there were scores of punk rock refugees for whom house, with its broadly anti-establishment message and DIY aesthetic, was a natural step—including Andrew Weatherall, Kris Needs, Mike Pickering, and others. It's patently visible in the artwork of the early Back 2 Basics flyers, whose promoter Dave Beer was a Wakefield, West Yorkshire, UK punk. His collaborative homages with designer Nic Gunn were so blatantly based on

Jamie Reid's work that they even held an exhibition in B2B to mark Reid's work. Sign of the Times, nominally a clothes store in Kensington Market where some of the best parties in London were thrown in the '90s, also drew water from the same well: "Keep warm this winter: MAKE TROUBLE."

At the opposite end of the Spectrum (pun intended) was Dave Little's iconic design for the eponymous club. With its rheumy eyeball and ornate framing, it was clearly designed with both Summers of Love in mind. Little credits US artist Rick Griffin as an inspiration. "I wanted to show a direct nod towards the first happenings with Ken Kesey, as I saw acid house as the fulfilment of what Kesey started twenty-five years previously." Another revival was the smiley face, which George Georgiou was primarily responsible for with designs for Danny Rampling's influential London club Shoom (although Alan Moore's twelve-issue comic book limited series *Watchmen* must be credited for its contemporaneous use as a cultural signifier).

Mark Wigan's accomplished work for the Brain, a club he ran with former JoBoxer band member Sean McCluskey for a few years around the turn of the '90s, was the culmination of the previous decade's work as an illustrator for both *i-D* and *NME* magazines, as well as several club commissions to paint murals (the Limelight in New York among them). Hailing from the north of England, Ian Swift also cut his teeth on London magazines, mainly *The Face* and *Arena*, but was responsible for bringing the ethos of Blue Note designer Reid Miles and mixing it perfectly with the typographic experimentalism of Neville Brody.

In the US, a rave scene blossomed, independent from the gay clubs that had sustained dance music through its postdisco years. These new nights were frequently the result of British DJs relocating to the US and bringing a template with them; thus, there would be frequent nostalgic nods toward the mother country. Johnny Dynell and Chi Chi Valenti's Jackie 60 weekly Tuesday club nights, and their subsequent tenure of the brilliant club named Mother, in Manhattan's meatpacking district, were neither gay nor straight, and somehow managed to attract everyone. Jackie 60 was what a club run by John Waters might look like.

OPPOSITE A George Georgiou design that shows the extensive influence of Blue Note designer, Reid Miles. Hardly surprising, given the many refugees from the pre-acid house soulboy scene that dominated clubs in the early '80s and included luminaries such as one of the featured DJs, Nicky Holloway.

ABOVE The godfather of hip-hop and father of the electrofunk sound, Afrika Bambaataa was, of all the early pioneers, the guy with the seriously deep crates. As likely to play the Monkees or the B52's as Parliament or Fatback Band, he was also instrumental in trying to bring peace to the warring tribes of the Bronx through dance.

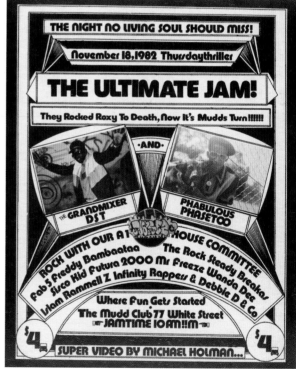

ABOVE LEFT Bronx-born Phase 2 (real name Lonny Wood) was hugely influential on the early graffiti scene, not least for being credited with inventing "softie" lettering (the cartoonlike, exaggerated lettering beloved by graff artists). Phase 2, alongside Buddy Esquire, was also the go-to designer for most of the great early poster and flyer art on the nascent rap scene as on this 1983 poster.

TOP RIGHT Negril was a small reggae club in downtown Manhattan, NYC, whose role in the birth of hip-hop was in introducing the rest of the world outside of the Bronx and Harlem to this new phenomenon, as shown on this 1982 poster. Run by British enthusiast Kool Lady Blue and former member of the Tubes, Michael Holman, it was the stepping-stone for Blue's tenure at the Roxy with Afrika Bambaataa.

BOTTOM RIGHT The Mudd Club, launched in 1978, became the yang to Studio 54's yin in Manhattan's nightlife, an antidote to the glitter and excess of Steve Rubell's club. This Phase 2-designed bill poster shows Grandmixer D. ST, already a rising star at the Roxy (and the man who put the scratches on Herbie Hancock's "Rockit") slam down at Steve Mass's club.

ABOVE *Graffiti Rock* was an ill-fated 1983 hip-hop TV show hosted by Michael Holman that was years ahead of subsequent efforts like *Yo! MTV Raps*. Based on other popular music shows, such as *Soul Train*, it's become—along with the seminal *Wild Style*—one of the few examples of early documentation of the growing hip-hop scene in New York. It never made it past the pilot episode, but it is now available as a DVD.

ABOVE LEFT Trevor Jackson's early work, from the late '80s, shows a clever molding of the early concepts of graffiti, with designs based on bold typography, combined with the same sense of fun that gave much of his work a Day-Glo, arresting feel, as on this 1988 poster.

TOP & BOTTOM RIGHT This pair of posters by Scrojo—from 2010 (top) and 2007 (bottom)—perfectly represents the *oeuvre* (if that's not too overblown a word to describe women with their kit off) of everyone's favorite ex-drug dealer, Snoop Dogg. It juxtaposes Snoop's own well-worn logo with an almost regal decal—or, as regal as you're likely to get with pneumatic girls perched atop.

ABOVE LEFT Given his relationship with the law—Ice T's metal band offshoot, Body Count, had its most controversial release with "Cop Killer"—the tongue is firmly in cheek for this FBI badge takeoff for Ice T's September 2010 show at Brooklyn's Knitting Factory by Two Arms Inc.

ABOVE RIGHT Scrojo's 2002 appropriation of the Russian type style, with its flavor of communism and subversion, is the perfect marriage for a poster featuring Public Enemy, whose outspoken frontmen Chuck D, Professor Griff, and their comic sidekick Flavor Flav, made them the most controversial band of the '80s.

TOP & BOTTOM LEFT A brilliant pair of posters from the enigmatic and highly prolific California-based artist Scrojo. Scrojo has now designed over one thousand posters for the Belly Up venues in Aspen, CO, and always seems able to capture something of the feeling of the band he's representing, while also offering glimpses of his inspirations, from Robert Crumb to Toulouse Lautrec.

ABOVE RIGHT These days, Ice Cube (former member of gangsta rap act NWA) is better known for his acting roles, his clothing line, and his love for the LA Raiders, than he is for being a rapper. This poster was created by Scrojo for Ice Cube's 2007 show at Aspen's Belly Up.

ABOVE LEFT Mitchy Bwoy's bold figurative posters have been instrumental in establishing strong public personas for the likes of Detroit's hipster Amp Fiddler and London collective Bugz in the Attic and, here, capturing the hippest hopper in the world, the Roots drummer Questlove at a 2001 show.

ABOVE RIGHT Blackalicious's poster by Scrojo promotes their third album, *Blazing Arrow*, at the Solano Beach, San Diego, CA, venue. The jutting breasts and lollipop phallus subscribe to the well-worn tropes of hip-hop iconography, which is somewhat at odds with the band's more meditative approach.

The Birth of Hip-Hop

The hip-hop of the 1970s, birthed in the projects of the Bronx, bears little resemblance to Rap Inc., 2011. In its original form, hip-hop was revolutionary, innocent, and fun, with few of its musicians having any ambition beyond being the best breaker at James Monroe High or the slickest MC at the Disco Fever.

Hip-hop was revolution by spray-paint, sweat, and turntables. It existed for years in its own small universe, long before the first record within the genre was ever made. Hip-hop eventually made it out of the projects, to downtown Manhattan and, propelled by the newfound respect of graffiti artists, ended up in the studios of Enjoy, Sugarhill, and Paul Winley. Its pioneer DJs turned the prosaic turntable into an instrument as potent as a Fender Strat or a Ludwig drum kit. Those early days are a far cry from the lyrically acquisitive cliché of modern rap, in which the DJs, graffiti artists, and breakdancers have walk-on parts in the story of the MCs' lust for Cristal, Swarovski, and ladies with generously proportioned bottoms.

Hip-hop is arguably the most revolutionary of all musical art forms, with its roots in the repurposing of other artists' records. It's certainly the most postmodern. As the former art student and DJ Johnny Dynell said upon seeing the early DJs: "They were playing the same records I was playing, but what they were doing was taking two copies and going back and forth and making this new thing out of them. Coming from the art world, I thought it was brilliant. It was like Marcel Duchamps."

First there was graffiti, which began to pockmark the walls and subway trains of New York City in the early '70s, making underground stars of TAKI 183, Tracey 168, Futura 2000, Dondi, Lee, and scores of others. Charlie Ahearn, who went on to make the influential early hip-hop movie, *Wild Style*, recalls his early fascination with Lee (Quiñones). "When I was in the Lower East Side, there were all of these murals all over. I really wanted to work with him, but he was really hard to find. What I found amazing was all the teenage kids were all completely in awe of this guy as an artist, yet the galleries had no idea he even existed."

In the Bronx, a giant DJ called Kool Herc played records in a totally new way. Led by dancers' reactions, he eschewed the meat of the song in favor of the breaks (the part where the drummer cuts loose from the rest of the band). Grandmaster Flash was an early disciple: "He was playing the music that I loved, but if he was playing duplicate copies of a certain section of a record they would have to wait until he mixed it, because it was never on time. I could see the audience in unison, then in disarray; in unison, then in disarray." It was Flash's genius to combine the funk records of Herc's sets with the smooth mixing techniques he'd heard from disco jock Pete DJ Jones.

In school gymnasiums and basketball courts or clubs like the Executive Playhouse, Hevalo, and Club 371 in the Bronx, Harlem World and the Black Door in Harlem, and the Aubudon Ballroom in Washington Heights, gigantic sound systems, inspired by Herc's own system Herculoids, sprouted like mini black skyscrapers, as DJs and kids would battle for the best breakers

and loudest sound system (Herc rarely lost). It all eventually coalesced in a little club in the Bronx.

"We were open seven nights a week," remembers hip-hop record executive Sal Abbatiello. "Monday was like a Saturday. We've got Grandmaster Flash on Monday, Lovebug Starski on Tuesday, I go get this other kid for Sundays called Eddie Cheeba, and now I give Kool Herc a night, he has a night with Clark Kent. And I always wanted to get DJ Hollywood, but Hollywood wouldn't come to the Fever, he just wouldn't come. Finally, I convince Hollywood and he does a Wednesday. And there's Jun-Bug. So I got everybody. The club was mobbed every night." For a few years, this limited-capacity nightclub—the Disco Fever—was the center of the hip-hop universe, before the news began to creep out in Manhattan.

Eventually, the dam broke. Early enthusiasts Kool Lady Blue, a British music nut, and Michael Holman, who was a member of art-rock band Gray, alongside Jean-Michel Basquiat and Vincent Gallo, brought the party downtown, first at the Negril and, more famously, later at the Roxy, where much of its culture arguably peaked and, for a brief moment, New York's tribes danced under one banner. "The mainstream music press was always

ABOVE The first act to have a rap hit with a song that many claimed (not without reason) was stolen from the rhyme books of Grandmaster Cas of Cold Crush. Given the fact that "Big Bank" Hank even spells out Cas's name (Casanova) in the rap, the cause for the prosecution against the Sugarhill Gang looks sound.

that it wasn't something they'd just thrown together. The crates of records that they were lugging down to these clubs spoke of a real connoisseur's knowledge of music that was deep and wide. Hearing those DJs made me think, 'Wow, it's not just throw your hands in the air.' These guys really had a deep knowledge of musical history."

By the turn of the decade, rap had finally made it onto vinyl and that early sweet scene was swiftly confined to history as the MC juggernaut consumed all before it, including its architects, the DJs, alongside the breakers and graffiti artists. Nothing was ever as revolutionary again. The story, once the rappers had found their voice, was about two things: guns and money. The party was dead.

THURSDAY OCT. 28th at midnite
¡ NEGRIL RAP NITES RETURN !

featuring..

"D.J. KOOL HERC"
the Godfather of Hip Hop Music

Africa Islam, RASTA D.J. Garfield SPUNK,

D.J. High Priest, and....

M.C.s; Rammellzee, Fab 5 Freddy
Lonny Wood, Word Up?!, and more.

five $'s adm.
located at 181 2nd Ave. & 11th st.

ABOVE LEFT The lo-fi flyer with the hi-powered lineup: Kool Herc, Fab 5 Freddy, Rammellzee, and Africa Islam; in other words, half the founders of hip-hop in one tiny club in downtown Manhattan. Note also the Letraset vibe on the flyer design, which is similar to a sixth-grade art project, and all part of the charm.

ABOVE RIGHT Kool Herc (left) and Grandmaster Flash receive their Pioneer awards at the Source's 1999 Awards ceremony, in a long overdue recognition of the work of the Bronx duo who, along with Afrika Bambaataa, are the holy trinity of hip-hop's conscience.

From **Manchester** with Love

TRANCE ATLANTIC TRIPOUT

TOP LEFT Mark Wigan's designs, pitched somewhere between Pablo Picasso and Keith Haring, helped define a particular era in club history during the '80s through his work at the Brain Club, which he also ran with former JoBoxer Sean McCluskey. This 1989 flyer was an invite for an evening of techno house with DJ Frankie Bones to promote the release of his compilation *Dance Madness and the Brooklyn Groove* (Wigan also designed the album sleeve).

BOTTOM LEFT The year 1986 was an interesting time for the Haçienda, when it had stopped being a hangout for small clutches of depressed students asking for Bauhaus, yet before it was drenched in sweat and ecstasy. It had finally found its feet as a club with help from DJs like Hewan Clarke and Mike Pickering, yet still had that cachet as an arty hangout, as demonstrated by design group 8vo's (de)constructivist poster.

TOP RIGHT Despite Chicago handing house music to the world, America's relationship with rave music happened largely because (primarily) white kids in Manchester and London exported it back. This 1990 primo event in Los Angeles was a classic example of dance culture being sold back to the US under the guise of bands like 808 State and Happy Mondays. Top one, nice one, get sorted.

BOTTOM RIGHT Stephen Hauptfuhr was scarcely out of his teens when he started throwing parties in Los Angeles during the rave explosion in the early '90s. In Hauptfuhr's 1990 flyer, using the pseudonym Mr. Kool-Aid, he was promoter, DJ, and designer of these early influential West Coast parties.

THE RETURN OF THE
HAPPY HAPPY
HAPPY HAPPY
HAPPY
SHOOM!!!
≡ CLUB

12 thro'5 Sat. Jan. 30
Fitness centre
Crown House
56-58 Southwark st.
SE1
Present invite plus £5

CHICAGO HOUSE & FRANKFURT BEAT
SPUN BY: **COLIN FAVER**
AND DANNY RAMPLING

All Night bar
NO RUFFIANS

TOMMOROWS WORLD + LIVE WIRE Crew · INVITATION TO A

WAREHOUSE PARTY

BANK HOLIDAY SAT 29TH + SUN 30TH APRIL
12 AM ONWARDS. MEET HOLBORN STN W.C.2

MR·C · CLEVELAND ANDERSON
DJ BONES · KID BACHELOR
SHOCK · TREVOR FUNG

TOP LEFT Club legend Nicky Holloway, who made a fortune and lost it, was the man behind the brilliant Special Branch parties in south London in the '80s, which had a full roll call of prefame DJs on the bill, including Pete Tong, Gilles Peterson, Danny Rampling, and Paul Oakenfold. George Georgiou designed the logo in 1987.

BOTTOM LEFT This 1987 flyer design launched a thousand smileys. George Georgiou's basic design was instrumental in reviving the smiley for a new generation of youth, while the club itself, Shoom—run by Danny and Jenni Rampling—was responsible (in London at least) for helping break acid house into the mainstream.

ABOVE RIGHT This primitive, yet alluring poster, captures the essence of much of the acid house era artwork, which was frequently created by enthusiastic amateurs armed with Letraset, magic markers, a grade C in Art O-level. The trend for warehouse parties had begun with promoters like the Dirtbox crew almost ten years earlier. The bill included Mr C, later to find fame with the Shamen, as well as house pioneers such as Kid Bachelor, former dancer Cleveland Anderson, and Ibiza veteran Trevor Fung.

WITH THE UN-SWEETN'D RETURN OF LOLLIPOP LEIGH AND SUGAR DADDY SEAN AT OUR DEAR MARSHA'S FRONT DOOR. ONCE INSDE WITNESS TOMAS BLISS AND THE "BALDY BUNCH" DO THEIR THING ON THE BED. DJ's MR. KOOL-AID (STEVE) AND MICHAEL (ALICE'S HOUSE, THROUGH THE LOOKING GLASS, AQUARIUS) SUPERSONIC SOUND BY CHRIS COMBS SPECIAL FILMING OF "THE MYTH OF HOLLYWOOD" A SWEDISH DOCUMENTARY AND YOU'LL BE IN IT!

THIS IS A PRIVATE PARTY
INVITATON ONLY
$10 ADMISSION

SATURDAY MAY 19th

FOR DIRECTIONS GO TO 5th AND ALAMEDA (BEHIND THE GAS STATION)
FURTHER INFO (213)281-1860

TOP LEFT Ian Swift has had a long association with Gilles Peterson and the London jazz scene, first designing the Talkin' Loud logo and then a proliferation of record sleeves, flyers, and posters that comprised a who's who of British jazz (and funkers), including this poster for the Talkin' Loud parties at the Fridge in London in 1992.

BOTTOM LEFT The designer, promoter, and DJ (who also happened to be the Mr. Kool-Aid of flyer legend) of this event was the multitasking Stephen Hauptfuhr. This party, from May 1990, was a series promoted by Hauptfuhr when he was still in his teens. Twenty years hence, LA resident Hauptfuhr is still throwing interesting parties, though these days without the assistance of either Mr. Kool-Aid or Marsha Brady.

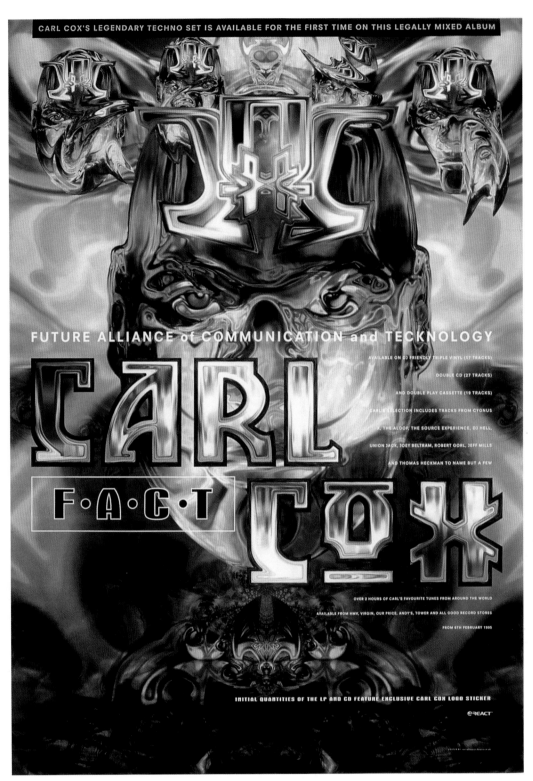

OPPOSITE, ABOVE RIGHT These days, for all of his Jamaican roots maneuvers, Jah Shaka is now as "London" as jellied eels and Pearly Kings. Shaka has been running sound systems in southeast London since the early '70s, and even portrayed himself in Franco Rosso's cult movie *Babylon*. Mitchy Bwoy's dynamic 1999 graphic perfectly captures the Shaka vibe.

TOP LEFT Creamfields, the festival which grew out of the Liverpool nightclub Cream, has long since outlasted its older brother, which ceased as a weekly night some years ago. The company now throws Creamfields festivals in locations all over the world, from Buenos Aires to Brisbane, although their powerbase is still the annual party on August bank holiday in the northern UK town of Warrington.

BOTTOM LEFT Sign Of The Times parties and flyers (designed by Paul Shobbrook) were a reflection of the wild eclecticism of Fiona Cartledge, whose Kensington clothes stall was the base of all activities. It was the sort of place where you could find rubber T-shirts, '60s hippie flares, Jackie badges, bondage trousers, and, of course, tickets for the next party. This flyer was advertising a 1991 party.

ABOVE RIGHT Now regarded as something of a techno classic, this 1995 album poster by Me Company's Paul White (who also worked on Björk's albums) displays all of the Detroit genre's obsessions with futurism and technology perfectly; the result is like a cross between *The Matrix* and *Total Recall*.

ABOVE LEFT Kate Moross's collaboration with Alex Sushon produced this enigmatically brilliant design for the Chromatics' April 2008 show in London, which would make Peter Saville blush with its charming lack of information. It's pure art (deco), but it suits the band's shimmering Italo sound perfectly.

TOP RIGHT It may have been 1992, but the punk influence is clear. So clear, in fact, that Jamie Reid, who created the famous ransom note lettering style on his work for the Sex Pistols, held an exhibition at the club. The Basics' slogans, too, are pure punk: "Two steps further than any other fucker." And, although it was largely a house music night, it was not unusual to hear the Clash.

BOTTOM RIGHT DJ Johnny Dynell, the promoter of the Night of a Thousand Stevies (NOATS) events, also designed this 2007 poster. Dynell (who comes from an art school background), alongside partner Chi Chi Valente, has been responsible for some of New York's more diverting and outrageous parties, from Jackie 60 to many varied evenings at their long-running venue Mother (sadly no more). NOATS, their most long-running party (now in its twenty-second year), even inspired a cult movie: Gypsy 83.

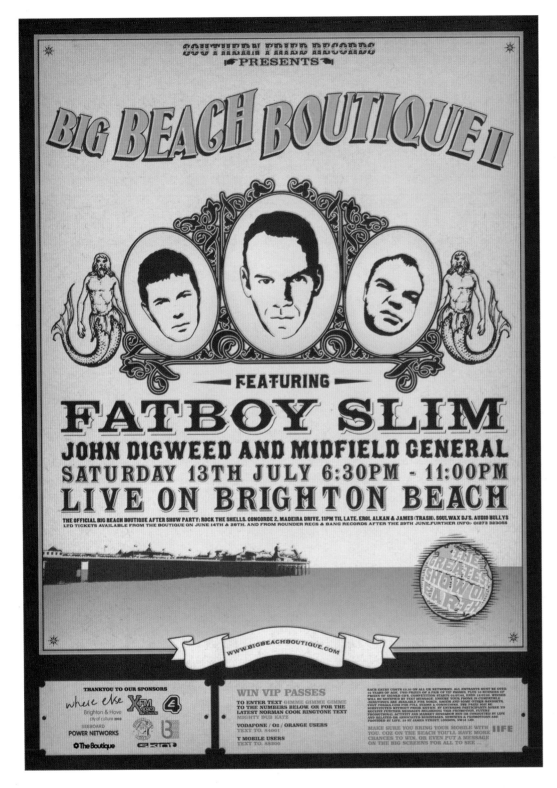

ABOVE LEFT The second and most controversial of Norman Cook and co's huge Brighton beach parties. Staged in 2002, the organizers anticipated a crowd of 60,000 but close to a quarter of a million people turned up, causing huge problems with traffic congestion. A nurse, Karen Manders, died as a result of a fall, and the party ended early, although the organizers were absolved of any blame.

ABOVE RIGHT Designer Trevor Jackson's work spans over two decades, and shows no sign of slowing down. Jackson, also a DJ and producer under the pseudonyms of Underdog and Playgroup, was responsible for a slew of graphically bold designs in the late '80s (mainly for indies like Gee Street and Champion). This barcode-inspired design is from Soulwax's 2004 album, *Any Minute Now*.

Dave Little

The designer Dave Little was responsible for some of acid house's most iconic and enduring images, among them the Spectrum "eye" design. The Geordie moved down to London in the early '80s and threw himself into the London club scene where he began producing graphic work for movers and shakers from Wag owner Chris Sullivan to the Boy's Own crew from Windsor. Little was also the in-house designer for Rhythm King during its late-'80s chart heyday.

There are many influences one might expect from the man behind one of acid house's most iconic designs, but Elton John's record sleeves are not among them. Dave Little, the designer of the famous "eye" logo for Spectrum—which was later used on the *Balearic Beats* album, as well as Electra's cover version of "Jibaro"—makes no bones about one of his design heroes. "I was really into Alan Aldridge, who did sleeves like Elton John's *Captain Fantastic and the Brown Dirt Cowboy*. All pen-and-ink and little watercolours. Beautiful man, fucking beautiful. He was a great airbrush artist."

In truth, acid house never had a signature style. It came from everywhere and everyone—stolen, created, or simply borrowed for the evening, like a druggy bridal gown. Ideas fetched in from the dying embers of punk and situationism, soul boys ripping off their favorite Blue Note sleeves, the dregs of 1980s Neville Brody fetishists. They were all present and correct. Acid house—entrepreneurial and anti-establishment, commune and profit center, drug-addled and drug-free—was all of these. Dave Little fitted right in.

Little studied art at South Shields Marine and Technical College, then headed for Hounslow, west London, where the snooty lecturers did not share his artistic passions. "I was really into airbrush art, which I'd taught myself. In those days there was no Photoshop, no computers, so if you wanted to retouch a photograph you had to wield an airbrush. By the time I was seventeen or eighteen, I was quite proficient and using Paasche Turbos and they could do a shine on a fly's eyeball." It was while out in the wilds of west London that he encountered the Clash photographer Pennie Smith, whose converted railway station studio in Hounslow was conveniently located at the end of his street. "She gave me a bullet that Joe Strummer had fired, which I wore as a necklace for years."

London clubs in the mid '80s were a melting pot of styles, sounds, and scenes, and the ebullient Little befriended some of its most notorious characters, among them Blue Rondo's Chris Sullivan, then owner of the Wag; Karl Bonnie of Renegade Soundwave; and Martin Heath, who had just started a record label, as had everyone then. "I did a sleeve for Renegade Soundwave on Rhythm King and Martin said to me, 'Oh, you're very good—I'll hire you on the spot.' Next thing you know, I'd done the sleeves for all these hits: S-Express, Bomb the Bass, Beatmasters. Classics of the time. It was a busy time between 1987 and 1990. Probably did some of my best work then, because there was an energy in London I don't think will ever be repeated." Eventually the spirit of acid house would be co-opted by the Post Office ("Sorted!") and diluted by endless corporate endorsements, but there

is still, somehow, something left in all of those whom it touched. "I think it changed the world," claims Little. "I don't think there's a nightclub around that hasn't been touched by acid house."

ABOVE Dave Little is a man of the old school, a gentleman-graphic artist whose skills were honed pre-Photoshop and Air Mac. Raised on the airbrushing skills of Alan Aldridge and Michael English, he was proficient with a Paasche Turbo before he was out of his teens, before going on to provide acid house with some of its most iconic imagery.

> "House only worked when you did the house dance, 'cos you couldn't do your old one. So you had all these people taking a new drug, doing a new dance, in their new clothes with their new mates."
>
> TERRY FARLEY

TOP LEFT It all looks a bit trite and dated, but for a short period those badly dressed ravers had done more to rock the fabric of British society than a thousand *Guardian* columnists. The yellow "smiley" logo, first created by Harvey Ball in 1963, has been revived numerous times, but nowhere more potently than in acid house's Watchmen-inspired love affair.

BOTTOM LEFT You don't have to think too hard to work out the inspiration for this Little-designed magazine cover. Alex and his droogs were perfect fodder for reappropriation on this hugely influential fanzine, published by the Boy's Own collective, whose numbers included DJs Andrew Weatherall and Terry Farley.

ABOVE RIGHT Dave Little's 1988 homage to the original Summer of Love was so effective that the idea was reused for the *Balearic Beats* album on the FFRR label and Electra's EP "Jibaro." Early acid house promoter Gary Haisman apparently suggested the eye logo, while Little's border was inspired by the graphic work of Grateful Dead designer Rick Griffin.

Alternative, Heavy Metal, Thrash, Grunge, Goth & Indie

1980s–2000

The Second Golden Age of Rock Poster Art

The '80s witnessed an explosion in styles and themes in rock art. While artists like Danny Garrett gave new life to the conventions of classic '50s poster iconography, heavy metal artists were drawing on the kind of sword-and-sorcery imagery that was patented by the artist Frank Frazetta in the '60s. The underground punk and hardcore scenes birthed an inventive approach to typography and logos—typified by Dave King's logo for Crass—while the first wave of affordable desktop publishing software allowed mainstream designers to create posters with a slick and polished appearance.

But in the '90s all this changed. Vinyl LPs were gradually replaced by CDs and MP3s, and as a result artists made the switch from designing lavish gatefold album sleeves to refocusing their creative efforts on the more traditional, silkscreened poster for advertising gigs. As baby boomers began to pay eye-wateringly high prices for mint originals from concerts at the psychedelic ballrooms of the '60s, rock poster art gained a new respectability; posters were being exhibited in renowned galleries alongside works by establishment painters, and collected and displayed by the Library of Congress, and at the Rock Poster Society's Festival of Rock Posters in San Francisco, established in 1999. America's rock poster art had entered its second golden age.

With this new-found status, rock poster design became the acknowledged successor to pop art, incorporating high- and low-brow themes into a vivid new American vernacular style. In the same way that Wes Wilson, Stanley Mouse, and Alton Kelley had incorporated motifs from art nouveau advertising into their work in the '60s, the posters designed by the new wave of American artists drew from the trash culture of the preceding four decades, reassembling the elements into something new, exhilarating, and quite postmodern: *Mad* magazine, horror comics, tiki and Polynesian kitsch, rockabilly and bowling iconography, custom-car and hot-rod design, Mexican Day of the Dead and *lucha libre* wrestling imagery, B movies, pinup girls, Hanna-Barbera cartoons, vintage pornography, Marvel comic books, Sailor Jerry tattoos, psychedelic poster art, steampunk and speculative fiction—it all went into the often eye-popping and lurid mix. The use of irony, juxtaposition, bricolage, and pastiche was the antidote to both the stylized blandness of pop and major label rock design, and the overblown sword-and-sorcery imagery of the heavy metal scene.

Instead, these new artists were inspired by the DIY impetus of early '80s punk and hard core, which provided many of them with the opportunity to start creating photocopied flyers and posters. Some, like Gibby Haynes of Texan psych-noise act the Butthole Surfers, came from working backgrounds in commercial art. Others, like Chuck Sperry or Emek, came from artistic families or studied printmaking at college, like Detroit's Mark Arminski. Most were self-taught, applying a kind of garage-band mentality to making art, learning the craft as they went along. Meanwhile, the period of inner-city

postindustrial decline opened up commercial spaces, allowing artists to create studios cheaply in old warehouses or garages, building homemade silkscreenprinting presses from industrial detritus, creating art from junk.

All of this activity would have gone unnoticed if the '90s hadn't also been the era when a new market for rock posters was being created. During the '80s promoters and record labels had begun to invest seriously in gig posters as merchandising opportunities, alongside T-shirts and tour programs, but in the following decade artists themselves became more entrepreneurial. Austin-based designer Frank Kozik, who had previously inked sleeves for the indie label Amphetamine Reptile, was the first to establish a new business model, contacting promoters and bands before shows and offering them one hundred free posters for upcoming concerts in return for the right to be able to sell five hundred of the same posters at the gig or by mail order afterward. This meant that fans no longer had to salvage posters from record-store walls or tear them down from the walls of clubs, complete with staple holes, but rather allowed them to order mint-condition posters after the actual concert. The most famous of these new artists—Kozik and Chris "Coop" Cooper, known for his buxom devil women—soon branched out into other media, designing T-shirts, action figures, shot glasses, and Zippo lighters. Some even began to create new posters for gigs that had taken place many years previously, while others began to experiment with new textures, combining the photo-offset lithographic printing process that had been used since the '60s with new digital tools, allowing artists to print on metal and vinyl plastic, or in 3-D.

The Internet also meant that what had previously been an impromptu patchwork of artists working on a regional level for local bands or promoters became a global phenomenon. The web inspired new levels of commercial and creative competition between artists, and also provided an outlet for fans worldwide to buy posters advertising gigs that they would not have been able to attend. In the twenty-first century, record labels would attempt to counter this with so-called 360-degree merchandising deals, controlling every aspect of a band's promotion, but some bands formed lasting relationships with favored artists—for example, Pearl Jam and Seattle's Ames Bros. design studios—in an attempt to maintain quality and creative control over the way that their gigs were presented. Until then, the new poster art scene blossomed, reaching new highs of artistic inventiveness and productivity. The rock poster artists, formerly marginal figures in the rock world, were now even developing cults around their work, while young people, who in the past might have bought a used guitar from a pawnshop and formed a band together, decided to teach themselves the rudiments of graphic design. In the '90s, the artist became the star.

ABOVE LEFT Harvey Kurtzman's cover art for issue eight (December 1953) of the widely read satirical comic book *Mad*. Kurtzman was the founding editor of the magazine in 1952 and its zany humor and graphic style attracted a large following among enthusiasts of alternative culture in the '60s and '70s, including rock music fans and graphic artists.

ABOVE RIGHT Mark Arminski's poster for a Nine Inch Nails' show in 1995. Inspired by fellow Detroit artist Gary Grimshaw and others, Arminski represents a bridge between Grimshaw's psychedelic era and the bleak industrial mood of the '90s. Here the muted colors and dark, squatting, Dickensian figure paint a picture of suitably gothic despair.

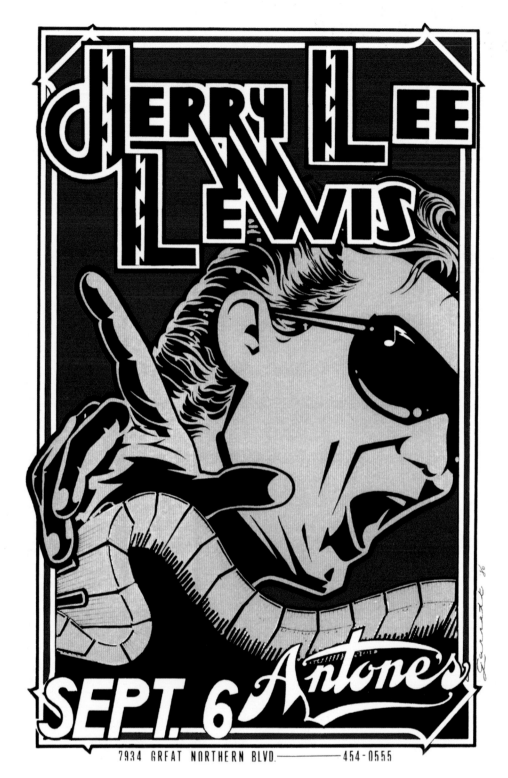

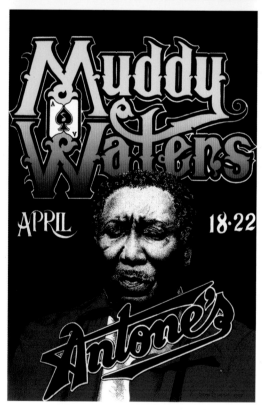

ABOVE LEFT Danny Garrett learned the art of rock poster design from Jim Franklin at Armadillo World Headquarters Club, in Austin, TX, in the '70s, after Franklin advised him to abandon his earlier ambitions to produce an underground comic. A comic strip sensibility still drives much of Garrett's work, such as in this 1986 poster for Jerry Lee Lewis's performance at Antone's.

TOP RIGHT Mick Haggerty's promotional poster for the 1980 Gamma album. The image is a typical example of Haggerty's photo-montage humor. The design was lampooned in the 1984 movie *This is Spinal Tap*, in which the cover of the fictional Spinal Tap's 1980 album, *Shark Sandwich*, has shark fins circling in a slice of bread.

BOTTOM RIGHT Danny Garrett's 1978 poster for a residency by Muddy Waters at Antone's blues club. Garrett's poster lends the elder statesman of the blues a totemic grandeur. The playing card in the guitarist's initials may be a reference to Waters's 1954 hit *I Just Want to Make Love to You*, with its line, "Don't want you runnin' around like the ace of spades."

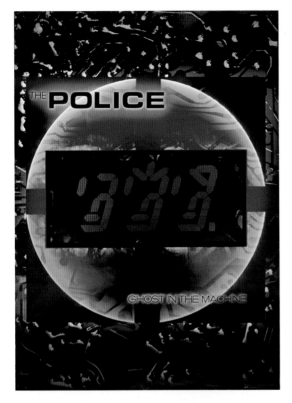

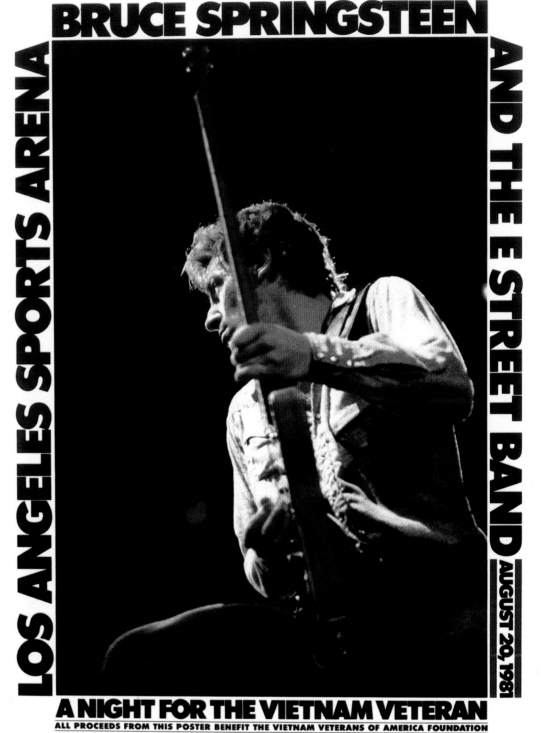

TOP LEFT Promotional poster by Mick Haggerty for the Police's fourth release, *Ghost in the Machine*, in 1981. The electronic display in the image is a digital representation of the three members of the band. The stark black and red of the album cover art is relieved here by images of circuit boards used on the inner bag of the original vinyl release.

BOTTOM LEFT A portfolio of end-of-year gigs promoted by Bill Graham Presents in 1981, advertised here in a poster by Arlene Owseichik. The design reflects the contemporary fashion for clear, precise graphics, a reaction to the anarchic cut-and-paste of punk. Owseichik, one of a very short list of women working as poster artists, was Graham's art director between 1985 and 2004.

ABOVE RIGHT Bruce Springsteen has written and sung in support of Vietnam veterans since his debut album in 1973. At this 1981 concert, all proceeds from poster sales were donated to a veterans' charity. The simple bold lettering of the design is pushed to the outer frame by the huge live presence of the mega star.

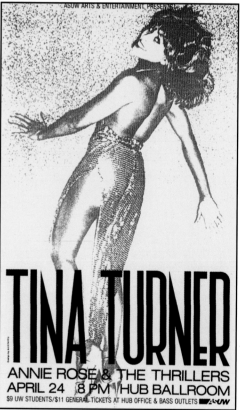

190 191 **ABOVE LEFT** One of the first multi-media artists to work in the music industry, Mick Haggerty's eye-catching designs for the Go-Gos' 1982 album *Vacation* captured their retro pop flavor. Inspired by a vintage postcard, Heggarty photographed a troupe of Florida water skiers and then replaced their heads with those of the band members.

TOP RIGHT Danny Garrett designed this poster for the owner of Antone's blues club, a venue that used his work in their advertising displays. Clifford Antone was serving a sentence for possession of marijuana, and promoted the 1987 concert as part of his community service. The 1930s Comanche Trail Park amphitheater was restored with the funds raised by the event.

BOTTOM RIGHT Art Chantry's clever design for a 1983 Seattle performance by Tina Turner. After a long decline since the days of the Ike and Tina Revue, the singer was on the verge of a spectacular revival of fortune. Chantry combined grungy Xerox chic with stylish retro lettering, and the glamorous image of a forty-three-year-old woman looking back, but moving forward.

ELTON JOHN

TOO LOW FOR ZERO

ABOVE LEFT Promotional poster for David Bowie's 1983 album *Let's Dance*. Mick Haggerty again appropriates vintage images—the letters of the title arranged like the printed instructions for '40s ballroom dance steps. The silhouette of Bowie as a light-footed boxer is reinforced by the graphics spelling out the singer's surname—a visual reference to the logo of '60s boxing brand, Lonsdale.

ABOVE RIGHT Elton John's 1983 album *Too Low For Zero* was Rod Dyer's seventeenth album artwork, with the same number of adaptations for promotional posters to his name. On the cover, the shapes comprised four dye-cut holes in the sleeve, which revealed colors printed as smears of ink on the inner bag. The album was a return to form for Elton, reunited with lyricist Bernie Taupin.

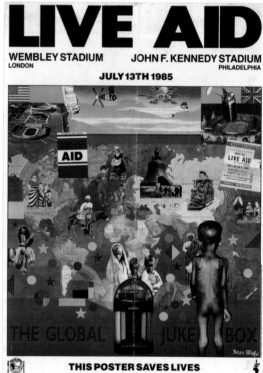

ABOVE LEFT Promotional poster for Bronski Beat's 1986 album *Truthdare Doubledare*, by British design team Peter Barrett and Andrew Biscomb. The pictogram and synthetic color scheme suggest the synthesized drum machine beat that was a feature of the Bronski sound. Barrett and Biscomb were much in demand in the '80s and early '90s by British bands from Simply Red to Suede.

TOP RIGHT The lush imagery of this promotional poster for Tears For Fears' 1989 album *The Seeds of Love* suggests the richness of their studio sound. The artwork, by Rob O'Connor of London design house Stylorouge, is a photo-collage reinvention of the fluid psychedelic posters of the '60s, chaotically packed with imagery.

BOTTOM RIGHT The original run of artist Peter Blake's *Global Jukebox* poster for the 1985 Live Aid event sold out within thirty minutes of the gates opening at London's Wembley Stadium. It has echoes of Blake's most famous work, the cover of the Beatles' *Sgt. Pepper* album, but shocks us with images not of the rich and famous but of the starving and dying.

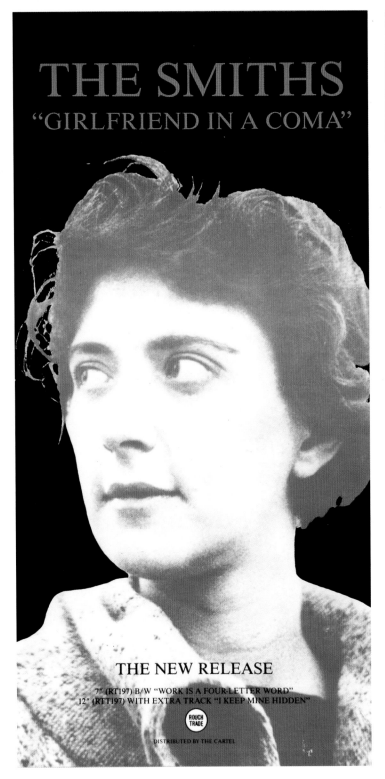

ABOVE LEFT & RIGHT A pair of promotional posters for 1987 singles by the Smiths. Lead singer Morrissey took creative control of the band's printed image. He selected old black-and-white photos that reflected his own eclectic and obscure passions and lent the band a serious, mysterious air. The 1961 portrait of playwright Shelagh Delaney is a case in point. Her first play, *A Taste of Honey*, was set in her native Salford, which borders the Smiths' home city of Manchester, and contains a sympathetic portrayal of homosexuality. The unfamiliar styling and thick eyebrows of Elvis Presley in 1954 are chosen to reflect Morrissey's own unconventional appearance, while the simplicity of the layout is reminiscent of Hatch posters from the dawn of rock 'n' roll.

PetShopBoys.

Behaviour.
PET SHOP BOYS

Performance

Blackpool Opera House May 27, **Glasgow S.E.C.C.** May 28, **Aberdeen Exhibition Centre** May 29, **Birmingham N.E.C.** June 1,2,3, **Whitley Bay Ice Rink** 5 June, **London Wembley Arena** June 7,8,9, **Belfast Kings Hall** June 13, **Dublin Point Depot** June 14.

194 195 ABOVE LEFT Promotional poster for the Norwegian band A-ha's 1988 world tour, based on the cover art of their current album, *Stay On These Roads*, by New Jersey photographer Jeri Heiden. Heiden was creative director at the group's label, Warner Brothers; there, and later at A&M, she was responsible for over 350 album covers, before founding Smog, her own studio, in Los Angeles.

TOP RIGHT A 1990 tour poster by Mark Farrow, who has developed a long working relationship with English electronic dance act the Pet Shop Boys. Farrow began his career in Manchester in the early '80s, creating artwork for the city's Factory Records and Haçienda nightclub. He has designed all but two of the band's studio releases.

BOTTOM RIGHT The logo and cartoon graphics for ABC's 1985 single *How to Be a Millionaire* are by Keith Breeden, who worked with the band on many releases. He forged similar long-term collaborations with others, including Fine Young Cannibals and Scritti Politti, and later designed the sculptures for Pink Floyd's *The Division Bell*.

TOP LEFT Commissioned by the promoter Final Solution, this thirty-by-forty inch brown-and-white poster for New Order's May 1982 gig at the National Ballroom in Kilburn, North London, features ghostly figures floating through a forest of trees—imagery fully in line with the Mancunians' stately image of the era.

BOTTOM LEFT This rare outing for 4AD act the Cocteau Twins at the exotic Bedford Boys Club came complete with a limited-edition run of two hundred twenty-by-thirty inch posters sold at the gig. The design was by Mick Lowe—a prolific sleeve designer in the indie music scene, and member of the Stylorouge design studio.

ABOVE RIGHT Design studio Stylorouge has enjoyed long-running relationships with dozens of British bands from the early '80s to the present day—among them, Simple Minds, whose campaign for their tenth studio album was given biblical undertones in common with much of their back catalog.

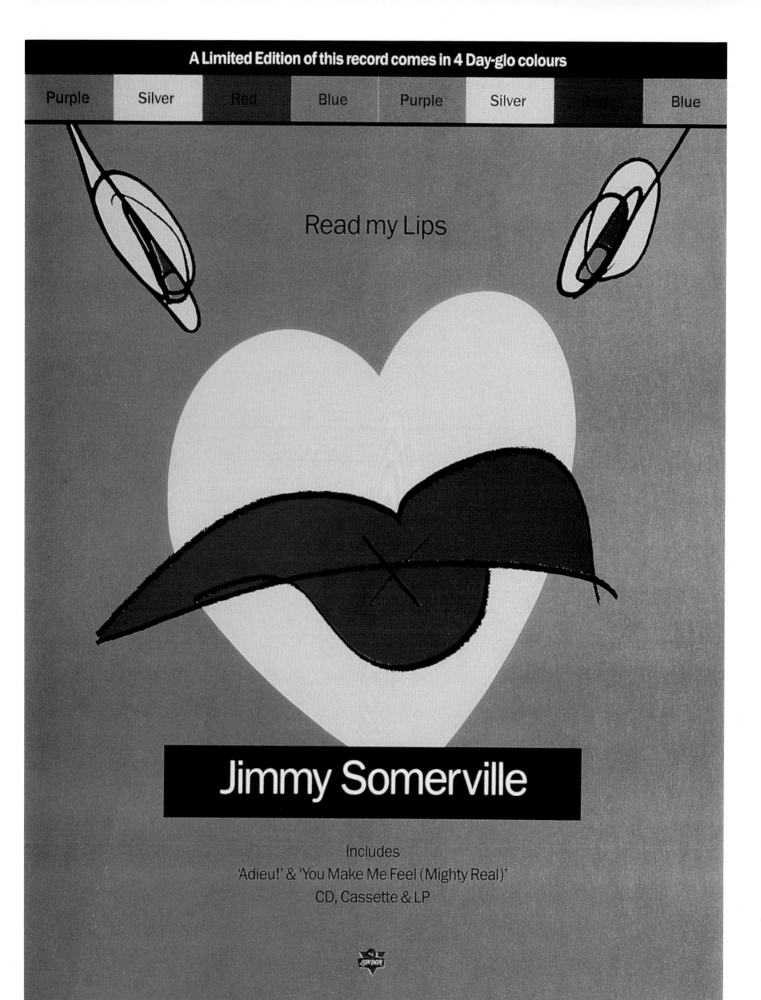

OPPOSITE The year 1989 saw the release of the first solo album by former Bronski Beat and Communards vocalist Jimmy Somerville, with artwork courtesy of the Me Company design studio. The bright, sketchy quality of the graphics captures the hi-energy, falsetto disco of the music on the album.

ABOVE LEFT In this promotional poster for Bowie's 1987 LP *Never Let Me Down*, Mick Haggerty reworks his cover design by cutting out and re-pasting elements from the cover for the poster. The album showed a carefully staged circus-ring scene, photographed by Greg Gorman; here, white space replaces the original colorful background. The result is visually complex and disorientating.

TOP RIGHT Bold graphics and lettering by Paul White, founder of London-based Me Company, for the Sugarcubes' 1992 album *Stick Around For Joy*—their third and last studio recording. White had also designed their first, and his company continued to produce work for the band's singer, Björk, for the next twenty years, as she embarked on a solo career.

BOTTOM RIGHT Stylorouge's design for Squeeze's "If It's Love" single was one of a series of domestic pet-friendly images used to promote the band and their album, *Frank*. The London-based design agency also created the video that promoted the single.

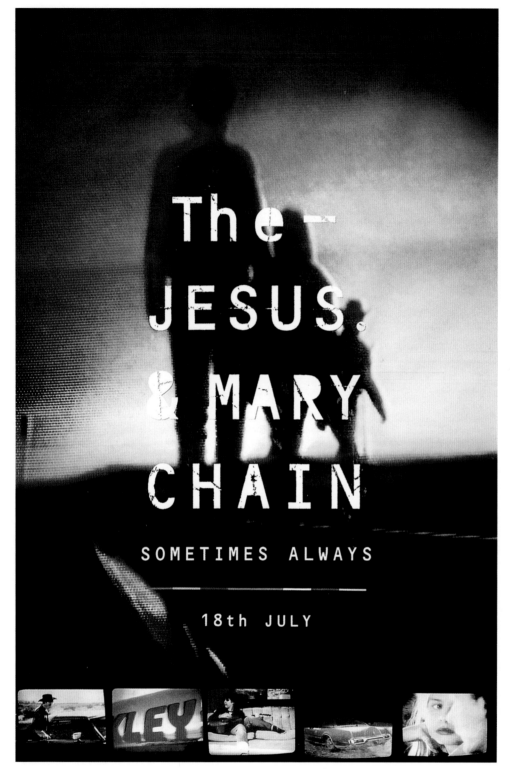

ABOVE LEFT Just as the Jesus and Mary Chain often blurred melody and noise, so Stylorouge's imagery for the band—such as this poster for their 1994 single, "Sometimes Always"—toyed with the focus of the viewer, here including stills from the road movie-themed video.

TOP RIGHT Jesus Jones's time as a hot act was long over by the time they attempted a Brit Pop era comeback in 1997 with the ironically titled single, "The Next Big Thing"—time had fared a little better to their Food label-mates Blur, of course. But at least they got some tasteful Stylorouge artwork for their troubles.

BOTTOM RIGHT Beyond the star attractions of Blur, Pulp, and Oasis the British guitar pop movement of the mid-'90s also spawned unlikely chart acts such as York's Shed Seven. Here, Stylorouge match the band's no-nonsense approach with some striking photography and full-impact type.

TOP LEFT The cover art for Kula Shaker's 1996 debut album *K* features on this promo poster, art directed and designed by Stylorouge, and incorporating artwork by comic-book artist Dave Gibbons. The various images and personalities in this work—from British comedian Ken Dodd to Krishna—all relate to the letter "K."

BOTTOM LEFT As well as designing the sleeve and poster artwork for Public Image Ltd, Mick Haggerty—one of the first designers to work across all media (print, video, and live shows)—also directed the promo video, and the Day-Glo multi-colors were prominent across both.

ABOVE RIGHT Paul White of Me Company was an early adopter of 3-D computer modeling (via Apple's Infini-D software) for use in 2-D images, as in this promo poster for Björk's 1995 single, "Army Of Me." Björk and her previous band the Sugarcubes recorded for the One Little Indian label, which White was involved in setting up in 1985.

The Debut Album • Out August 30th

AVAILABLE ON ALL FORMATS

Includes smash hits Supersonic, Live Forever and Shakermaker

a creation records product

NEW SINGLE

ROLL WITH IT

OUT 14.8.95

ABOVE LEFT Shot in the living room of band member Paul "Bonehead" Arthurs's house, Brian Cannon's cover for Oasis's debut album (with photography by Michael Spencer Jones) featured signifiers of the band's influences and passions— including a photo of Manchester City footballer Rodney Marsh. The photo used for this poster was actually the image on the reverse of the album sleeve.

ABOVE RIGHT British designer Brian Cannon, best known for his Microdot design company, became strongly linked with Oasis. This image, also by Spencer Jones, was shot on the beach at Weston Super Mare in the West of England for the band's "Roll With It" single, and captures the "mad-for-it" spirit of lead singer Liam Gallagher. The track was one half of the chart battle with Brit-Pop rivals Blur.

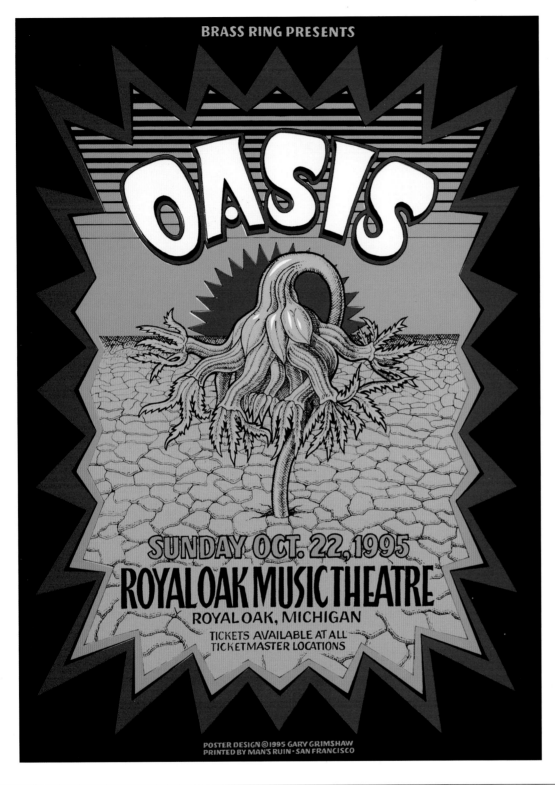

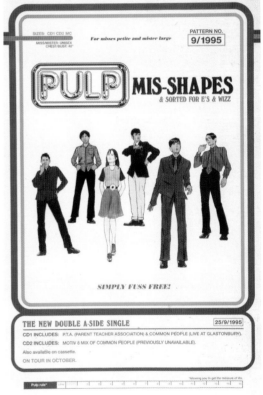

ABOVE LEFT Poster by Gary Grimshaw for a 1995 show by Brit-Pop giants Oasis, as part of their third North American tour. The image of a green shoot in a desert was a very literal interpretation of the band's name, if not of its swaggering, aggressive reputation. The poster by the Detroit veteran was printed in a limited edition of 425 copies.

TOP RIGHT Stylorouge brilliantly echoed their own album cover artwork for Blur's 1994 *Parklife* album (which featured a photo of two racing greyhounds at a dog track east of London) for this poster advertising the band's 2009 comeback show in Hyde Park. The band's return to the limelight—without new material—was very much a celebration of their Brit-Pop period.

BOTTOM RIGHT Design company Blue Source had caused a minor frenzy in the British tabloid press with their sleeve for Pulp's double A-sided single, "Sorted For E's and Whizz" and "Mis-Shapes," since some commentators thought the "wrap" in the artwork encouraged drug use. The alternative imagery, seen here—based on '70s sewing pattern packaging— upset no one.

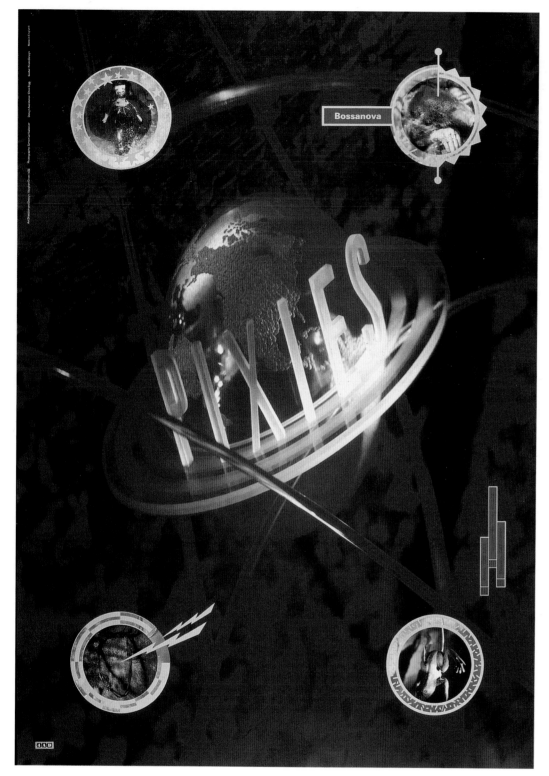

ABOVE LEFT Graphic designer Vaughan Oliver and his company 23 Envelope had a close relationship with London's 4AD record company and designed the artwork for most of their releases, including this poster for the Pixies' album *Bossanova*. As with many of Oliver's images for the company, the art is rich in iconography.

TOP RIGHT Vaughan Oliver worked together with photographer Simon Larbalestier for this promotional poster for the Pixies 1990 single "Velouria." Oliver's graphic style had a huge influence on the post-punk generation, encouraging designers to experiment with the relationship between text and photography.

BOTTOM RIGHT A photograph by celebrated music photographer Kevin Westerberg featured on Vaughan Oliver's and design partner Chris Bigg's sleeve design for the Breeders' 1990 album *Pod*. Urban legend has it that the blurred image is actually of a naked Oliver doing a fertility dance with eels strapped to his waist.

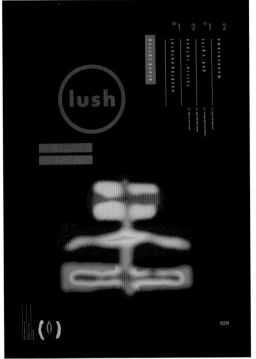

TOP LEFT Manchester design company Central Station Design—consisting of brothers Pat and Matt Carroll, together with Karen Jackson—created artwork for several Factory Records' artists and became closely associated with their fellow Mancunians the Happy Mondays.

BOTTOM LEFT Lush's 1991 *Black Spring* album release came with a poster by Vaughan Oliver that played with the conventions of graphic design by tipping the message sideways. The poster marked a move away from Oliver's usual "dark" style toward a lighter color palette.

ABOVE RIGHT A cropped version of this painting, showing Happy Mondays' singer Shaun Ryder (a cousin of designers Pat and Matt Carroll), featured on the cover of the band's album *Bummed*. For this promotional poster Central Station Design zoomed out to show the entire portrait.

The New Masters

From his first concert in December of 1965 up until his death in a helicopter crash in October of 1991, the promoter Bill Graham held a virtual monopoly on live music in San Francisco. Under the aegis of art director Arlene Owseichik, his company Bill Graham Presents also acted as a hothouse for some of the most important poster artists of the 1990s, allowing them to get a break and earn a crust by working full-time on their designs at a time when the decline of traditional media meant that commercial magazine illustration work began to dry up.

Chris Shaw designed his first poster for Bill Graham in 1992 after training at the California College of Arts and Crafts and creating huge murals for nightclubs, later going on to create posters for Pearl Jam, Foo Fighters, Hole, and the Vans Warped Tour. Shaw's use of bright coloring and distended fonts for his Bill Graham Presents posters sits in stark contrast to his regular work for the jam band Moonalice, as well as his political posters, which use much more subdued textures and colors. Meanwhile Shaw's separate endeavors in fine art subvert religious iconography by fusing it with pop-cult symbolism: a Madonna holds a television set where her child would normally be, or a penitent Elvis bleeds from stigmata and his crown of thorns.

Ron Donovan and Chuck Sperry met while working at Bill Graham Presents in the mid-'90s. Shortly afterward, Sperry joined Donovan's Psychic Sparkplug silkscreen poster company, where the pair built a reputation for their witty and knowing juxtaposition of iconic '60s imagery with garish post-punk fluoros. While working on restoring a mural depicting striking workers during the 1934 San Francisco General Strike, Sperry was introduced to a local fire chief who offered the pair the lease on an abandoned fire station on the fringes of the well-to-do Pacific Heights neighborhood of the city. For four years between 1997 and 2001, Sperry and Donovan operated out of the building, naming their collaboration the Firehouse Kustom Rockart Company in tribute to the place and creating more than five hundred posters, as well as printing posters for Frank Kozik, Stanley Mouse, Alton Kelley, and Victor Moscoso. Both Donovan and Sperry were inspired by situationist theory and the desire to take back the graphic environment of public space, reclaiming it from bland corporate advertising—and this political impulse is key to the work of all three artists. Sperry produced political cartoons for his college magazine while studying at the University of Missouri School of Journalism and contributed to the politicized underground comics *World War 3 Illustrated* and *Last Gasp Comix & Stories*. Both Donovan and Shaw cut their teeth in the guerilla and street art movement, with Shaw producing many anti-Bush and Reagan flyers and handbills. From the late '80s onward, the nexus between politics and underground rock grew stronger until Shepard Fairey (most famous for his ubiquitous *André the Giant Has a Posse* posters and stickers) was commissioned to create the iconic, and often imitated, Barack Obama *Hope* poster for the 2008 presidential campaign).

In line with continued interest in rock posters as a serious art form, all three artists have been active in supporting and recognizing peers and forebears. In the mid-'90s Sperry and Donovan hosted poster art exhibitions at the Off the Wall Gallery on San Francisco's former hippie hub, Haight Street, featuring art by Gary Grimshaw, Victor Moscoso, Frank Kozik, Coop, Emek, Dennis Loren, John Seabury, and others. Sperry has become a global authority on the art of poster design, offering young artists from around the world the opportunity to work as apprentices at Firehouse and opening Firehouse Europe in Milan in 2006. Alongside peers like Kozik and Lindsey Kuhn, Sperry and Donovan have done much to act as ambassadors for the

> "The telephone poles around San Francisco were thick with posters and there were no rules around postering then. It was like an outdoor gallery, and all the poster artists checked out each other's work on the poles, and we all knew each other from their work there."
>
> TERRY FARLEY

form, inspiring and mentoring young artists and ensuring that the artists who inspired them received the credit that they so deserve. "The Fillmore Poster Series is a great San Francisco tradition," said Sperry in an interview in 2010. "The great 1960s artists—Wes Wilson, Stanley Mouse, Alton Kelley, Victor Moscoso, and Rick Griffin—started it out, and the artists David Singer, Randy Tuten, Randall Chavez, Gary Grimshaw, and others continued the tradition. The new Fillmore artists continue this tradition with me and Ron Donovan and Chris Shaw and Rex Ray, among others. It is a great club to be part of. And it made me take my poster work seriously."

ABOVE A gathering of greats in the Firehouse (left to right): Ron Donovan (with his Clapton 2011 tour poster), Chris Shaw (with Bad Religion), Alexandra Fischer (Jewel), John Seabury (the Damned's thirty-fifth anniversary), Dennis Loren (Yes and Asia at the Warfield, SF), and Firehouse cofounder Chuck Sperry (Warren Haynes Band).

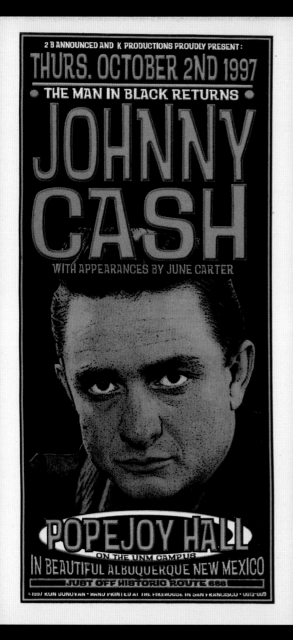

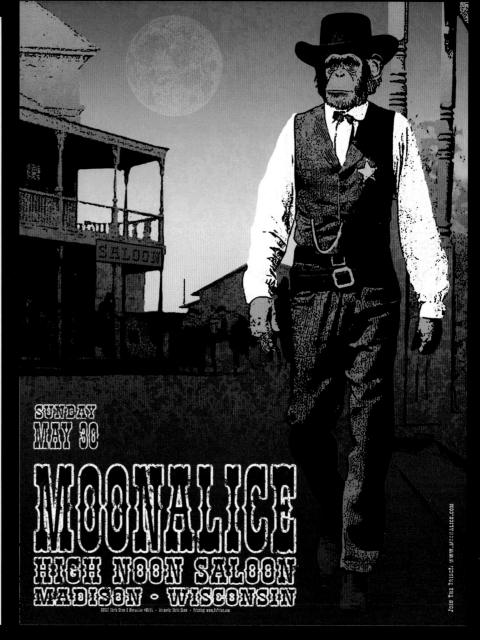

ABOVE LEFT Ron Donovan of Firehouse created this poster for a 1997 performance by Johnny Cash. The direct gaze of the poster image reinforces Cash's new role as an authoritative country-rock veteran; his career spanned the entire period of rock 'n' roll, and at this time he was enjoying a late-in-life revival with his album series for American Recordings.

ABOVE RIGHT Drawing its inspiration from the venue rather than the band, this 2010 Chris Shaw poster starts out with a classic image of Gary Cooper from the movie *High Noon*, adding a playful high *moon* for good measure. Chris Shaw's direction of the Moonalice poster campaign has been an important force in developing rock poster art for the twenty-first century.

ABOVE LEFT After graduating from the Art Institute of Pittsburgh, Thomas Scott worked at various Florida art studios creating images for the theme park industry. In the late-'80s, he began producing offset lithographs under the name Eye Noise for local shows, such as this playing card-inspired poster (two-color offset on yellow stock) for a 1993 double header by Belly and Radiohead.

TOP RIGHT Thomas Scott's marker pen drawing (re-drawn using Adobe Illustrator software) of a Chevy truck is the highlight of his 1997 poster for lo-fi legends Pavement. The image was inspired by the band's song "Heaven Is A Truck" taken from their *Crooked Rain, Crooked Rain* album. The Pavement type was hand drawn, while the Trickhouse font was used for the support band Royal Trux.

BOTTOM RIGHT The Pixies' track from their *Doolittle* album was the inspiration for this clean and simple design by Thomas Scott/Eye Noise 1991 gig poster. The seventeen-by-eleven inches, two-color offset was produced on inexpensive paper stock.

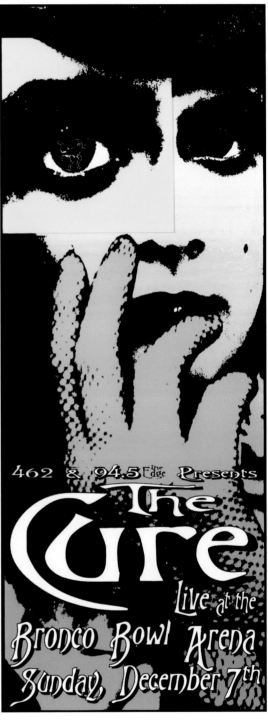

ABOVE LEFT Lindsey Kuhn's 1993 six-color screen print, for a show by US rockers Rocket From the Crypt, is one of several he designed for a band whose strong '50s-influenced sound inspired numerous classic gig posters. A limited run of two hundred made this pin-up-inspired poster highly collectible.

ABOVE RIGHT A poster by Lindsey Kuhn advertising a 1997 show by the Cure at the Bronco Bowl in Dallas, TX. The colors and Kuhn's collaging technique brilliantly match the band's uncompromising, often macabre and melancholic sound. In the mid-'90s, Kuhn managed to combine his passions of skateboarding, music, and art, and started designing his own skateboard decks.

ABOVE LEFT 1960s San Francisco music promoter and one-time manager of Janis Joplin, Chet Helms was often referred to as the father of the hippie Summer of Love, and many acts from that period lined up to thank him at a 1994 tribute show. The poster's artist, Jim Phillips, began work as an illustrator for surfing magazines, before combining his love of rock and skateboards by designing skate decks and music posters.

TOP RIGHT One of the classic '60s Filmore artists, David Singer moved from poster design to illustrating album sleeves, book jackets, and magazines. He returned to rock posters with this design for a Paul McCartney show at Berkley's Memorial Stadium in March 1990.

BOTTOM RIGHT Harry Rossit became a staff artist at Bill Graham Presents in 1991. He has a reputation for a sense of humor, often using his own face on background figures, concealing a 3-D image or incorporating a yellow smiley face within the detail of his posters. The hieroglyphic border of this 1995 poster offers plenty of opportunity for such hidden amusements.

ABOVE LEFT Concert poster for Buddy Guy's 1995 appearance in Ann Arbor, MI, by Detroit artist Mark Arminski. Arminski studied printmaking and computer art before establishing his Phoenix Impressions Studio in 1984, producing fine art images of the human form. He began producing rock posters after his 1989 exhibition of nude images, Untamed Eroticism, scandalized local religious groups.

ABOVE RIGHT The bold graphics, hand-drawn lettering and rich colors of this 1994 Stone Temple Pilots poster confirmed Mark Arminski's debt to the psychedelic artists who inspired him as a teenager. Born in 1950, Arminski combines that '60s sensibility with the darker realities of the '90s, using threatening, aggressive images such as the airborne skulls seen here.

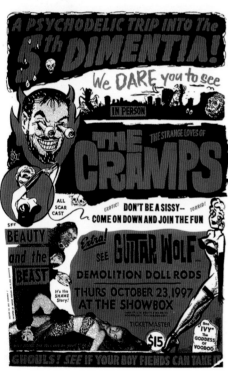

TOP LEFT This 1991 one-color concert poster connects directly to the boxing-style posters of the '50s, and represents a conscious attempt to return to no-frills rock after the excesses of '80s stadium rock and heavy metal. The inclusion of a handwritten scrawl, printed over the typeset text, is a sign of the (unknown) designer's post-punk sensibility.

BOTTOM LEFT "Every client you meet introduces you to their world," says Seattle's Art Chantry. "Getting to know that world well enough to do the assignment requires a huge learning curve." Few poster designs match the band's world better than this Chantry collage for the Cramps from 1997, mixing elements of forgotten B-movie posters with a style learned from Kustom Kar artists such as Ed Roth and Kenny "Von Dutch" Howard.

ABOVE RIGHT A five-color, twenty-one-by-twenty-six inch silkscreen print for the July 3, 1996 Smashing Pumpkins show with Garbage, at the Gund Arena in Cleveland, OH. Legendary poster artist Lindsey Kuhn featured a suitably twisted clown–vampire hybrid. During high school, Kuhn began making posters for the skate contests he was promoting, while at the University of Alabama he began working with local bands.

TOP LEFT Chris Shaw looked to hot-rod decoration and tattoo art as sources for this 2000 Deftones concert poster for the promotion company Bill Graham Presents. The image of a haloed nude, often with flaming tattoos, has become a recurring motif of his more recent artwork, painted in the style of religious art or stained glass.

BOTTOM LEFT A 1996 concert poster for glam-rockers Kiss, by Chris Shaw, at that time a staff artist for Bill Graham Presents. The lurid mixture of sex and violence in the poster befits the image of the band, who sported heavy, stylized makeup masks and elaborate leather-and-steel costumes combined with footwear onstage. Shaw also designed stage sets for the band.

ABOVE RIGHT One of his first posters for Bill Graham Presents, this design by Chris Shaw for three Pearl Jam shows in October 1993 provides a distinctive psychedelic variation on classic Tiki art of the '50s, combining fluoros with warped Polynesian imagery.

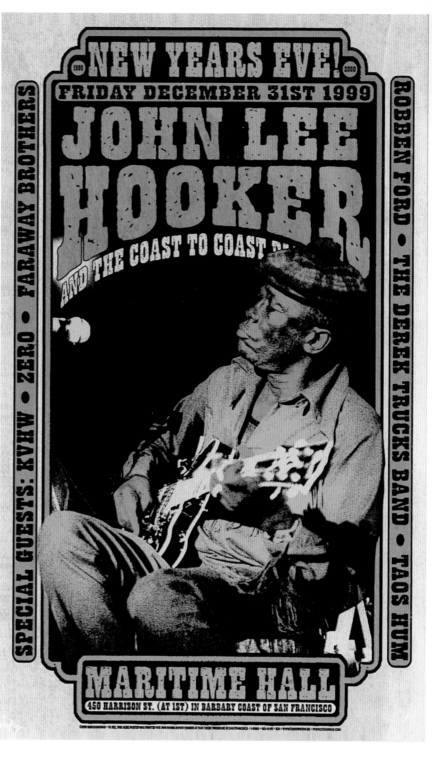

ABOVE LEFT After a period of designing posters in Hollywood (for *Back to the Future III* and *Total Recall*), Bob Masse returned to rock poster art in the early '90s. This poster for a Black Crowes show at Stubb's BBQ in Austin, TX, as part of the South By Southwest festival, was a notable return to his '60s form, updating his style for a new generation.

ABOVE RIGHT Poster for a 1999 end-of-the-year show, designed by Ron Donovan of Firehouse. The tinted photograph and nineteenth-century playbill lettering add a vintage sheen to the work, giving age and weight to Hooker's blues heritage and emphasizing the imminent passing of another century. Hooker himself passed away only eighteen months later, at the age of eighty-three.

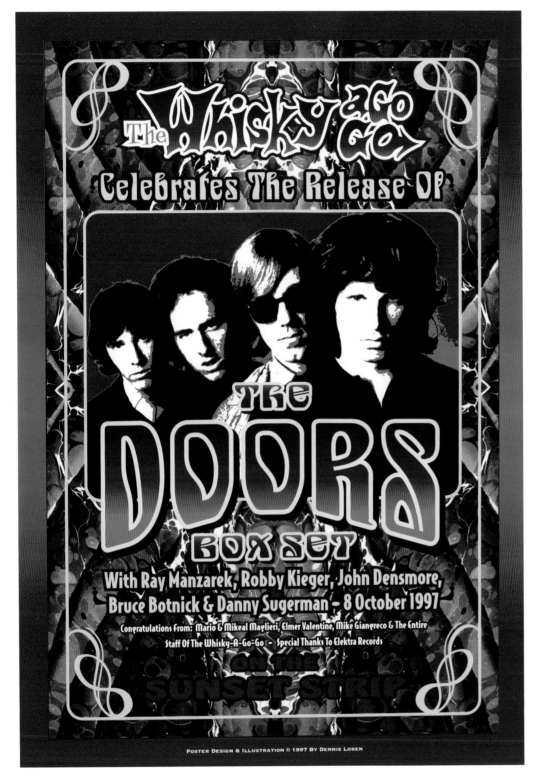

ABOVE LEFT When Elektra Records released the first Doors box set in 1997, the Whisky A Go Go hired Dennis Loren to design this poster for the celebration. Loren was chosen for the project because of his previous poster designs for the club, including gigs by the Velvet Underground and Chicago in 1968.

TOP RIGHT An early Ron Donovan design for Firehouse, founded in 1997, promoting a concert the same year by US-Belgian techno outfit Lords of Acid. The threatening, unfamiliar alien image set against hallucinogenic swirls is a good match for the industrial electronica of a band whose very name celebrates mind-altering drug culture.

BOTTOM RIGHT 1997 concert poster designed by Dennis Loren for a performance by Bob Dylan in LA's art deco El Rey Theater. It is a perfect example of Loren's art: The juxtaposition of strong, opposing colors; the graphic development from a photograph of the performer; and the use of mirror images—all of which are his trademarks.

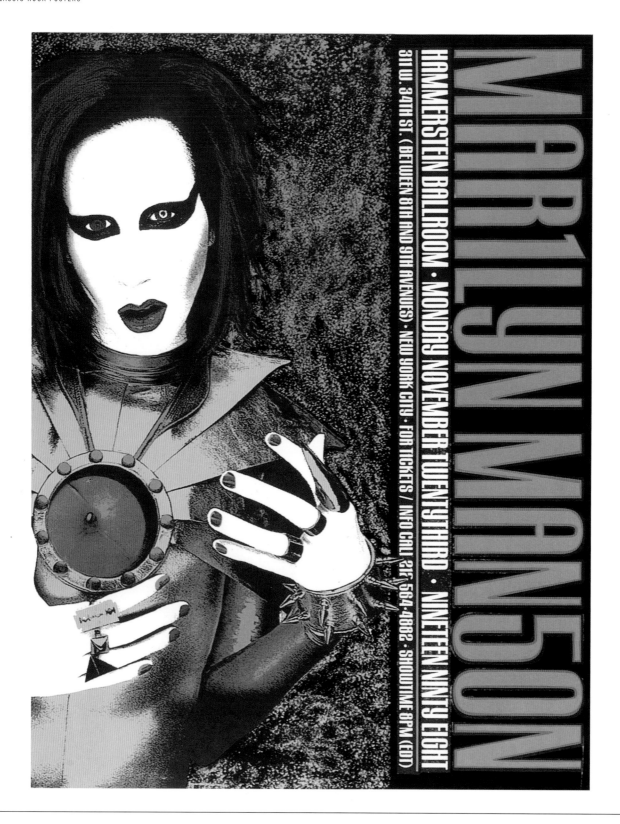

MARILYN MAN5ON

311 W. 34TH ST. (BETWEEN 8TH AND 9TH AVENUES) · NEW YORK CITY · FOR TICKETS / INFO CALL 215 564-4882 · SHOWTIME 8PM (CDT)

HAMMERSTEIN BALLROOM · MONDAY NOVEMBER TWENTYTHIRD · NINETEEN NINTY EIGHT

214 215 ABOVE Marilyn Manson's music played with the senses and so did Ron Donovan's silkscreen print for his Hammerstein Ballroom headline show, tipping the print sideways, like a skyscraper. Seeing numerological significance in his name and birthday (January 5, 1969) Manson incorporated a one and five into his name during this period—a touch noted by Donovan.

OPPOSITE LEFT In this 1999 concert poster Mark Arminski focuses on the art-nouveau elements of the psychedelic art that first inspired him. A romantic, sorrowful female figure, who could have been a model for Alphonse Mucha, averts her eyes. She puts the viewer in the mood for the soulful rock ballads that were, by the late '90s, the stock in trade of both Journey and Foreigner.

OPPOSITE RIGHT As the resident artist at Detroit's Grande Ballroom, Gary Grimshaw developed a style that eschewed the psychedelic excesses of some of his contemporaries and favored stark and dramatic, two-color designs that suited the raw energy of the Detroit scene. This poster for a concert by Wayne Kramer and John Sinclair in 1997 is an exemplar of that style.

Grunge vs Brit-Pop

As heavy metal and mainstream rock were swept aside by grunge in the early '90s, a new aesthetic in poster art began to emerge. Its pioneer was Frank Kozik, who had settled in Texas's capital, Austin, while stationed in the US Air Force in the early '80s. Kozik was beginning to frequent hardcore punk gigs while at the same time making frequent trips out into the desert to trip on peyote. "It didn't matter what kind of weird music you like[d]," he remembers. "We were all weirdos. You'd go to the punk rock club and all the gays and old stoners and freaky cowboy dudes were mixing with the punkers and new wavers."

The merging of punk and psychedelia in Kozik's subsequent art reflected the music scene at the end of the decade: disaffected suburban kids mixed FM rock hooks with punk angst and metal's heaviness to create a completely new sound. In Seattle, WA, the location most closely associated with grunge, the city fathers responded to the sudden interest in their town by banning the flyposting of gig posters or handbills to telegraph poles, lampposts and traffic lights, with fines for both the poster's creator, the band the poster was advertising, and the promoter of the concert. The ordinance was in place for ten years before finally being repealed in 2004; in the meantime, artists were forced to create ever more garish, outrageous, and eye-catching designs to make their posters stand out on the increasingly crowded walls of venues and record stores.

In the United Kingdom, the '90s had kicked off with a revival of interest in pop art, surrealism, and the psychedelic posters of the '60s as rave promoters employed graphics that self-consciously mined the imagery of artists such as Rick Griffin for inspiration. Despite the work of Paul Cannell for Primal Scream, Stylorouge for Blur, or the Manic Street Preachers' association with respected Brit artist Jenny Saville, much of the iconography surrounding Brit-Pop was a reaction to the perceived American dominance of the airwaves, reveling in a jingoistic and functional style that often had recourse to mod imagery or the union jack. Microdot's Brian Cannon, who designed sleeves and an early logo for Oasis, navigated this line better than many of his peers, forging a visual style that smartly connected past and present, rooting his clients in a lineage of classic British rock while never seeming less than contemporary.

Bucking the trend were Jamie Hewlett (who graduated from being a comic book artist with the magazine *Deadline* to creating sleeves and gig posters, before defining the visuals of Gorillaz in the early twenty-first century) and the Welsh artist Pete Fowler, whose association with the Super Furry Animals led to commissions for other bands, as well as toy and comic strip design.

> "I had been doing mail art, where people would make weird art and mail it back and forth. We had this little mail-art collective going on, and we would also do weird 'punk' comics and posters, just random street art sort of stuff."
>
> FRANK KOZIK

OPPOSITE LEFT & RIGHT Although both Grunge and Brit-Pop were long-overdue reactions to the shallow excess of much rock and pop in the '80s, they took very different forms. In the UK, bands such as Oasis and Blur (with singer Damon Albarn, far left) expressed their dissatisfaction with the dominant influence of American culture with a reinvention of British Pop for the '90s.

Meanwhile, in the US, groups such as Pearl Jam and Nirvana (led by Kurt Cobain, left) in the Pacific Northwest combined a stripped-down heavy metal with the region's proto-punk garage tradition. The result was a grubby, defiantly untheatrical expression of youthful rejection.

ABOVE LEFT Frank Kozik's five-color screenprint for a 1992 grunge double bill. The woman at the center is Maria Liljedahl, whose image Kozik saw on a poster for a 1968 Swedish soft-porn movie. The initial print run of 450 was soon followed by a second edition of 2,500 copies. The design has since become an icon of the grunge movement.

ABOVE RIGHT Julian Opie—one of the biggest names in contemporary British art—designed the cover art and poster for Blur's 2000 The Best of collection. In Tate magazine, James Hall commented that "Opie has actually made art to be displayed on billboards . . . [His] paintings and sculptures play complex perceptual games, yet stylistically they evoke cartoons and children's toys."

Modern Era

2000—2012

From Dance Halls to Facebook Walls—Posters in the Digital Age

Listen to the wrong voices, and it would be easy to assume that the first decade of the twenty-first century marked the painful death of rock 'n' roll. Its killer? The Internet, hung and executed without a fair trial.

But those unhappy doomsayers were usually connected to the old music industry—an industry from a not too dim and distant past in which the only way to own music was to buy it first. Increasingly, actually purchasing the music you listen to has become a very old-fashioned concept indeed; as old-fashioned as reading the liner notes of an album cover as you listen to your favorite band. The old music industry—whose companies once had complete control over which artists they signed, what music they released, and how much money they charged fans for the privilege of collecting—has become virtually powerless. Whatever the "old" music industry now is, it is certainly not cool; it is not only seen as a lumbering old oil tanker, unable to turn itself around and navigate the new world, but it is also viewed as the enemy of fun, as a clumsy giant that wants to stop people from listening to music, rather than as a provider of the bands and songs they love.

With hindsight, it is easy to see where the music industry went wrong. It failed to embrace the Internet and fast-changing digital technology by shutting down the first peer-to-peer networks, such as Napster in 2001 (instead of realizing that it was being offered a brand-new distribution model), and attempting to outlaw downloading music by threatening legal action against an entire generation throughout the decade.

There is no doubt that the Internet has led to a shrinking of the music industry and has made earning a living from recorded music more challenging for artists; but rather than mark the end of music, the Internet has in fact led to its explosion. It is easier to make music, it is easier to promote music, and it is easier to hear music. The only problematic part is making money from music. Nonetheless, the music from 2000 to 2012 will be viewed in the future as the music of a decade of boom—remembered less for acts such as Arcade Fire, the Strokes, the National, and Gorillaz, and more for the technology that made and played the music, for the rise of the iPod, of Auto-Tunes vocals, and of the iTunes music store. Another reason why musicians make less money today than perhaps they did in the '70s, '80s, and '90s is that there is more music available. Much, much, more.

This tsunami of musical availability—which has given everyone with a broadband connection the same access to new music (access once enjoyed only by *NME* journalists or DJs in the mold of John Peel)—has had a number of side effects. One is that genres have become blurred, and just as it is no longer unusual to find a hip-hop artist such as Kanye West working with a folk-rock artist like Bon Iver, it is common for a fan of heavy metal to admit to a fondness for drum 'n' bass, or for a drum 'n' bass DJ to attempt a remix of a chart pop act. No one likes just one thing any more.

The second biggest effect is that seeing artists perform live has replaced owning their music as the priority for music fans. In fact, you can't really count yourself as a fan of a musician or band unless you've seen them live, and this appetite has led to a vast increase in the number of gigs and festivals.

In the '60s, when Bill Graham was putting on concerts at the Fillmore in San Francisco and the underground newspaper *International Times* was organizing fourteen-hour love-ins at the Alexandra Palace in London, live concerts were rarer. Today, there is a gig on every city street corner every night of the week, and there aren't just one or two festivals to last the whole summer—there are dozens every weekend. So how do bands and promoters make these events unique? The answer: our old friend, the poster.

The part played by the Internet in the story of the music poster revival is not without its own irony. Just as the music industry had suffered, so had print publishing, and many senior artists feared that an entire generation of illustrators would be lost because of the decline of print. Instead, however, the music poster boom has given an outlet and income to tens of thousands of artists who might not otherwise have been noticed. And although computer technology has played a major part (today's posters are more likely to be seen on Facebook walls than pasted to brick or concrete ones), the scene has helped to keep screenprinting very much alive; just as music has diversified to include a broader range of influences than ever before, so has music poster art.

The rock music poster has evolved and come full circle since its inception as a promotional tool for touring rock 'n' rollers—today, posters are regarded both as promotional "product" and as works of art in their own right. Increasingly, fans no longer buy posters because of the bands they advertise or as a souvenir of a night out; instead, it's because they like the print or follow the designer's work. At one time, rock posters were artifacts and mass-produced ephemera, pasted to a wall one day and pasted over the next. Today, they are handmade, collectable pieces of art.

"More and more bands want a big poster and they don't want it mass-produced," says the legendary artist Emek, whose designs for Erykah Badu, the Flaming Lips, and Tool, among others, have helped to raise the bar for gig poster art. "What they say is that they want to be part of the golden age —'We want to belong to that pantheon of cool bands that had cool posters.'" And who wants to be in a band and not be cool?

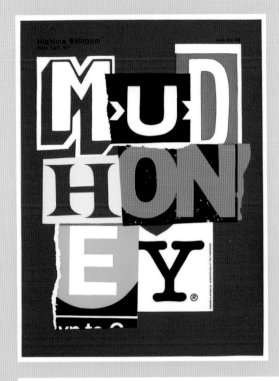

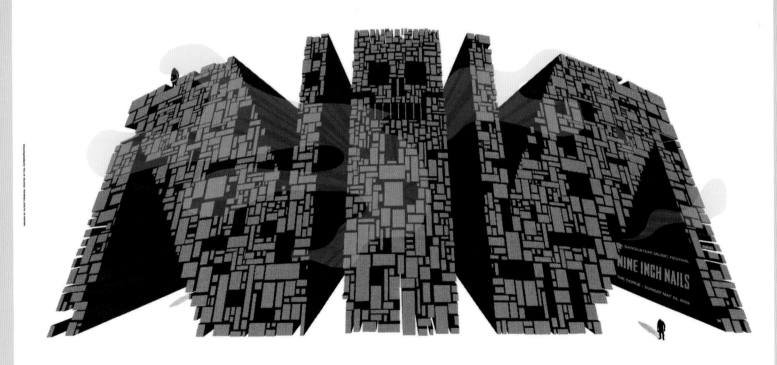

TOP LEFT As well as designing rock posters, San Francisco's Alan Hynes works on branding and corporate identity for commercial clients. His interest in packaging is reflected in this striking and deceptively simple piece of collage work for a Mudhoney concert at New York's Highline Ballroom.

TOP CENTER A nine-color silkscreen poster by Emek for Soundgarden's reunion gig at the 2010 Lollapalooza Festival in Chicago. Emek's artwork suggests the fleeting nature of live events; moments which are over so quickly that only a robot could capture them—or are so momentous that only robots will be left to capture them.

TOP RIGHT Todd Slater has to date designed three posters for Las Vegas' the Killers and, like much of his work, this poster centers on a clever visual pun in the juxtaposition of the ram's horns with a woman's head.

ABOVE Patent Pending's Jeff Kleinsmith and Jesse LeDoux teamed up for this monumental poster for a Nine Inch Nails' show at the Sasquatch Music Festival in 2009. As well as a regular thirty-six-by-eighteen-inches silkscreen print on heavy paper, the Seattle duo also produced a badass, limited-edition twenty-four-by-twelve-inches run on steel.

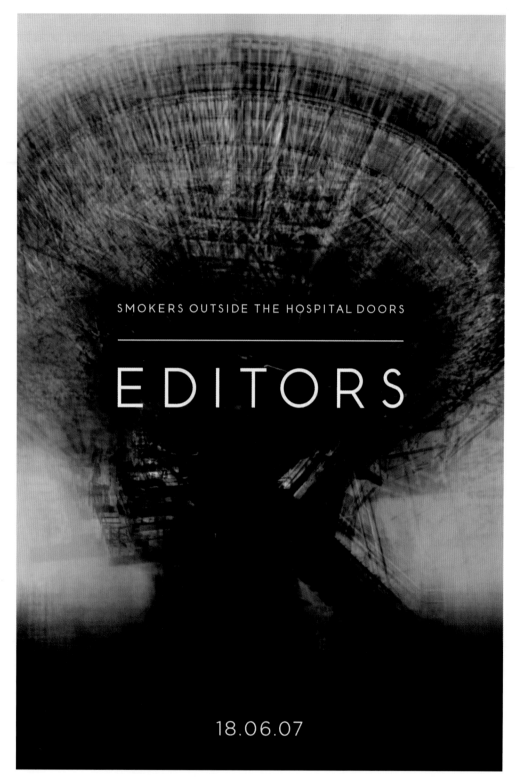

SMOKERS OUTSIDE THE HOSPITAL DOORS

EDITORS

18.06.07

GRACE JONES
HURRICANE
03/11—08

WWW.WALLOFSOUND.NET
WWW.THEHURRICANEISCOMING.COM
WWW.MYSPACE.COM/GRACEJONESOFFICIAL

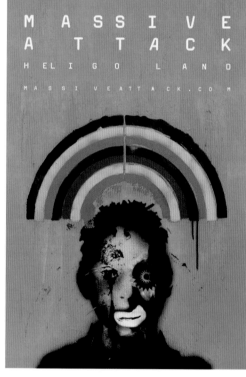

MASSIVE ATTACK
HELIGOLAND
MASSIVEATTACK.COM

ABOVE LEFT Established in 1997 by the former in-house designer at London's legendary Blue Note nightclub, Tom Hingston Studio is an independent, multi-disciplinary design agency that has worked on visuals for clients as disparate as global fashion groups to Hollywood movie makers—a mark of how far rock poster design has traveled since its early days.

TOP RIGHT After almost two decades, Grace Jones's 2008 comeback album required a forceful visual identity from Tom Hingston to compete in a world where rock sleeve art has to function across a variety of media—from advertising billboards to images the size of thumbnails for display on websites.

BOTTOM RIGHT Based on a painting by Robert Del Naja, a member of Massive Attack and former graffiti artist, Tom Hingston's second design for Massive Attack's 2010 album sleeve had to be altered substantially in order to be posted on London's underground system. The poster contravened London Transport's guidelines, since the image looked too much like opportunistic street art.

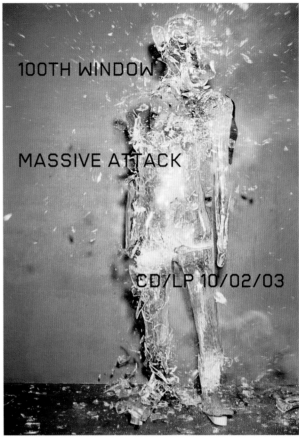

100TH WINDOW

MASSIVE ATTACK

CD/LP 10/02/03

GNARLS BARKLEY ST. ELSEWHERE
THE ALBUM – INCLUDES THE NO.1 SINGLE CRAZY – OUT NOW

ABOVE LEFT Although he worked in print as an apprentice to *The Face*'s designer Neville Brody, Tom Hingston uses high-end commercial design software to achieve effects such as this hyper-real aquatic universe for dance duo the Chemical Brothers.

TOP RIGHT Once again demonstrating how far rock design has come since the days of the boxing-style poster, Tom Hingston's design for Massive Attack's *100TH Window* sleeve artwork utilized state-of-the-art computer software to generate the imagery for the band's fourth album in 2003.

BOTTOM RIGHT Following a design brief that stipulated that the album sleeve was not to feature a photograph of the band, but instead reference classic '60s pop-psychedelia, Tom Hingston drew upon Cuban movie posters of the early '70s for inspiration for his Gnarls Barkley 2006 artwork.

DON'T LOOK BACK CONCERTS PRESENT

TEENAGE FANCLUB

PERFORMING THEIR ALBUM BANDWAGONESQUE

WITH THE BEVIS FROND · 24 JULY · 2006 · THE FORUM · LONDON

SUPERGRASS
LIFE ON OTHER PLANETS

**THE ALBUM - OUT 30TH SEPTEMBER.
CD & LIMITED EDITION GATEFOLD VINYL.
FEATURES THE SINGLES
'NEVER DONE NOTHING LIKE THAT BEFORE' & 'GRACE'.**

OCTOBER LIVE DATES: 15 NOTTINGHAM ROCK CITY. 16 NORTHUMBRIA UNIVERSITY. 17 GLASGOW BARROWLANDS. 18 LEEDS UNIVERSITY
20 MANCHESTER ACADEMY. 21 BIRMINGHAM ACADEMY. 22 BRISTOL ACADEMY. 24 SOUTHAMPTON GUILDHALL. 25 CARDIFF UNIVERSITY
27 CAMBRIDGE CORN EXCHANGE. 30 LONDON SHEPHERDS BUSH EMPIRE

WWW.SUPERGRASS.COM

OPPOSITE Although based in Portland, OR, Guy Burwell's distinctive pen-and-ink designs are highly regarded across Europe, where his work is often exhibited. Burwell has drawn campaigns for M&M's and Nickelodeon, and this poster for Teenage Fanclub's performance of their album *Bandwagonesque* at London's Forum in 2006 draws upon classic '50s commercial design.

TOP LEFT Designed by Guy Burwell, this 2004 poster for a Kings of Leon concert was produced shortly before the release of the band's second album, *Aha Shake Heartbreak*. The design reflects the band's ramshackle country-rock roots—at this point the Nashville, TN, group had yet to become a slick stadium rock act.

TOP RIGHT Among the influences of the fourth Supergrass album, in 2002, was the band's love of the trippy 1980 TV documentary series *Cosmos*, which featured celebrated astronomer Carl Sagan. The influence manifested itself in this mirror-image design, created by the Designers Republic (tDR), on the tour poster, which is illustrated with the colors of the rainbow arching above the cutouts of the four members. Far out.

ABOVE Ian Anderson founded the Designer's Republic in Sheffield, England, in 1986. TDR's work for the Warp, R&S, and Tresor labels over the next ten years defined the visual language for much of the ambient/electronic/techno output of the period. This 1988 poster for Moloko's second album, *I Am Not A Doctor*, illustrates their fun aesthetic, inspired by '60s kids' TV show *Heidi*, Milka chocolate wrappers, and '50s glamor.

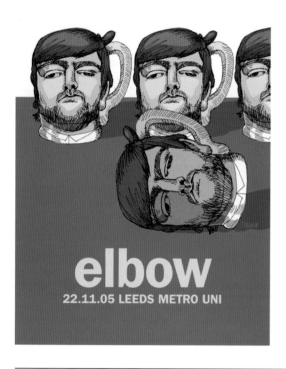

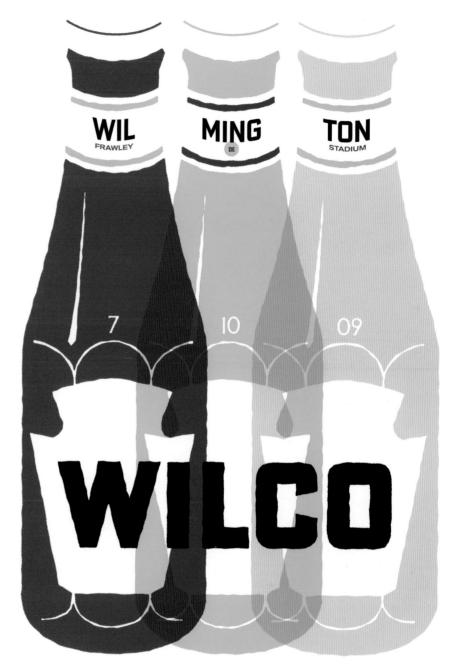

TOP LEFT Describing his work as "courageously silly," south London-based Luke Drozd is an artist who stumbled into making gig posters after illustrating a poster for an art exhibition. Drozd sees every piece of work as a link to the next one, including this 2010 tri-colored screen print for Circa Survive, featuring a chilled-out monkey king on a throne of building blocs.

BOTTOM LEFT Matthew Ferres designed this 2005 screen print for English rock band Elbow. Ferres, based in the city of Leeds in the north of England, sells limited-edition prints of his rock art online. With a background in commercial graphic and web design, he has created artwork for bands including the Arctic Monkeys and the Flaming Lips.

ABOVE RIGHT The three ketchup bottles promote a July 10, 2009 summertime show by alt-country legends Wilco. A wonderful riff on Andy Warhol's pop art homages to great American brands, the four-color silkscreen print by Heads of State was intended to evoke a backyard barbecue using the iconic Heinz bottle.

OPPOSITE Jason Kernevich and Dustin Summers have been working together under the Heads of State moniker since 2002, when they began to create gig posters for Philadelphia's indie scene. This deceptively simple design advertises an R.E.M. concert on June 17, 2005, in Manchester, UK.

TOP LEFT Sometimes artists are given ludicrously short spaces of time in which to turn around a poster design; such was the case with this print for a "secret" MySpace show by Bullet For My Valentine on April 26, 2010. Created by Adam Pobiak, it was designed and printed in under six hours, from the initial email, outlining the task in hand, to delivery.

BOTTOM LEFT Motörhead's famous "war dog" logo, created by Joe Patagno for the British heavy metal legends' debut album in 1977, was given a stunning remix by Adam Pobiak in this poster for the band's show in Weismain, Germany, on June 17, 2011. The snaggle-toothed hot-rod comes equipped with two other icons of significance to fans of the band: spades (after the band's most famous track,

"Ace of Spades") and the insignia of the *Luftwaffe* (after the title track of their album *Bomber*). The silkscreened poster also came in a very limited run, with gunmetal replacing the red.

OPPOSITE ABOVE RIGHT The imagery for Adam Pobiak's silkscreen prints comes from a variety of sources, including photographs—such as photo-portraits of Britain's Queen Elizabeth II—and hand-drawn type. The psychedelic British monarch promotes a pair of Flaming Lips' shows in London in November 2010.

TOP LEFT Combining hand-rendered illustration techniques with work on iPad, London-based designer Dan Mumford's poster for a Dingwall's matinee show by Gallows, in 2010, is unusually straightforward. His other work, such as his range of T-shirt designs, draws upon more "baroque" '80s heavy metal influences and fantasy role-playing imagery.

TOP RIGHT This 2010 poster for Pulled Apart By Horses was designed by Alex and Chris White of We Three Club, who are also the organizers of Poster Roast—an annual festival intended to foster community among gig poster artists in the UK. It was screen printed in two colors by East London independent screen printers, Loligo.

ABOVE In 2006, Nick Rhodes (aka Switchopen) created several gig posters that cast lead singer Pete Doherty as a bohemian chameleon. At the time, Doherty was in the media because of his after-hours activities and on-and-off relationship with British model Kate Moss. Rhodes captured the moment of Kate leaving Pete in a comical way, with the model recast as a fly escaping from the reach of our rock 'n' roll amphibian.

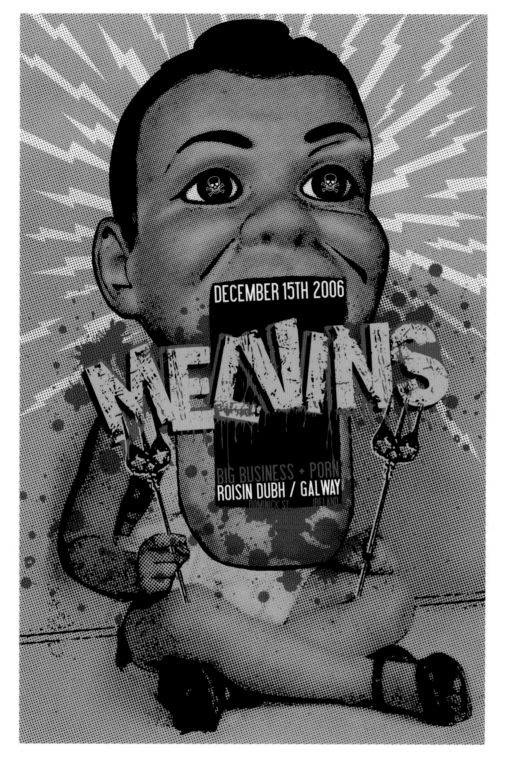

ABOVE LEFT Belfast artist Glyn Smyth (aka Scrawled Design) is celebrated for imagery that draws upon folkloric influences. But for legendary US band Melvins, the poster incorporated the macabre and the playful to create a possessed doll—a surreal juxtaposition of styles that matched the band.

TOP RIGHT This 2004 poster for Manchester band Elbow was Switchopen's first-ever screen print. Nick Rhodes set out to produce a design that would look like a lion, but instead created the "face" of the lion using goldfish. "I wanted to portray the feeling of Elbow's music. They can be as calm as a fish, but some of Guy Garvey's lyrics can cut to the bone, just like a lion," explained Rhodes.

BOTTOM RIGHT A commercial artist based in Nottingham in England's Midlands, Michael Cowell is influenced by the more "eldritch," or otherworldly, comic and fantasy art, as demonstrated by this poster for Queens of the Stone Age in 2011.

OPPOSITE LEFT Stephen Keane (Chaos vs Cosmos) produced a suitably freak-out four-color screen print for psych experimentalists, Clinic. The mutant sea vegetable creature that advertised the band's gig at the Half Moon in Herne Hill, south London, in May 2010 was only the second poster Keane had created.

OPPOSITE RIGHT Tom Lacey, a singer with Brighton-based hardcore punk act Ghost of a Thousand, also designs posters and album sleeves. Lacey mainly uses Adobe Illustrator software to create his artwork, as in this extremely limited-edition—only thirty were made—design for one of his band's final shows in 2010.

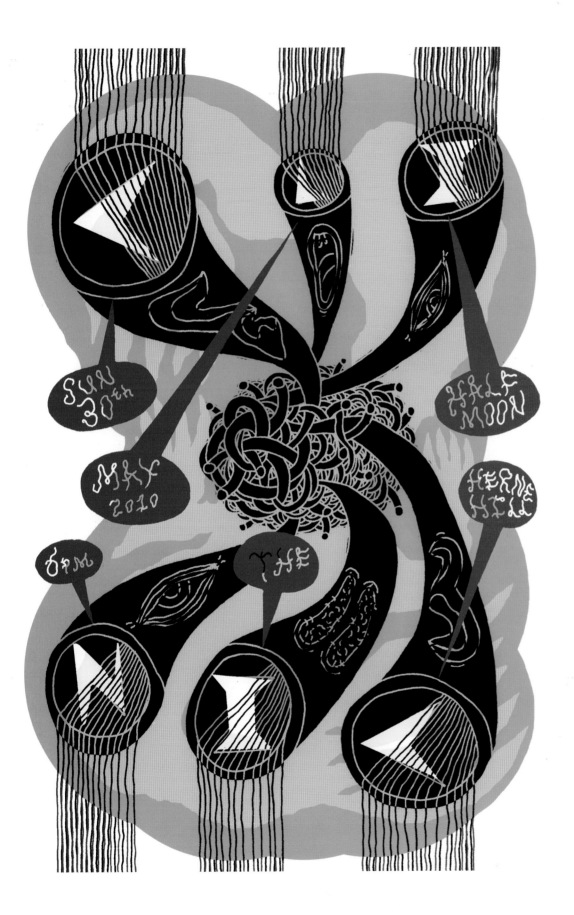

good shoes

art & print by Mara Piccione www.piccione.nl

Alter Schlachthof, Lingen 28/07/2011

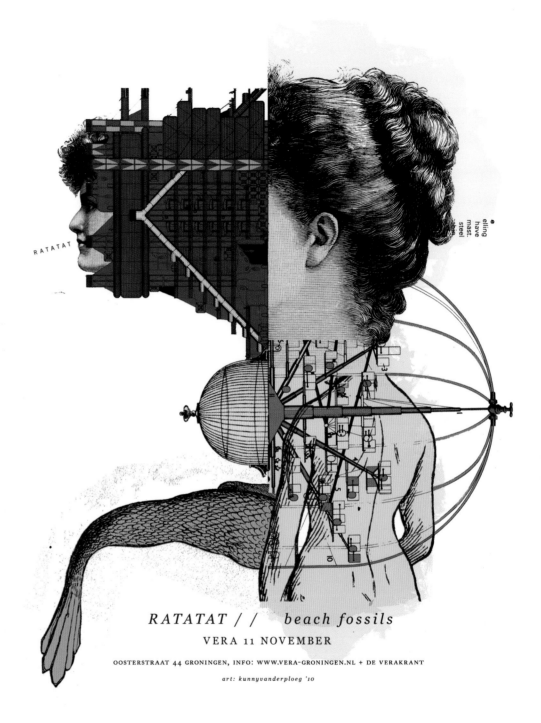

RATATAT // *beach fossils*
VERA 11 NOVEMBER

OOSTERSTRAAT 44 GRONINGEN, INFO: WWW.VERA-GRONINGEN.NL + DE VERAKRANT

art: kunnyvanderploeg '10

OPPOSITE Dutch illustrator and designer Mara Piccione's work routinely takes the forms and color palette of children's book illustrations, subverting it with often nightmarish imagery. However, this 2011 design for British indie band Good Shoes showcases the flip side of Piccione's style: playful and cartoonish, but no less unsettling for all that.

TOP LEFT Spanish-born and London-based artist Diego Mena earns his living from fashion-related design work, but his numerous designs for East London underground promoters Upset the Rhythm fuse hand-drawn illustration with computer-manipulated images— a perfect match for Dan Deacon's electro-indie.

BOTTOM LEFT Based in Tortona, Italy, the Malleus collective produce some of the most imaginative—and collectible—posters around, infusing the kind of art-nouveau influences that inspired the San Francisco artists with an otherworldly and surreal sensibility, typified by their work for the legendary Italian horror movie maestro, Dario Argento.

ABOVE RIGHT Mixing analog and digital techniques with collage and "found" illustrations, this witty design for Ratatat, from 2010, is typical of Kunny van der Ploeg's style, which involves much ransacking of flea markets and antique-reference books to create something new and striking from the unrelated detritus.

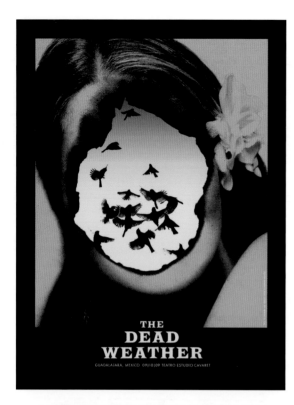

TOP LEFT Artists collaborating on any of Jack White's various musical projects are obliged to conform to his strict aesthetic guidelines. In the case of the Dead Weather artwork, the artist, Alan Hynes, was told only to use black, white, and yellow for this surrealistic 2009 image.

BOTTOM LEFT As with his poster for Mudhoney (see page 221), Alan Hynes's four-color design for a Primus show at Pittsburgh, PA, Stage AE venue draws on packaging design as inspiration for the collage-style rendering on the side of his mechanical fish.

ABOVE RIGHT An unsettling image from Eye Noise (Thomas Scott), this 2007 poster for Dinosaur Jr. takes the veteran alt-rock band away from their scrappy '80s DIY roots with a move to clean lines and abstract imagery.

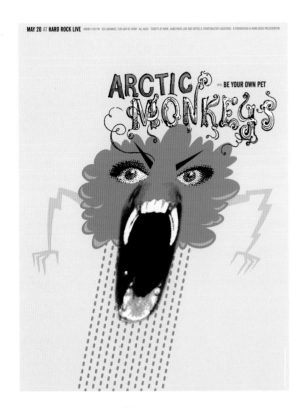

TOP LEFT This pop art-indebted poster from Eye Noise, designed for English indie rock act Arctic Monkeys, shouts out the quirky sense of humor that typifies much of Thomas Scott's work.

BOTTOM LEFT Eye Noise's idiosyncratic and highly distinctive technique of overlaying illustration on to pointillated backgrounds is shown off to good effect in this 2006 poster for the Yeah Yeah Yeahs.

ABOVE RIGHT Casey Burns riffed on Sonic Youth's Sonic Nurse for this three-color screen print poster for a 2004 gig. "This poster was huge for me," explains Casey. "Simply because it was the best I had ever done at the time, plus it was for a band that had a huge impact on me from a young age." Striking and sexy without being stupid, the print chimed perfectly with the cool aesthetic of the band's album cover artwork.

The Art of Emek

If you had to name one artist whose work represents the current rock poster renaissance, that artist would be Emek. More than just advertisements for gigs, his work is often layered with hidden details and messages that are sometimes fun, sometimes political, and always smart and inventive, while the technical expertise is staggering. In the past few years, he has become the most collected poster artist in America, with the *Oregonian* newspaper noting the snaking queues to buy his work at a poster fair and describing him as "a savior of rock 'n' r oll." The self-effacing Emek—whose YouTube channel is filled with demos and jokes, such as a screen-printed poster made from ketchup and beans—is embarrassed by the accolades and would rather hang out at a gallery than a rock show, but his peers are equally complimentary.

Speaking in the 2009 documentary film *American Artifact: The Rise of American Rock Poster Art*, '60s psych designer Gary Grimshaw called Emek's work "astounding."

Emek's posters for the likes of Radiohead, Queens of the Stone Age, Pearl Jam, and PJ Harvey have, like the designs that defined live '60s rock, become synonymous with the times and as iconic as album sleeves were for previous generations. He's also stretched the limits of what a rock poster actually is, making 3-D posters such as the alien *Gig Fossil* for The Flaming Lips and the circuit-board print for Thievery Corporation, as well as creating a stamped metal poster for a Foo Fighters and Motörhead show last year.

Born Emek Golan in Israel in 1970 and raised in California, he would sit round a table as a young kid and play drawing games with his younger brother and sister. His parents were artists and their home was filled with art, but of all his parents' possessions, Emek says it was his father's old rock posters that had the biggest influence on him.

"I loved the '60s posters," he says. "I always gravitated to the art that also had text on it. It made it seem urgent, like a newspaper headline."

He started making posters for imaginary rock bands when he was nine years of age, and then when his friends started punk rock bands he designed their flyers. After graduating from California State University, Northridge, with, he says, "a major in art and a minor in unemployment," he got his first commission.

"It was in the days after the L.A. Uprising in 1992," he remembers. "It was for a unity rally and concert held on Martin Luther King Day. People started stapling [the poster] to burnt-out buildings, and newspapers carried the image.

"It was then that I realized that the posters illustrated an historical event, and they were in the moment, bold, and important. Suddenly, the idea of the poster as something wholly dispensable, printed to promote a friend's punk band, and left to flap in the wind after the show, seemed myopic. Posters are the people's art. So, why shouldn't a limited-edition silkscreened gig poster be an art form more worthy of a living room wall than a telephone pole?"

Most musicians that commission Emek give him free rein to let his imagination run riot. With soul singer Erykah Badu (for whom he designed her stunning 2005 tour poster and later the amazing artwork for her album *New Amerykah Part One* [4th World War]), Emek's had a long-term collaborative relationship that's extended far beyond the usual lifespan of a musician and poster artist relationship, which usually lasts the length of a phone call.

As the album sleeve disappears further into memory, one reason Emek's posters are so revered and so popular is that they are a reminder that rock 'n' roll is cooler if it comes packaged with cool art, whether you hold it in your hands, stare at it in a book, or tack it to your wall.

"I am allowed to dip into the recesses of my imagination and see what spills out onto the page. Today's disposable culture paves the way for tomorrow's collectable nostalgia . . . I'm just trying to make it interesting."

EMEK

ABOVE Emek was born in Israel while his parents were working there on a kibbutz. He was heavily influenced by the '60s poster art on the walls of his parents' Californian home, and the punk designs of the '80s. Now his work is influencing a whole new generation of artists.

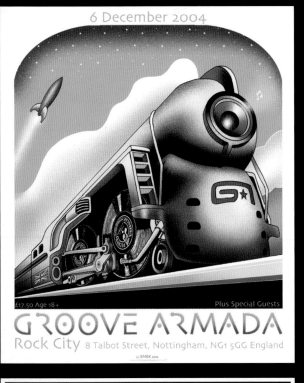

6 December 2004

£17.50 Age 18+ · Plus Special Guests

GROOVE ARMADA
Rock City · 8 Talbot Street, Nottingham, NG1 5GG England

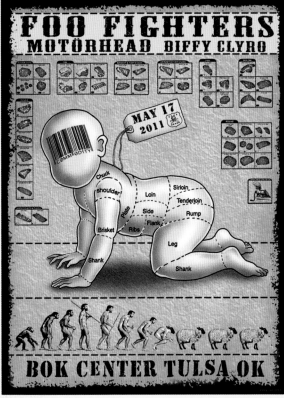

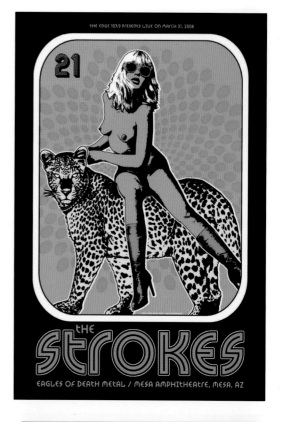

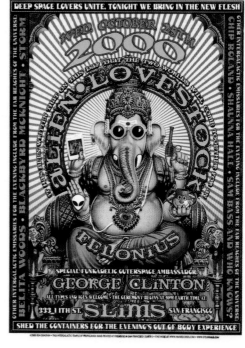

ABOVE LEFT Detroit-born graphic design legend Dennis Loren struck up a friendship with the White Stripes after he designed a poster for an early gig in Seattle. He established an illustrative style that used the band's chosen color scheme of red, black and white, and for this show incorporated a zebra after he saw a stuffed zebra feature as part of the band's stage-set appearance on a David Letterman TV show.

TOP RIGHT Of the third or fourth-wave of poster artists, Arizona-based James Rheem Davis has one of the most distinctive styles, blending together pastel colors and unusual fonts. This Strokes poster from 2006 is atypical of his work, being much cleaner and less impressionistic.

BOTTOM RIGHT Ron Donovan of the Firehouse Kustom Rockart Co. is the artist behind this stunning thirteen-color silkscreen poster for an impromptu live show featuring Funkadelic outer-space ambassador George Clinton on October 25, 2000. The work began as an art print—everything Ganesha is holding belongs to Donovan—before being adapted for the show.

OPPOSITE ABOVE LEFT One of a paired set of posters for two back-to-back shows in 2009 by emo rockers Fall Out Boy by Jeral Tidwell. Tildwell became a music poster artist after being inspired by the work of Frank Kozik. Calling his style "Kentucky fried," in 2003 he diversified his tattoo-style graphics into skateboard decks for the Reliance Skateboard Co.

TOP RIGHT Leia Bell started making posters as a teenager in her parents' garage in Utah, making flyers and handbills of punk shows for all ages in Salt Lake City. Her later work draws on images from nature, such as this illustration for a Decemberists show in Dublin, Ireland, in 2007.

BOTTOM RIGHT Many of Leia Bell's posters are based on photographs she takes of family, friends, or crowd members at local concerts, and then rendering them as illustrations—such as this 2008 poster for the Dandy Warhols.

TOP LEFT Chuck Sperry and Ron Donovan of the Firehouse Kustom Rockart Co. in San Francisco have been responsible for plenty of Eric Clapton tour posters (ten, at the last count). This ten-color silkscreen masterpiece commemorated the guitar legend's eleven-show run at the Royal Albert Hall, London, in May 2009, and stars a suitably cosmic Routemaster double-decker bus.

BOTTOM LEFT Inspired by the art nouveau style of the late '60s San Francisco scene, Justin Hampton's limited-edition silkscreen for Wolfmother matched the Australian band's hairy retro rock styling perfectly. Known for his comic book style, Hampton got his design break in the Seattle grunge scene of the early '90s.

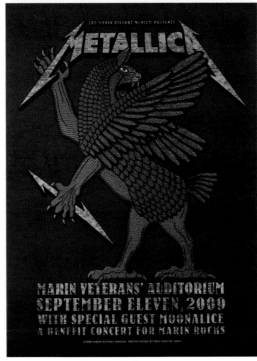

©2003 · GARY HOUSTON · MIKE KING · VOODOOCATBOX ✦ HAND PULLED AT GH DESIGN · PORTLAND, OR · WWW.VOODOOCATBOX.COM

OPPOSITE TOP RIGHT This 2011 poster for Pearl Jam was created by Frank Kozik. Born in Spain, Kozik moved to the US in 1976 at the age of fourteen, and found himself drawn to poster art through the Austin, TX, punk scene. He temporarily retired from the music industry in 2001 to develop several series of collectable vinyl art toys, including Smokin' Labbit—a rabbit with a tobacco habit.

OPPOSITE BOTTOM RIGHT Alice Cooper has been a patron of rock poster artists for four decades. His image is so familiar worldwide that his name no longer needs to be legible; the face says it all. This poster is for a gig at the Warfield, a former vaudeville theater and cinema in San Francisco, which launched as a rock venue in 1979 with a two-week season by Bob Dylan.

ABOVE LEFT Although he paints and draws, Portland, OR's Gary Houston is most famous for his designs that use scratchboard, such as those for the city's annual Waterfront Blues Festival, or this 2003 poster for BB King. A popular technique for illustration up until the '50s, it involves etching into fine white china clay with a blade, and then printing.

TOP RIGHT Boston-born Chris Shaw's 2003 poster for this heavy metal bill shows his debt to the psychedelic era. Yet like many contemporary poster artists, Shaw was first inspired by the punk movement of the early '80s. He studied printmaking in California, and since 2007 has been art director for a series of more than 450 posters for the band Moonalice.

BOTTOM RIGHT This 2009 Metallica poster by Dave Hunter was published as a 500-copy, limited-edition, six-color, silkscreen print using—appropriately for the headline act—silver, copper, and gold metallic inks. Hunter worked for four years at the Bill Graham poster archives in San Francisco, and regularly designs posters for support act Moonalice, who commission new artwork for every gig.

ABOVE LEFT An antique black-and-white military photo gets a fiery illustrative intervention in this poster by Jeff Matz for a gig by alt-country wild men O'Death on February 5, 2009. The Florida-based Matz worked as a creative director for an advertising agency before setting up his own agency in 1998.

TOP RIGHT AIDS Wolf are a Canadian noise-rock band who got their name from the urban myth that wolves carry AIDS and pass it on to house pets, who then pass it on to people. Jeff Matz's distorted three-color screen print for a 2007 show in his native Orlando, where he runs Lure Design, captures a metamorphosis between man and beast.

BOTTOM RIGHT Jesse LeDoux's cartoon fantasies have graced numerous album sleeves, including Death Cab For Cutie, for whom he also designed this 2005 concert poster commissioned by the House of Blues. A partner in Patent Pending, LeDoux is best known for his Grammy Award-winning artwork for the Shins album, *Chutes too Narrow*.

ABOVE LEFT Mind-f**k freak rockers Flaming Lips get the screen print they deserve with this mind-bending blast of metallic silver, fluorescent pink, fluorescent blue, and black. If fans' minds weren't blown away by the music, then perhaps Jesse Le Doux's poster would do the trick.

TOP RIGHT Greg "Stainboy" Reinel describes himself as an entertainer rather than an artist. His brash repurposing of pop-cult iconography employs the most eye-popping fluoros and the most buxom women in its effort to get noticed. Here, Disney's Goofy character gets a Third Reich makeover

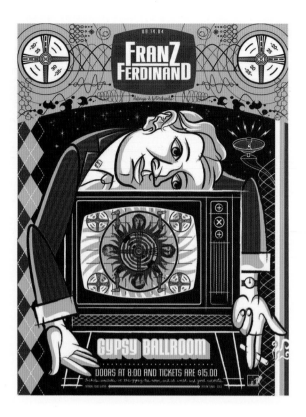

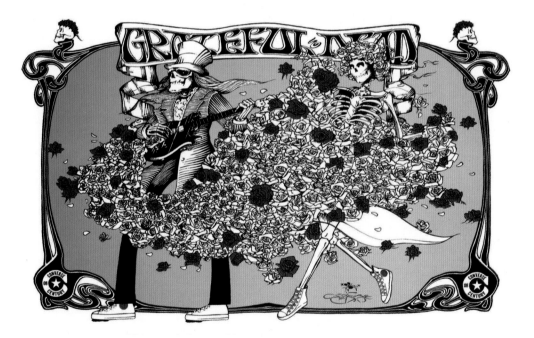

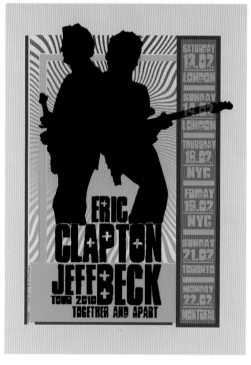

TOP LEFT One of the biggest names in rock poster art, Austin's Todd Slater has only been designing since the middle 2000s, but his bold use of color has won fans among the Black Keys and the Dead Weather, for whom he has designed record sleeves—as well as Franz Ferdinand, for whom he produced this 2004 poster.

TOP RIGHT This scratchboard-style design for a Kings of Leon show at Philadelphia's Spectrum club in 2009 contains a neat visual pun from Todd Slater. Because the concert was staged by the international promoters Live Nation, the run was slightly bigger than usual, with a set of two hundred signed and numbered prints.

ABOVE LEFT Along with Alton Kelley, Stanley Mouse created the Grateful Dead's iconic skeleton and roses design. The design is revisited on a 2008 poster—almost four decades after Mouse's association with the band began.

ABOVE RIGHT The type on this poster by Ron Donovan for this three-city 2010 tour by two veterans of the British blues scene is almost superfluous: the silhouette profiles of Beck and Clapton are distinctive enough to sell the concerts, while the red, gold, and green color scheme is a subtle nod to Clapton's association with Bob Marley.

TOP LEFT Lindsey Kuhn produced two versions of this poster for art rock legends Devo at the Coors Amphitheater in Englewood near Denver, CO, in 2005. The show, which also featured A Flock of Seagulls, was billed under the banner of Lost '80s and Kuhn returned to his roots to incorporate a skateboard as a focal element of the four-color screen print.

BOTTOM LEFT In 2009 Lindsey Kuhn produced a numbered, signed limited-edition run of ninety-nine three-color screen prints, featuring a dude-mobile worthy of a double bill of Aerosmith and ZZ Top. Kuhn also produced a single serigraph on aluminum version.

ABOVE RIGHT This 2007 poster is the most recent of a handful of posters that Lindsey Kuhn has produced for West Coast rappers Cypress Hill. The legendary Swamp designer also sold this five-color silkscreen print as a progressive proof set, with five separate proofs.

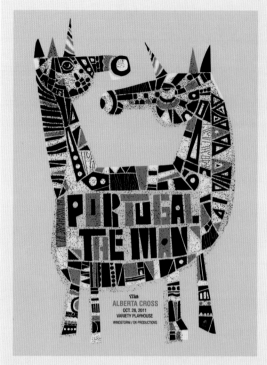

ABOVE LEFT Methane Studios got their turnaround in the late '90s, when the duo of Mark McDevitt and Robert Lee began designing silkscreen posters for the East Atlanta club the Echo Lounge. McDevitt is responsible for this four-color print for Sonic Youth.

TOP RIGHT A 2011 blend of '50s graphic design and '60s psychedelia by Robert Lee for the band Portugal. The Man. Lee founded Methane Studios in 1998 with fellow Columbus, OH, art student Mark McDevitt. At college they majored in illustration, and their work draws more on vintage fine art and design than the bold traditions of rock posters. Methane is based in Sharpsburg, GA.

BOTTOM RIGHT This two-color screen print by Robert Lee was for a day of live music at the South by Southwest festival in Austin, TX, in 2011. As with many of Methane Studios' rock posters, there's a mix of art and subtle humor going on.

ABOVE LEFT Portland, OR-based artist Mike King started out making posters and handbills for punk shows in his hometown in the '90s, and is now one of the most prolific and highly regarded artists around today. The detail on this limited-edition and hand-drawn silkscreen poster for a Vampire Weekend appearance, in 2009, shows a debt to Victoriana that is typical of his work.

TOP RIGHT If you look closely, you can just about make out one of artist Paul Imagine's trademark skulls on the heel of this diabolical-looking stiletto on a 2006 poster for Californian garage-soul act the Bellrays.

BOTTOM RIGHT Sacramento's Paul Imagine is inspired by early '80s skateboard and punk flyer art, and his hand-drawn designs capture some of the same kind of reckless and anarchic spirit— forsaking computerized fonts, his skeletal and mohawked pterodactyl on this poster for British punks, the Exploited, has a raw energy.

248 249 **ABOVE LEFT** Jeff Kleinsmith is the co-owner of Patent Pending Design, the collective behind hundreds of posters and album covers, as well as the creative director at influential record label Sub Pop Records. This striking print for R.E.M. is typical of a bold style that makes a rock-concert announcement appear as if it is a message from some shadowy secret force.

TOP RIGHT & OPPOSITE Along with the Mars Volta poster (opposite), this design showcases Tara McPherson's love of manga comics and Japanese *anime*. Her depiction of women sits in stark contrast to the buxom mannequins and scantily clad devil women beloved of many her male counterparts.

BOTTOM RIGHT Brooklyn's Two Arms design team consists of Michael Tabie and Karen Goheen. The duo's style draws on the commercial art and design of the '40s and '50s, as in this silkscreened design for a Guided by Voices festival in McCarren Park, Brooklyn, in 2012.

The Art of Collecting

Several years ago in the British *Guardian* newspaper, music journalist Jon Wilde, noting the renaissance in music poster art, confessed that he had become so infatuated that he had spent fourteen hours gazing at GigPosters.com and had forgotten to brush his teeth, eat, and even walk the dog. "With apologies to my cocker spaniel," Wilde wrote, "I'd reached nirvana without going to the trouble of snuffing it—that's how astonishingly great gig poster art is right now."

It's true, gig poster art right now is amazing and as close to the DIY spirit of punk rock as music gets. And now, thanks to new media and websites such as GigPosters.com, you don't have to live in New York or Nottingham or Brisbane to see the concert posters that date back to the '60s, '70s, and '80s (which would be seen only on the walls of the towns where the venues were) or appreciate the local artists in those particular towns. Music is everywhere and thanks to the wonder of the web, music poster art is everywhere, too. You didn't have to go to Bon Iver's show at the Zorn Arena in Eau Claire, Wisconsin, to buy the poster; hell, you don't even need to know where Eau Claire is.

Back in the early days of GigPosters.com's online life as a store and community for poster artists, a debate raged about what exactly defined a gig poster. Did uncommissioned posters count, where artists had taken it upon themselves to produce a souvenir poster of a concert in their town? Were commemorative prints valid, where an artist produced a poster of a gig or festival now long gone?

Writing on a forum in 2004, Texas poster artist Jermaine Rogers, responsible for plenty of iconic prints including the wonderful illustration of Morrissey sitting between James Dean and Marc Bolan, which was used to promote a live date in El Paso, summed up the general mood: "Part of why concert posters are so cool to me is that they mark a place in time. They capture the aesthetic of said band and event in a snapshot."

Indeed, the artwork is only a part of what makes current concert posters so collectible. The other part is that most posters are hand-crafted limited editions, and because only, say, 250 copies are made, each copy automatically becomes more special and cool. A similar thing has happened with vinyl releases in this era of MP3s: bands release a small pressing on vinyl and, unlike a mass consumer CD release, it not only feels unique but it also grows in value. But if a poster wasn't commissioned or even used to promote a gig, it feels worthless.

What is remarkable about GigPosters.com is that every day an increasing number of posters are uploaded by more than 20,000 different artists. And this site isn't alone—there are plenty of others around the world, including Lone Star Posters in America and the Richard Goodall Gallery in the United Kingdom as well as dozens of smaller sellers, bloggers, and galleries, trying to carve out their own niche in this expanding scene.

While most contemporary posters are deliberate limited editions, the scarcity of posters from the '60s and '70s stems from an entirely different situation. Original gig posters—particularly those for British concerts—were designed to be ephemeral, and most were trashed right after a gig. Even if some posters did find their way into the possession of fans, print runs were short and few were produced with an eye for being sold commercially. This wasn't always the case, however; posters for '60s gigs at the Fillmore in San Francisco were often given away, and such was their popularity that there would be numerous print runs.

It is because of such varying values that Mike Bloomfield of memorabilia site rockpopmem.com sticks with UK posters. "It is difficult to become an

> "The MP3 has no album art at all. So people are actually hungry for art; it's an innate thing within them. They respond to posters, and why else then would there be this enormous renaissance of poster art."
>
> PAUL GRUSHKIN (COAUTHOR OF *THE ART OF MODERN ROCK*)

expert across too wide a range," he says. "The problem with US posters, for instance, is that the US has long been more commercially astute than us in the UK. Therefore, gig posters in the US were designed not only to promote a specific gig but also to be sold at a later date for commercial benefit. Some iconic US psych posters of the '60s have been reprinted twenty to thirty times, and you really need to be on top of lots of arcane information to know whether you're buying a first print or the twenty-third! In the UK it is much easier to determine what are originals and what are modern repros."

Auctions by Christie's and Bonhams over the past two decades have helped give poster collecting credibility in Europe. Stephen Maycock, entertainment memorabilia consultant at Bonhams, began his career as rock 'n' roll memorabilia specialist at Sothebys in 1990. He now conducts regular valuation sessions around the world for Bonhams in conjunction with the Hard Rock Café. At these self-styled Antiques Rockshows, members of the public are encouraged to bring in their own treasured items from rock's past. Maycock acknowledges the role of the internet in raising awareness of the desirability, availability and value of rock poster art. In an interview for memorabilia website www.retrosellers.com, Maycock comments "There are sites that are just specifically for information, there are business sites who are buying and selling . . . There's just a mind-boggling amount of information there that wasn't available before."

Online poster site Wolfgang's Vault started out as a poster archive with the acquisition of the Bill Graham Presents posters and related assets, including live recordings. Wolfgang's (Wolfgang was Graham's real first name) is now home to a library of concert posters from the circus and boxing-inspired bills of the '50s through to punk's provocative cutups.

While many of these vintage prints can fetch up to $12,500, part of the appeal of poster collecting and another reason for the booming market in online sales is its modest entry level. Unlike fine art, you can start collecting original, limited-edition gig posters for $15 and in many cases own something totally unique.

One effect of the awareness generated by online sales and information sites has been the steady growth of rock poster collectors' fairs and festivals, at which enthusiasts and artists can meet one another face to face. The chance to discuss an artwork with its creator and come away with a signed example enhances not only the experience of collecting posters, but also the value of any collection.

TOP Mike Bloomfield is the founder of rockpopmem.com. A Cambridge University, England, history graduate and former investment banker, Bloomfield turned his rock poster hobby into a business in 1997. Early posters such as these are so valuable because they were never meant to last; more recent posters are collectable precisely because they *are* designed to be retained long after the event they advertise.

ABOVE Alida and John Van Hamersveld on their stall at the fortieth anniversary of the Summer of Love music festival in Golden Gate Park, San Francisco, in 2007. John made his name with the artwork for the Beatles' *Magical Mystery Tour* album. He moved into industrial design in the '80s and '90s, but returned to rock in 2005 with a poster for the Cream reunion gigs in London's Albert Hall.

Index

Credits

Front cover credits
Top, L-R: Dennis Loren; Brian Pike; © Martin Sharp; Roger McNamee Collection / www.moonalice.com. © www.wolfgangsvault.com
Bottom, L-R: Micael Priest, courtesy of the South Austin Museum of Popular Culture, www.samopc.org; © Live Nation, courtesy of Chris Shaw; Arlene Owseichik © www.wolfgangsvault.com; Dennis Loren.

Courtesy of Adelita: 97BL, 114BL, TL, R, 150BL, TL, R.
© Apple Corps Ltd: 66L.
© Mark L. Arminski: 187R, 209L, R, 215L.
Richard Barnes: 41.
© Mark T. Behrens: 86L, 106BR.
Leia Bell: 239BR, TR.
Russell Bestley: 140BR, 145L, 152L.
Tony Booth: 30TR, 33R.
Barney Bubbles: 97BL, 114BL, TL, R, 150BL, TL, R.
Casey Burns: 235R.
GUYBURWELL-guyburwell.com: 224, 225TL.
Camera Press / Caroline Coon: 142BL.
Brian Cannon / Microdot. Photography by Michael Spencer Jones: 200R, L.
Copyright Central Station Design Manchester / centralstationdesign.com / richardgoodallgallery.com: 203R, TL.
Design by Art Chantry: 154BL, 190BL, 210BL.
Chaos vs Cosmos – Stephen Keane / www.chaosvscosmos.blogspot.com: 231L.
Corbis / Bettmann: 74.
Glenn Cornick Collection: 98TR.
Art Director David Costa, illustration George Rowbotham: 108BL.
Michael Cowell: 230BR.
Roger Crimlis: 135R, BL, TL, 136L, BR, 144TR, 145R.
Painting and logo by and © copyright Roger Dean 1974 rogerdean.com: 111B; Painting and Greenslade logo by and © copyright Roger Dean 1971 rogerdean.com: 113L.
The Designers Republic™: 225B, TR.
Detroit Annie: 93TL.
Ron Donovan Collection: 160L.
Luke Drozd / www.lukedrozd.com: 226TL.
Colin Duffield: 40TR.
Rod Dyer: 103BR, 104L, 106TR, 109BL, 120TR, 191R.
Johnny Dynell / The Jackie Factory: 180BR.
EMEK (emekstudios.com): 221TC, 236, 237TL, TC, TR, BL, BR.
© EMI Records: 104BR.
© Michael English: 72, 73TR.
David Ensminger: 147L, 149R, L.
© David Fairbrother-Roe: 64TR, L.
Matt Ferres – www.ferres.co.uk / info@ferres.co.uk: 226BL.
Photography by Danny Fields: 137TR.
The Firehouse Kustom Rockart Company / Ron Donovan: 205L, 212R, 213TR, 214, 238BR, 240BR; Ron Donovan & Chuck Sperry: 240TL.
Jim Fitzpatrick / www.jimfitzpatrick.com: 120 BR, L.
Terence Flynn / Portal Publications: 85BL.
Jim Franklin: 99R, 106L.
Lalo Garcia Collection: 91L.
Danny Garrett / www.dannygarrett.com: 188 L, BR, 190TR.
Design by Malcolm Garrett (Assorted Images): 143TR; Design by Malcolm Garrett (Assorted Images). Photograph by Jill Furmanovsky: 143BR.
George Georgiou. Promoter Nicky Holloway: 177TL; Promoter Nicky Holloway at the Milk Bar: 166; Collaboration with Danny Rampling: 177BL.
Getty Images / Richard E. Aaron/Redferns: 162R; David Corio/Redferns: 167; Kieran Doherty/Redferns: 216L; GAB Archive/Redferns: 27, 133BL; Hulton Archive: 9TR, 26L, 187L; Alastair Indge/Photoshot: 216R; Michael Ochs Archives: 18, 26R, 38, 50, 62, 75L, 128; Al Pereira/Michael Ochs Archives: 174; Steve Pyke: 146L; Time & Life Pictures: 9R; WireImage: 146R; Vinnie Zuffante: 175R.
Globe Poster Printing Corp. / Globe Collection & Press at MICA www.mica.edu/globe: 20, 23BR, TR, 24BL, TL, 28L, TR, 29BL, 29R, 29TL, 44; Photograph by Kyle Van Horn: 34L.
© Martine Grainey / www.martinegrainey.co.uk: 107TL, 123.

© Rick Griffin: 76BR, 76TR.
© Gary Grimshaw: 73BR, 86TR, BR, 88L, TR, 89R, BL, 101R, 201L, 215R.
Art and design by Mick Haggerty: 126L, 188TR, 189TL, 190L, 191L, 197L, 199BL; Design by Mick Haggerty and John Kehe: 115.
JC Hall Collection: 161TR.
Design and Photography – Geoff Halpin: 111TL; Design – Geoff Halpin, Art Direction – Michael Ross: 154TR.
Justin Hampton: 240BL.
© Hapshash and the Coloured Coat: 49R, 63R, 68, 69BR, TR, 69L, 70L, 92, 93R.
Courtesy of Harvest/EMI Records: 97TL.
Hatch Show Print www.hatchshowprint.com. Courtesy of the Country Music Hall Of Fame: 23L, 34R, 35R, 35L, 56TL.
Stephen Hauptfuhr: 176BR, 178BL.
The Heads of State: 226R, 227.
Art direction and design: Tom Hingston Studio / Illustration: Idris Khan: 222L; Photography: Nick Knight: 223TR; Illustration: Kam Tang: 223BR; Photography: Cover art Robert Del Naja: 222BR; Photography: Jez Tozer: 223L; Photography: Jonathan de Villiers: 222TR.
Gary Houston Design: 241L.
Dave Hunter: 241BR.
Design by Alan Hynes: 221TL, 234TL, BL.
Paul Imagine: 247TR, BR.
Michael Jackson: 204.
Barry Jones: 136TR.
K&K: 33L.
© 1982 Alton Kelley: 109R; © 1976 Alton Kelley & Stanley Mouse: 113R.
Image from King Crimson Archive courtesy of DGM Ltd © Robert Fripp, www.dgmlive.com. Designed by Barry Godber, 1969: 108R.
Design by Jeff Kleinsmith: 248L; Design by Jeff Kleinsmith (Patent Pending): 14BL; Design by Jeff Kleinsmith and Jesse LeDoux (Patent Pending): 221B.
Marijke Koger / Fool Collective: 66TR.
Frank Kozik © 2012: 161L, 217L, 240TR.
Lindsey Kuhn www.swampposters.com: 207L, R, 210R, 245TL, BL, R.
Tom Lacey Art & Design / cargocollective.com/tomlaceyart: 231R.
Design by Jesse LeDoux (Patent Pending): 242BR, 243L.
© Dave Little Design: 183BL, R.
© Live Nation: 241TR.
Mark London Collection: 87.
Dennis Loren: 105R, 121R, 213L, BR, 238L, 251B (photographer).
Gary Loveridge: 137L, 142BL, 144L, 150BL, 155TR, 156L.
© Carl Lundgren: 86TL, 90BR.
Mike Malignant: 138, 159.
Malleus Rock Art Lab – www.malleusdelic.com: 233BL.
© Jim Marshall Photography LLC: 112L.
Bob Masse: 212L.
Jeff Matz: 242L, 242TR.
Roger McNamee Collection / www.moonalice.com: 13L, 78TL, 78R, 79R, 79BL, 79TL, 80, 81TR, 81BR, 81L, 82BR, 82L, 82TR, 83, 84R, 84L, 86BR, 88TR, 88BR, 89TL, 89R, 89BL, 90BR, 93BL.
Tara McPherson: 248TR, 249.
Design by Me Company / www.mecompany.com: 179R, 196, 197TR, 199R.
Diego Mena www.didacus.co.uk: 233TL.
Alexander Mertsch: 32.
Methane Studios, Inc: 246TR, 246L, 246BR.
www.mikemcinnerney.com: 70BR.
mitchybwoy.com: 173L, 178R.
© Morrissey: 193L, R.
© Pat Moreno: 152R.
Designed by Kate Moross & Alex Sushon, commissioned by Ali Warm / studiomoross.com: 180L.
© 1967 Stanley Mouse: 63BL; © 1976 Stanley Mouse & Alton Kelley: 113R; © Stanley Mouse & the Grateful Dead: 244BL.
Dan Mumford – www.Dan-Mumford.com: 229TL.
Bill Narum: 127BL.
Courtesy of Nashville Convention & Visitors Bureau www.visitmusiccity.com. Photo: Robin Hood: 19.
Albert Neiman Collection www.visualtransformation.com: 54R, 58R, 59R, 85TL, 113R, 127R, 208TR, 210TL.
© Neon Rose 1967, www.victormoscoso.com: 78TL
Art direction and design: Vaughan Oliver, photography: Jim Friedman: 203BL photography: Simon Larbalestier: 202L; 202TR; photography: Kevin Westerberg: 202BR.
© Julian Opie. All Rights Reserved, DACS 2012: 217R.

Tony Ortiz: 99TL.
Alec Palao Collection: 47L, R.
Designed by John Pasche. © 1970 John Pasche: 102; © 1970 John Pasche: © 1971 John Pasche: 103L; © 1973 John Pasche: 119TL; © 1975 John Pasche: 117TL.
© Raymond Pettibon. Courtesy the artist and Regen Projects, Los Angeles: 147L, 149R.
Phase 2: 168L, BR, TR.
Jim Phillips: 127TR, 208L.
Kevin Phillips Collection / www.sf-texposters.com: 20, 21BR, 21L, 21TR, 22R, 23BR, 23TR, 24BL, 24TL, 25TR, 25L, 28L, 28TR, 29TL, 45TL, 45BL, 45R, 52TR, 55TL, 55R, 56R, 85BL, 86TR, 88L, 100TR, 106L, 112L, 119R, 127BL, 160R, 161BR, 161L, 188L, 188BR, 190TR, 208BR.
Mara Piccione, www.piccione.nl: 232.
Brian Pike: 51.
Adam Pobiak: 228TL, BL, R.
Jamie Reid, courtesy Isis Gallery UK: 139T, BL, BR, 140TR, BR, L, 141B, 147R, 148L.
Greg "Stainboy" Reinel • stainboy@stainboyreinel.com: 243R.
Rex Features / Rick Colls: 183TR; Everett Collection: 163; Mike Hollist / Daily Mail: 133R; Ben Smith: 162L.
© Rhino Entertainment Company. Used with permission. All rights reserved. www.familydog.com: 75R, 77, 78R, 79R, BL, TL, 80; artist Victor Moscoso, www.victormoscoso.com: 93BL.
Art by Nick Rhodes at Switchopen.com: 229B, 230BR.
Rockpopmem.com: 10TR, 30L, BR, 31TR, BR, 43TL, BL, 46, 65TL, BL, 66BR, 99BL, 100BR, 100L, 101TL, 104BR, 107TR, 108TL, BL, 109TL, 110TR, 111TR, 118, 122R, 124T, 126BR, 153T, 192BR, 194L, TR, 195BL, TL, 251T.
Don Rogers Collection: 52L.
© Peter Saville: 158BR, L, TR.
Ron Schaeffer Collection: 103TR.
Design: Thomas Scott, Eye Noise: 206TR, BR, 234R, 235TL, BL, 206L, Illustration: Billy Davis: 14BC.
© Scrojo. Courtesy of D.King gallery, dking-gallery.com: 170TR, BR, 171R, 172R, TL, BL, 173R.
© Martin Sharp: 67, 70TR, 71BL, TL, R.
Artwork © Chris Shaw & Moonalice: 127TL, 205R; Courtesy of Chris Shaw: 211TL, 211BL, 211R, 241TR.
Gilbert Shelton: 90L.
Todd Slater: 221TR, 244TL, TR.
Design/Photography © Bill Smith for BSS, London: 151L.
Glyn Smith: 230L.
Design Stylorouge: 156BR, 195R, 198L, 199TL; Photography Daniel Greene: 201TR; Photography George Logan: 198BR; Photography Trevor Rogers: 197BR.
Photography David Scheinmann: 192TR; Illustration Blaise Thompson: 198TR.
Design by Storm Thorgerson: 124B; Storm Thorgerson / Hipgnosis: 124T, 125R; Storm Thorgerson & Aubrey Powell / Hipgnosis: 97R.
Jeral Tidwell – www.humantree.com: 239L.
Triangle Productions – Bruce Cohn: 104TR.
Randy "Biscuit" Turner: 160R.
Two Arms Inc. Michael Tabie, and Karen Goheen: 171L, 248BR.
Design by United Artists, based on sleeve design by Malcolm Garrett (Arbitrary Images). Montage by Linder: 143L.
© Universal Records: 194BR.
Kunny van der Ploeg, www.kunnyvanderploeg.nl: 233R.
© John Van Hamersveld: 91TR, BR.
John Van Hamersveld Collection: 14BR.
Dave Walters Collection: 13BR, 55BL, 56BL, 57BL, 58L, 59L.
© Warner Bros. Records: 107B.
Anthony Weller/Archimage: 112R.
WeThreeClub: 229TR.
© Copyright 2012, Paul Whitehead. All rights reserved: 14T, 98BR, 108TL.
© Wes Wilson: 13L, 81TR, 81R.
© www.wolfgangsvault.com: 13TR, 81L, 82BR, L, 82TR, 83, 84L, 85R, 100TR, 103TR, 116, 119R, 121TL, BL, 122L, 125L, 126BR, 129L, 189BL, 208TR, BR, 211TL, BL, R.
Kent Wood Archives / www.cahootsgraffix.com: 24R, 86L, 101BL, 105L, 106BR.

Authors' Biographies

Dennis Loren was born in 1946 in Detroit, Michigan. Dennis began designing concert posters in 1967; his first posters were produced for Muddy Waters, the Youngbloods, and the Jimi Hendrix Experience, as well as for legendary venues such as the Matrix, the Fillmore Auditorium, the Avalon Ballroom, and the Whisky A Go-Go. From 1977 to 1992, Dennis served as the art director for a succession of music magazines, including *Blitz!*, *Goldmine*, *R.P.M.*, *Creem*, and *Metal*. During his career he has created artwork for numerous record labels and recording artists, from Frank Zappa and Otis Redding to Rick James and Roky Erickson. Although he now lives in the San Franciscoco Bay Area, he maintains a strong connection with his Detroit roots, which can be seen in his concert poster designs for younger bands such as the White Stripes, the Dirtbombs, the Detroit Cobras, and the Go. Some of his concert poster work appears in *The Art Of Modern Rock* by Paul Grushkin and Dennis King. Dennis and his art have also appeared in the 2009 documentary film *American Artifact— The Rise Of American Rock Posters*.

Mick Farren learned his trade as a writer in the heady days of the underground press, and at the *NME* in the 1970s. Mick created *Get On Down*, the very first collection of rock posters, in 1979. He has also published more than a dozen non-fiction works that range in subject from music to drugs to conspiracy theory, and include the bestselling *Elvis And The Colonel*, *The Black Leather Jacket*, and autobiographic *Give The Anarchist A Cigarette*. He has also published twenty-two novels that include the psychedelic fantasy of *The DNA Cowboys Trilogy*, the neo-gothic *The Renquist Quartet*, and the far-future militarism of *Their Master's War*. An unreconstructed rock and roller, he continues to work as a recording artist and songwriter, with more than a dozen CDs to his credit.

Contributors' Biographies

Russ Bestley is a lecturer in Graphic Design at the London College of Communication, London, England. He has co-authored and designed a number of books, including *Visual Research* and *Up Against the Wall: International Poster Design*, and has contributed articles to journals including *Eye*, *Zed*, *Émigré*, *The National Grid*, and *Punk & Post-Punk*.

Bill Brewster is a music writer and DJ. His work has appeared in *The Guardian*, *Time Out* and *Mojo* and he is also the co-author of *Last Night A DJ Saved My Life*, the history of the DJ.

Nigel Cross founded *Bucketfull of Brains* magazine and has contributed to various publications including *Sounds*, *The History of Rock*, *Forced Exposure*, *Ptolemaic Terrascope*, and was co-editor of the German-based zine *Hartbeat*. He set up Shagrat Records, a label that issues obscure vinyl artefacts from the first underground era by acts such as Mad River, Screw, Bridget St John, Formerly Fat Harry, and ex-Moby Grape singer Bob Mosley. Nigel is currently researching a book on British rock and the music hall tradition.

Johnny Dee promotes gigs and ran a fanzine in Brighton before becoming a music journalist for *NME*, *Smash Hits* and *Q*. He now writes for *The Guardian* and edits "The Vinylist" blog.

Michael Heatley has authored more than one hundred biographies, and was editor of *History of Rock* partwork (1981–84). His acclaimed biography of late DJ John Peel sold in excess of 100,000 copies, while *Michael Jackson— Life Of A Legend 1958–2009* topped the *Sunday Times* bestseller lists, and has been widely translated. His book on Jimi Hendrix's guitars, *Hendrix Gear*, was among the most celebrated music books of 2009.

Colin Salter is a graduate in applied art and design, a former tour manager, and a popular music historian with a particular interest in '60s soul and '70s rock. He has published articles on transport posters of the '30s, record labels of the '50s, and synthesizer pop of the '80s. His work also appears in two books about classic pop songs, a history of stage musicals, and several encyclopedias of rock biography.

Wolfgang's Vault

Wolfgang's Vault contains the greatest collection of finely curated live concert recordings and memorabilia representing the history of live music of the past fifty years. In its Concert Vault, music fans find audio and video, which has been painstakingly restored and digitized for a unique online live music streaming experience. Browsing the Wolfgang's Vault store, collectors and music fans explore the great vintage concert poster collections, fine art concert photography by the most celebrated photographers, vintage concert T-shirts, retro rock clothing, and millions of treasures of live music memorabilia. A rare archive with a highly engaged worldwide community of live music fans and a unique retail entertainment experience, Wolfgang's Vault *is where live music lives*. **www.wolfgangsvault.com**

This book would not have been possible without the support and generosity of the following people and organizations:

Ron Donovan, Lulu Ehrhard, Kent Wood, Chuck Sperry, Roger and Ann McNamee, Cindy Poon, Peter McQuaid, Ben Kranich, Cyndie Berg, Mark London, Mike Giangreco, Steve Stanley, Alec Palao, Kevin Phillips, Kay Cavallero, Merle Becker, Wade Goring, Arlene Owsiechik, J.C. Hall, Chris Shaw, Alexandra Fischer, Carolyn Ferris, John Seabury, Winston Smith, Wendy Wright, Wes Wilson, Stanley Mouse, Victor Moscoso, Justo Moscoso, Lee Conklin, David Singer, Gary Houston, Bob Masse, Alida & John Van Hamersveld. Steve Keyser, Mark T. Behrens, Tsvi Deer, Bill Ham, Reggie Williams, Albert Neiman, Bruce Dauser, Ellen Harmon, George Hunter, Michael Wilhelm, Country Joe McDonald, Barry Melton. Peter Lewis, Jerry Miller, Omar Spence, Sam Andrew, Peter Albin, Dave Getz, Pete Sears, Ray Manzarek, Cyril Jordan, Prairie Prince, Laney and Paul Kopf, Marguerite Kelley, Ida Griffin, Randy Nauer, Gordon T. McClelland, John Helms, Dolly, Jim & Jimbo Phillips, Laura & Gary Grimshaw, John Sinclair, Mark Arminski, Michael Erlewine, Michelle & Carl Lundgren, Scott Dedenbach, Meg White, Jack White, Ben Blackwell, Dennis King, Ron Schaeffer, Walter Medeiros, Mark Weiman, Eric King, Boots Houston, Dusty Houston, Richard Goodall, Jud Cost, Eve & Paul Imagine, Brianna & Jon-Paul Bail, Freddie "Steady" Krc, Cam King, Carol & Alex Del Zoppo, Fred Herrera, Nancy Nevins, Debbie Jacobson, Phil Cushway, Paul Grushkin, Jorge E. Gamboa, Vince Duggar,

Kris Mikkelson, Clara Bellino, Nick Cernak, Jeff West, Mark Rodriquez, Mary Hohn and all the members of The Rock Poster Society (www.trps.org), Nels Jacobson, The American Poster Institute (www.aip.org), Clay Hayes (www.gigposters.com), Sherman Au, Brandon Newton, Rickie Fontenot, Voltaire Jayme, Charles Dudley, Larry Finn, Mike & Anja Stax, Jason, Candance & Sheppard Soloman for all of their help, memories and historical information.

Tony Molatore and Lalo Garcia (of Berkeley Giclee) for photographing many of the poster images appearing in this book. Megan McKearney at ScanArt in Emeryville, CA for scanning additional posters. Jennifer Cornett and Janet Hunter at Chromatics in Nashville, TN for scanning the Hatch Show Print slides. Loretta Baraona for access to her photographs from The Rock Poster Society events and Flatstock 25. And photographers Kyle Van Horn, Robin Hood, David Wilds, Michael Jackson, Herb Greene, Gene Anthony, Jim Marshall Leni Sinclair and Anne Kransdorf.

To the following individuals, collections, copyright holders and organizations that allowed us access to their collections or provided valuable historical information:

Jim Sherraden of Hatch Show Print (www.hatchshowprint.org), The Country Music Hall Of Fame (www.countrymusichalloffame.org). Chuck Creasy of the Nashville Convention & Visitors Bureau (www.visitmusiccity.com), Bob

Cisero, Ray Allen, Mary Mashburn, Gail Deery and Jessica Weglein of the Maryland Institute College of Art and the Globe Poster Printing Corp./Globe Collection & Press at MICA (www.mica.edu/globe). William Sagan and Katherine York of Wolfgang's Vault (www.wolfgangsvault.com), Rhino Entertainment (www.rhino.com), Arlene Owsiechik (www.bigpicturedesign.com), Michael Bailey of Bill Graham Presents/Live Nation (www.livenation.com), Roger McNamee (www.moonalice.com), J.C. Hall (www.idealposters.com), Kent Wood Archives (www.cahootsgraffix.com), Kevin Phillips (www.SF-TEX.com), Dennis King (www.dkinggallery.com), Reggie Williams (www.thestraight.com), Albert Neiman (www.visualtransformation.com), Leea Mechling and Henry Gonzalez of the South Austin Museum of Pop Culture (www.samopc.org), Freddie "Steady" Krc, (www.steadyboyrecords.com), Mark London Alec Palao, Café Au Go Go (www.originalcafeaugogo.com), Tom Flynn of Portal Publications, The Don Rogers Collection. The Dave Walters Archives, The Don "Lucky" Lockhart Archives.

And to all of the artists whose poster designs appear in this book. Thank you for your art, cooperation and contributions.

And anyone else we may have unfortunately forgotten to mention.